Answers to Distraction

■ ■ ■

Answers to Distraction
...

Edward M. Hallowell, M.D.
and
John J. Ratey, M.D.

Pantheon Books

NEW YORK

Grateful acknowledgment is made to the following for permission to reprint previously published and unpublished material: *American Psychiatric Association*: Excerpts from the Diagnostic and Statistical Manual of Mental Disorders, 4th ed., Washington, D.C.: American Psychiatric Association, 1994. Reprinted by permission. *Ronald C. Hume*: Description of the Learning Disabilities Association Screening Program. Reprinted by permission of Ronald C. Hume, Learning Disabilities Association of Washington. *Mary Alice King*: Letter from Mary Alice King to Edward M. Hallowell, M.D. Reprinted by permission of Mary Alice King.

Library of Congress Cataloging-in-Publication Data

Hallowell, Edward M.
Answers to distraction / Edward M. Hallowell and John J. Ratey.
p. cm.
ISBN 0-679-43973-0
1. Attention-deficit hyperactivity disorder—Miscellanea.
I. Ratey, John J., 1948–   . II. Title.
RJ506.H9H3448   1995
616.65'89—dc20
[616.85'89]   94-34578
CIP

Book design by Cathryn S. Aison

Manufactured in the United States of America

First Edition

2   4   6   8   9   7   5   3   1

This book is dedicated to the millions of people who have worked to help those of us who have ADD, and to one of those individuals in particular, an unacknowledged hero of this world (or any other):

Sandra Freed Thomas, R.N.

Contents

■ ■ ■

APPENDIXES

Preface

■ ■ ■

Not long ago John Ratey and I wrote a book entitled *Driven to Distraction: Recognizing and Coping with Attention Deficit Disorder from Childhood through Adulthood*. This book is based upon questions we've been asked about ADD since the publication of *Driven to Distraction*.

We are fortunate to live in a time of great advances in the field of the scientific understanding of the brain. One of the areas that has benefited particularly is the study of how people learn. It was only a few decades ago that most people thought the main learning disability was simply stupidity, and the main treatment was to try harder. People had heard of dyslexia, perhaps, but the term didn't carry much weight. As for attention deficit disorder, a few decades ago the term hadn't even been invented; back then what we now call ADD was referred to as "minimal brain dysfunction." Over the past twenty years we have learned a great deal about how people learn—and how they fail to learn.

Norman Geschwind, and later his colleague Albert Galaburda, pioneered the research that now gives us the biological, anatomical basis of dyslexia. The research into ADD dates back to the beginning of this century when the British physician George Still speculated that certain kinds of disruptive behavior in children may be caused by brain problems, rather than by moral failings, as was usually held. It is a great black mark in human history that up until this century, and even into this century in some places, the "diagnosis" of children who acted up was that they were in some way "bad." The "treatment" prescribed by medical, religious, and lay leaders alike was to punish the child, usually by beating him or her. Make no mistake about it: we have brutally abused our children, particularly our "overactive" children, throughout human history.

Mercifully, our understanding of the brain has led us to view these children differently in this century. From George Still in Britain, to Charles Bradley in this country in the thirties and forties, and on to Virginia Douglas in later years in Canada, the concept of the hyperactive child evolved into the idea of the child whose main problem was in focusing attention. By the time the term "attention deficit disorder" was born in the seventies, we had developed a number of safe, effective treatments for these children using both medication and nonmedication approaches.

Since the seventies, research into ADD has mushroomed. It is by now one of the most rigorously studied of all syndromes in medicine. Led by Russell Barkley, Joseph Biederman, Judith Rapoport, Paul Wender, and Alan Zametkin, the research into ADD has freed hundreds of thousands of children from painful disability and stigma. Furthermore, Wender, Leopold Bellak, Hans Huessy, and others pioneered the work that led us to identify ADD in adults as well as in children. Now adults who had thought they were simply lazy, stupid, or "spacey," are finding ways of achieving their potential.

Driven to Distraction was an introduction to the world of ADD. In that book we told stories that had been told to us by our patients, stories of the struggle to learn and to focus, stories of lives gone off track because of missed connections or a missing diagnosis. We also told stories of triumph in that book. Both John Ratey and I were students when the great research into ADD was getting started. We grew up professionally as ADD was coming of age. Using the knowledge given to us by the researchers in the field, we have felt the great joy of seeing our patients get better. We have also felt the excitement of seeing the current understanding of ADD take shape.

Our patients, time and again, gave us a special kind of privileged information; they gave us the most precious of medical messages: their histories. They asked us to pay attention to attention itself. When our patients told us, "I can't focus on one job; I daydream all the time," we took what they said at face value and asked them to tell us more. When they went on to say they had been like this since they were a child, and when they told us of other symptoms such as impatience, impulsivity, mood swings, and the love of highly stimulating situations, we knew from the medical research what they were talking about.

Now ADD is almost a household word. One sees it lampooned in cartoons, hears it debated on daytime radio, sees it on the cover of *Time* and *New York* magazines, and encounters arguments over it in newspaper editorials. This is good news and it is bad news.

The good news is that thousands of children and adults are at last getting the help they need. Parents who had not understood why their children were underachieving at last understand. Those children at last have a better chance to fulfill their potential. Adults who had thought they were stupid or hopelessly disorganized now more often get the proper diagnosis and treatment and have a chance to turn their lives around. Physicians, teachers, and other professionals are diagnosing ADD more, now that they have the knowledge to recognize it. The workplace, thanks in part to the Americans with Disabilities Act, is becoming friendlier to people with ADD. Schools, colleges, universities, and professional schools are offering accommodations to their students with ADD.

While at times people are hostile to whatever is new, we have not found this to be the case with ADD. In the main, people have been curious and inquiring. What little jeering has occurred has been drowned out by intelligent dialogue among many thousands of individuals.

The bad news is that there is still a great deal of misinformation to be countered, some of it being offered by pro-ADD enthusiasts who see ADD everywhere, and some of it being offered by anti-ADD zealots who debunk the validity of the diagnosis and decry its various treatments, particularly the medications.

We are radical moderates. We feel radically about the importance of keeping a moderate position. Both John and I are general psychiatrists, and I have specialty training in child psychiatry as well. Both John and I treat a wide variety of conditions, from major mental illness like schizophrenia to problems of everyday living. Both of us trained at the Massachusetts Mental Health Center in Boston, where the overriding principle was to listen to the patient first. We have taken with us the value of remaining loyal to no dogma other than the open inquiry into our patients' pain. We do not, therefore, see ADD everywhere. We try to see it where it is, and only where it is.

We take great care to retain a balanced view, not swearing allegiance to any camp or sect. Our allegiance is to our patients and to science, the rational pursuit of truth. Our radical moderation does not mean we do not feel passionately about the importance of correctly diagnosing and treating ADD. We do. It is precisely because we feel so strongly that we do not want to see the diagnosis either trivialized by overinclusiveness or excluded by deaf skepticism.

The enthusiasts who see ADD everywhere bring to mind the remark, "If you give a man a hammer, pretty soon he thinks everything looks like a nail." ADD is such a seductive diagnosis that once you understand what it is you have to be very careful not to see it in everyone you know. Everyone does have some of the symptoms of ADD some of the time. However, we do not all have ADD. In fact, only about 5 percent of us do.

On the other hand, just because the diagnosis is seductive, just because it can be overused, that does not mean it should be thrown away altogether. The backlash against ADD derives mostly from ignorance; people who do not know what ADD is hear a few phrases about it and say, "That's ridiculous," or "That's just the latest excuse for getting out of work." Once they understand the facts, they usually retract those remarks.

The backlash also derives from a misguided notion that the diagnosis of ADD undermines the work ethic. Most of us in America believe deeply in the formative value of work. As a nation, we work hard, harder than almost any other nation in terms of hours worked per week and length of vacation per year. Some of our beliefs may have crumbled over the past few decades, but our belief in work has not. Work may be the most widely agreed-upon value we hold. We recoil at anything that might undermine that belief.

For example, when *Time* magazine ran its cover story on ADD (July 18, 1994), one of the letters to the editor it provoked spoke for the way many people feel:

> The excusing of America is a growth industry. I doubt that there is a single human failing that has not been diagnosed, labeled, and treated with drugs. Doctors constantly invent new ailments to explain away irresponsibility and failure, and there is no end in sight.

I wonder if the person who first described nearsightedness met with the same response. "Just another trumped-up excuse for failure," a skeptic might have said. "If you can't see, squint harder, but don't invent some new ailment to explain away your failures." Indeed, ADD has a lot in common with nearsightedness. Both are invisible problems, apparent only to the person who has them. You can't tell by looking at someone if he is nearsighted or if he has ADD. And both nearsightedness and ADD result in problems with focusing. The nearsighted person has trouble focusing his vision; the person with ADD struggles to focus his attention.

But no one doubts the validity of the diagnosis of nearsightedness, nor does anyone object to a person's wearing glasses to improve his or her eyesight. ADD, however, still contends with some opposition, despite an abundance of scientific evidence establishing its validity. Why? I think it is because people like the man who wrote the letter to *Time* fear that the diagnosis of ADD will undermine our work ethic. In an age when so many people seem to have an excuse, these people fear that ADD is just one more dodge.

However, it is a misconception that the diagnosis of ADD undermines an individual's obligation to work. Treating an individual's ADD may make her work more productive, her labor better focused, but it does not in any way reduce the necessity of industry.

In fact, most people with ADD are by nature hard workers. They are full of energy and they are eager to achieve. They want to do well. Like the nearsighted person who can't see clearly but must strain to read the blackboard, the person with ADD must strain much harder than most people to stay on task and to inhibit distractions. People with ADD don't want to make excuses; all they want, and deserve, is proper diagnosis and treatment.

ADD should not be a diagnosis influenced by morality or politics but by science. ADD should not be associated with liberals or conservatives; it has nothing to do with liberal or conservative thinking. Everyone, after all, is in favor of proper medical treatment.

In order to provide that treatment to all who need it, the job of education must continue. We have been deeply satisfied by the number of people who have responded to *Driven to Distraction*. Through their comments, questions, and anecdotes, they have raised new issues and taught us a great deal. Now that there is more general knowledge of ADD, people are asking increasingly probing questions. We never seem to have the time or the forum to answer them.

At the end of one lecture I gave in Wilmington, Delaware, I was handed a particularly thick stack of index cards bearing questions. There were about a thousand people in the audience, and each person must have written a question. I couldn't have got through more than twenty of them before time ran out.

The next day Mary Ellen Foulds and her husband, Rick, the organizers of the conference, came up to me. Mary Ellen said, "We think we know what your next book should be."

"Yes?" I responded, and smiled politely, less than eagerly awaiting the reply.

"We think you should take that stack of index cards you were handed last night and answer all the questions, instead of just a few, and make the answers your next book. It would be the perfect format for the reader with ADD. Questions and answers. Q and A. It's ADD heaven. No wasted time. Get to the point. Read a little bit here, a little bit there. Skip around. No need to stay in order. Perfect."

What had been a polite smile on my face became a real smile. "Yes," I said, wheels whirring, eager now.

"Just start collecting questions everywhere you go," Mary Ellen said. "Divide them into categories. You can answer them in writing and make a book out of your answers. You can call the book *An-*

swers to Distraction. You can make some answers short and some long, some funny and some serious, some about children, some for adults—you know, cover the waterfront like you did last night."

I discussed the idea with John Ratey. He liked it. So did the people at Pantheon. So we took the many questions we'd collected, sorted through them, and answered them. A few of the questions were posed by us. They are questions we wish we'd been asked and want to answer. But the great majority of the questions come from real audiences of people interested in ADD. We are glad to have the chance to answer them here.

John and I are practicing psychiatrists, both of us are on the faculty of the Harvard Medical School, and both of us have attention deficit disorder ourselves. John has written most of the answers to the questions in chapters 5, 6, and 12–16; I have written the rest.

But the entire book is the result of a true collaboration, not only between John and me, but among John, me, the scores of professionals who have helped us by sharing their research and their experience, the hundreds of patients who have taught us and guided us by sharing with us their own lives, and the thousands of listeners and readers who have contributed ideas, questions, and anecdotes. This book and its predecessor are collaborations through and through. This book, especially, is shaped as much by its audience as by its authors.

—EDWARD M. HALLOWELL

Answers to Distraction

■ ■ ■

.1.

You Mean There's Actually a Name for It?

TOWARD A DEFINITION OF ADD

■ ■ ■

Q: Can you tell me *in brief* what I need to know about ADD?

A: I can try. ADD is a neurological syndrome that is usually genetically transmitted. It is characterized by distractibility, impulsivity, and restlessness. In ADD these symptoms are present from childhood on, and with a much greater intensity than in the average person, so that they interfere with everyday functioning. Diagnosis is made primarily by reviewing one's history; there is no foolproof "test" for ADD. Great care must be taken to make an accurate diagnosis and to look for other problems that may occur along with ADD, such as low self-esteem, depression, substance abuse, or family turmoil.

Treatment includes education, structure, coaching, and medication. With treatment, the prognosis is usually good.

Both diagnosis and treatment should always be done under medical supervision. ADD is a tricky diagnosis and the treatment is not always simple. You should *never* diagnose or treat yourself.

■ ■ ■

Q: Are there any advantages to having ADD?

A: Yes. There are many.

To the extent that there is such a thing as the ADD personality—and I believe that there is—it has its pluses and its minuses. The pluses are not usually discussed much because books and articles about ADD naturally tend to focus on problems and solutions rather than advantages. But the advantages deserve prominent mention. They include:

- High energy
- Creativity
- Intuitiveness
- Resourcefulness
- Tenacity
- Hardworking, never-say-die approach
- Warmheartedness
- Trusting attitude (sometimes too much so)
- Forgiving attitude (sometimes too much so)
- Sensitivity (often can hurt as well as serve the person)
- Ability to take risks (again, a double-edged sword)
- Flexibility
- Good sense of humor
- Loyalty

Lest the skeptic think this sounds more like the Boy Scouts' oath than a legitimate list of traits, let me hasten to add that not all people with ADD have all these qualities, nor can I prove the scientific validity of the list itself. However, based upon my experience with thousands of individuals with ADD, and based upon my conversations with many other authorities in the field, this list of positive qualities does fairly describe the advantageous side of the ADD personality.

People with ADD do tend to be warm, creative, flexible, loyal, innovative, hardworking, and the rest of the qualities on that list. However, the problems their ADD causes can be so severe that these positive qualities never gain full expression or recognition. The negative qualities can be so toxic and self-defeating that the strengths are wasted.

Once the person gets proper treatment, the negative aspects of ADD recede, and the positive can flourish.

People with ADD remind me of the bumblebee. The bumblebee should not be able to fly. Its body is too big and its wings are too short. Scientists say it should not be able to fly. Aerodynamically, it should be impossible. The physicists agree—the design of the bumblebee is incompatible with flight. Its balance should be all off. So how does the bumblebee fly? We don't know. But it does fly. That much we do know.

■ ■ ■

Q: Is there a hallmark of ADD, a single core trait that defines it best?

A: In our opinion, yes there is. It is a relative lack of inhibition. People with ADD tend to be more spontaneous than the average person. They speak freely, at times too much so. They think freely, at times creatively, at other times chaotically. They act unpredictably: often even they do not know what they're going to do next. They do not inhibit their responses as stringently as most people do. They often lack the intermediate reflective step between impulse and action. This can be charming and innovative, or it can be annoying and disruptive, depending upon the impulse and the action.

People with ADD neither inhibit nor shape their responses as automatically as those who do not have ADD. This leads, directly or indirectly, to almost all of the other symptoms associated with ADD, including disruptive behavior, impulsivity, restlessness, uneven attention span, disorganization, tactlessness, irritability, impatience, and risk-taking behavior. It also leads to many of the positive qualities of ADD, such as creativity (because creativity depends upon some degree of disinhibition), spontaneity, high energy, and openness (people with ADD do not inhibit responses long enough to close down and become guarded). Most treatment aims to increase inhibition where needed, without imposing unwanted limits.

■ ■ ■

Q: What is the best definition of "attention deficit disorder"?

A: We do not know exactly what attention deficit disorder is. The most official definition is found in a volume entitled the *Diagnostic and Statistical Manual of Mental Disorders,* published by the American Psychiatric Association. The first edition of this manual was published in 1952. It has been updated several times since then. Its most recent incarnation, the fourth, was published in 1994. For short, it is called DSM-IV. Here is how DSM-IV defines ADD:

A. Either (1) or (2):

1. Six (or more) of the following symptoms of *inattention* have persisted for at least six months to a degree that is maladaptive and inconsistent with developmental level:

> a. often fails to give close attention to details or makes careless mistakes in schoolwork, work, or other activities
> b. often has difficulty sustaining attention in tasks or play activities
> c. often does not seem to listen when spoken to directly
> d. often does not follow through on instructions and fails to finish schoolwork, chores, or duties in the workplace (not due to oppositional behavior or failure to understand instructions)
> e. often has difficulty organizing tasks and activities
> f. often avoids, dislikes, or is reluctant to engage in tasks that require sustained mental effort (such as schoolwork or homework)
> g. often loses things necessary for tasks or activities
> h. is often easily distracted by extraneous stimuli
> i. is often forgetful in daily activities

2. Six (or more) of the following symptoms of *hyperactivity (a to f)-impulsivity (g to i)* have persisted for at least six months to a degree that is maladaptive and inconsistent with developmental level:

a. often fidgets with hands or feet or squirms in seat

b. often leaves seat in classroom or in other situations in which remaining seated is expected

c. often runs about or climbs excessively in situations in which it is inappropriate (in adolescents or adults, may be limited to subjective feelings of restlessness)

d. often has difficulty playing or engaging in leisure activities quietly

e. is often "on the go" or often acts as if "driven by a motor"

f. often talks excessively

g. often blurts out answers before questions have been completed

h. often has difficulty awaiting turn

i. often interrupts or intrudes on others (e.g., butts into conversations or games)

B. Some hyperactive-impulsive symptoms that caused impairment were present before age seven years.

C. Some impairment from the symptoms is present in two or more settings (e.g., at school [or work] and at home).

D. There must be clear evidence of clinically significant impairment in social, academic, or occupational functioning.

■ ■ ■

Q: What do you think of DSM-IV?

A: DSM-IV, like its predecessors, has come under attack for being generated more by politics than by science. However, this is a problem inherent in psychiatric diagnosis itself. When you are classifying people's behavior, when you are trying to draw lines between what is normal and what is abnormal behavior or what is a normal or abnormal personality, it is impossible to avoid the appearance, at least, of political or cultural bias. Probably the most famous example of this was the inclusion of homosexuality in the 1952 version of the DSM as a pathological condition.

DSM-IV goes to great lengths to avoid such bias. It is based upon extensive empirical fieldwork and a tabulation of all research. More analysis of data went into the compilation of DSM-IV than perhaps any document in the history of the American Psychiatric Association. The current DSM has its flaws—none as egregious as the 1952 version—but it is, in the main, a fair attempt to system-atize a field that is almost impossible to systematize. Thanks to DSM-IV, we at least have one standard for diagnosis, and a basis of communication between professionals. We may argue with DSM-IV, debate it, and get angry at it, but we at least have it as a refer-ence point. It helps bring order to what would otherwise be greater chaos in psychiatric diagnosis.

When I was a resident at the Massachusetts Mental Health Cen-ter, I was trained in the tradition of the "empathic diagnosis," and I believe in its usefulness to this day. This tradition was championed by the great teacher Elvin Semrad, and it has influenced psychiatrists nationwide, since Massachusetts Mental has been a leader in train-ing psychiatrists for many decades. The empathic diagnosis is based upon the doctor's empathic response to the patient. It is a wonder-ful tool, and it is a tool modern medicine is in great danger of losing to technology. However, it is necessarily subjective. I am much safer in using my empathic diagnosis if I can *also* make an objective diag-nosis based upon a standard, such as DSM-IV, to which others can refer in order to confirm we are talking about the same entity.

Without DSM-IV, or something like it, diagnosis in psychiatry risks being so vague as to be meaningless. Indeed, before the field tried to become more rigorous about diagnosis, most people admit-ted to psychiatric hospitals in this country were diagnosed schizo-phrenic without a second thought. Today this does not happen, and we have, in large part, DSM-IV and its forebears to thank.

■ ■ ■

Q: Does ADD have different degrees of severity?

A: Yes. ADD exists on a spectrum from mild to moderate to se-vere. At the mild end of the scale we see the gray area where it is

hard to tell at what point normal, everyday distractibility or scat-
teredness leaves off and ADD begins. At the severe end of the scale
we see children who cannot function outside a hospital and adults
who are incarcerated or who cannot hold jobs or stay in relationships. Most people with ADD fall somewhere in between.

ADD is not a condition, like pregnancy, that one either has or
does not have. Instead, it is a condition, like depression, that occurs
in varying degrees of intensity.

■ ■ ■

Q: Can you "come down with" ADD as an adult?

A: No. There must be evidence of ADD in childhood for the diagnosis to be made as an adult. There need not be a history from
childhood of an actual diagnosis, as the diagnosis may have been
overlooked. However, the clinician should be able to draw out of
the patient a history of symptoms typical of ADD from childhood.

If no such history exists, if the symptoms suddenly appear in
adulthood, one must search for some cause other than ADD. Probably the most common other cause is not a medical diagnosis at all,
but what I call "pseudo-ADD" or culturally induced ADD. We live
in an "ADD-ogenic" society. The fast pace, the quick sound bites,
the need for instant gratification, and the abundance of high-tech
communication tools all tend to shape us along ADD contours. If
you do not have ADD when you are born, and you grow up in an
urban environment, chances are you'll *look as if* you have it by the
time you're fifteen.

But this is not true ADD. One way to tell ADD from pseudo-
ADD is as follows. If you take an individual with pseudo-ADD and
put him on a farm in Vermont, in a few months his symptoms will
have subsided. If, on the other hand, you take a person with true
ADD and put him on that same farm, in a few months the farm will
really be hopping.

Aside from pseudo-ADD, there are other causes of the emergence of ADD-like symptoms in adulthood. Among these are
agitated depression, mania (as the manic phase of bipolar or

manic-depressive disorder), substance abuse, excess caffeine intake, withdrawal from nicotine, generalized anxiety disorder, or posttraumatic stress disorder. These are just a few of the more common causes. They should underscore the wide range of possible diagnoses signaled by the emergence in adulthood of symptoms associated with ADD.

■ ■ ■

Q: I have been told by some people that ADD does not exist in adults. When I tell them it does, they say the DSM does not recognize it. Is this true?

A: ADD does exist in adults. DSM-IV specifies no upper age limit for making the diagnosis, and it specifically includes terminology that includes adults. For example, it states that hyperactivity, "in adolescents or adults, may be limited to subjective feelings of restlessness." Therefore, although there is no separate category for adult ADD in DSM-IV, adult ADD is most certainly recognized.

Furthermore, the clinicians and researchers who work with ADD now agree that the syndrome does indeed sometimes appear in adulthood. The old teaching that ADD always disappeared in childhood is obsolete.

■ ■ ■

Q: My husband seems to have ADD only when he comes home from work. He totally ignores me at these times. Is it possible to have ADD at home but not at work or anywhere else?

A: No. The intensity of the symptoms may wax and wane during the day, but one cannot have ADD at home and not have it at work. Similarly, in children one cannot have ADD at home but get over it at school. The symptoms may be worse at home (or, on the other hand, at school) due to differing environments and management techniques used at each place, but you have ADD—or you do not have ADD—no matter where you are.

■ ■ ■

Q: Is there such a thing as "silent ADD"? In other words, if I identify with the symptoms of ADD, but they aren't bothering me in any way, do I really have ADD?

A: Your question is almost philosophic. It is like asking, "If ADD falls in the forest, but no one is there to hear it, does it make a sound?" I would dodge the question by answering that it doesn't matter. If you pressed me, I would say, "No, you do not have ADD." Unless there is some impairment in your functioning, then you do not have the symptoms severely enough to qualify for the diagnosis.

■ ■ ■

Q: Why is attention deficit disorder called what it is?

A: It really shouldn't be. Attention *deficit* is a misnomer. It should be attention *inconsistency* or attention *variability*. People with ADD, children and adults alike, can pay attention extremely well at times. At times they can focus with great intensity. This is when they are highly motivated or captivated by a situation full of novelty.

■ ■ ■

Q: How many people in the United States have ADD?

A: Probably between 8 million and 15 million, depending upon whose figures you believe. The sure fact is that ADD is not rare.

■ ■ ■

Q: When I read your descriptions of ADD, I get confused because there seem to be so many contradictions. You say there may be hyperactivity, but then you say there may not be. You say the person may be distractible, but then you say he may pay attention very well. Are these contradictions mistakes on your part or are they part of ADD?

A: Actually, the contradictions are part of ADD. Dr. Elizabeth Leimkuhler has called ADD "the syndrome of paradoxes," and it is that indeed. You pointed out two of them. There may be hyperactivity or its opposite, a daydreamy quietude. There may be close attention or its opposite, distraction.

Other paradoxes are often found in the same person with ADD. He or she may be exquisitely sensitive and attuned to the feelings of other people at times, while at other times be oblivious to interpersonal dynamics. She may be highly creative in a certain situation while a few minutes later be utterly devoid of new ideas. She may be steady under pressure one hour, a surgeon in the operating room, and the next hour be flighty and unreliable. She may be optimistic in one conversation and pessimistic in the next, warm one day, cold the next.

These paradoxes go beyond changing moods. They include contrary tendencies in the same person. This is one reason it can be difficult to describe a person with ADD. The person can vary so much that paradox must become a central part of his or her description. Intimate one moment, closed off the next. Good at math one day, bad at math the next. Same person, same brain, different program.

This tendency is so pervasive that any description of ADD that does *not* contain contradictory symptoms is not a complete description of ADD.

■ ■ ■

Q: Is ADD more common in this country than in Europe?

A: The reported rates of diagnosis of ADD in the U.S. are higher than in Europe. Some people believe that this is due to our over-diagnosing the condition. However, I believe that the incidence of ADD truly is higher in the United States than it is in Europe. This is because I believe our gene pool is loaded for ADD. If you think about what sort of people colonized this country, and what sort of people immigrated over here, these were people who didn't want to toe the line, who didn't want to sit still, who were willing to take a big risk, who were in search of something new. Not all colonists had ADD, but one can fairly speculate that a disproportionate number did.

■ ■ ■

Q: I have heard you describe ADD as a metaphor for contemporary American society. What do you mean by that?

A: ADD is like life these days. I don't want to sound too high-flown in my claims, but I do believe that this medical syndrome meshes with the gears of current American culture. The fast pace of everyday life, the search for the sound bite, the love of fast food and instant gratification, the proliferation of fax machines, cellular telephones, computer networks, bulletin boards, and E-mail systems, our appetite for violence and action and adventure, our rush to get to the bottom line, our widespread impatience, the boom in gambling, our love of extremes and of danger—all these very American traits are also very ADD-like.

This may help explain why ADD is fascinating to so many people, and why it is a seductive diagnosis. When you hear a description of ADD, it can sound like a description of urban life in this country. Doesn't everyone in Los Angeles or Manhattan have ADD? It can seem that way. Of course, it is important to underline that they *do not*. But it would be fair, I think, to diagnose our urban culture as inducing an ADD-like syndrome, or what I call pseudo-ADD.

Pseudo-ADD means having many of the symptoms without the actual diagnosis. Millions of Americans have pseudo-ADD.

But numbers aside, ADD is a compelling diagnosis in a way most medical diagnoses are not. We can sit and ponder ADD in a way we would not ponder many other medical or psychiatric conditions. We can wonder whether a person has ADD or is just afflicted with modern life. That is an interesting differential diagnosis.

■ ■ ■

Q: I have read that ADD is high among criminals. Is this true?

A: Yes. We don't have reliable statistics, but most authorities would agree that ADD is higher among the criminal population than among the general population. This makes sense when you consider that poor impulse control is a core symptom of ADD.

■ ■ ■

Q: Since ADD is higher among criminals, do any court systems screen for ADD?

A: All should, but few do. It would be a wise allocation of funds to put money into screening for ADD (and LD, since learning disabilities are also a risk factor for criminal behavior) in the court system so treatment could begin then and there. This would save money down the line. As it is now, these people rarely get diagnosed early. They are thought of as criminals, not undiagnosed patients. But if they could be diagnosed, treatment would greatly reduce the likelihood they would return to jail after they served their initial sentence.

The most innovative program in the criminal justice system that I know of is in the Seattle area, in Redmond, Washington. A district court judge there named David Admire has teamed up with Ronald Hume, head of the Learning Disabilities Association of Washington to set up a program that could serve as a model in other states. At my request, Mr. Hume gave me the following description of the program:

> As a result of having two children with multiple learning disabilities, Judge David Admire of Northeast District Court in Redmond, Washington, became concerned that

many of the defendants appearing before him also had learning disabilities. This was especially evident from the frustration that boiled over and the inappropriate behavior displayed by certain defendants that he recognized as similar to his sons' reactions. When he asked the mother of one defendant whether her son had learning disabilities, the woman began to cry and said that no one had previously cared enough to ask.

Believing that the number of learning-disabled defendants could be significant, Judge Admire contacted the Learning Disabilities Association of Washington to devise a method to verify and address this situation. In conjunction with the Learning Disabilities Association, a six-week test period was established during which every defendant who pled or was found guilty was tested to determine if an in-depth evaluation for learning disabilities was warranted. Thirty-seven percent of those individuals tested were found to be candidates for further testing.

Based on these preliminary findings, Judge Admire felt it would be appropriate to test future defendants for learning disabilities and refer them to appropriate programs. However, no such program existed. Judge Admire and the Learning Disabilities Association worked together to establish and implement the Life Skills Program to assist offenders with learning disabilities (LD) and/or attention deficit disorder (ADD). For those offenders who are placed on probation, the judges of the King County District Court, Northeast Division, have directed that a condition of probation requires that defendants be tested for learning disabilities and, if appropriate, complete the Life Skills Program of the Learning Disabilities Association. Failure to do so places a defendant in violation of the terms of his sentence, which can result in the imposition of jail or other punishment.

The program targets LD and/or ADD misdemeanor and gross misdemeanor offenders between eighteen and forty-five years of age. The program provides:

1. Initial screening to determine if the client/offender possesses the basic tendencies, behavior, and history consistent with LD and/or ADD
2. Testing to confirm the diagnosis
3. A fourteen-week (twenty-eight-hour) instructional class geared specifically toward the needs of the LD and ADD clients

The Life Skills Program is designed to address the offenders' difficulties in personal interactional skills, anger control, and problem-solving. It also provides information on learning and attentional disabilities, offers suggestions on specific coping mechanisms, and provides community resource information. A supplementary manual for both clients and instructors has been developed. The clients' manual includes cartoons that have been drawn by a young man with learning disabilities. Enrollees seem to identify with the feelings expressed in the cartoons, and the manuals also make the program easier and more standardized. The focus of this program is not to address academic problems, as the development of personal interactional skills is seen as a prerequisite to addressing academic weaknesses. Clients are provided with information and referral sources to help in academic areas.

As a result of the program, clients become aware of the personal characteristics that are related to or are the result of their LD or ADD; they learn how to process information; and they develop specific skills to assist in anger management and appropriate social interaction.

After completion of the Life Skills Program, the recidivism records of offenders are reviewed at six months, one year, eighteen months, and two years. Present data indicate a recidivism rate of 67 percent without the program, 45 percent for offenders who start but do not complete the program, and a drop to only 27 percent for individuals who complete the entire fourteen-week program.

This program benefits the offender-participants by teaching them skills to improve their social functioning and to stay out of jail; it benefits the court system by reducing the clogging that occurs with repeat misdemeanor offenders; and it benefits the general public who pay taxes that fund the court system or who may be victimized by the behavior of one of these offenders.

I met with Judge Admire and Mr. Hume, and I was greatly impressed by their can-do approach to what many regard as a can't-do situation. Put an LD/ADD screening program in the courts? Negotiate that bureaucracy, cut through all that red tape merely in the name of learning disabilities? Easier to pass a camel through the eye of a needle.

Yet this is exactly what Judge Admire and Ronald Hume have done. What a stroke of good sense it would be if other states would follow their lead!

■ ■ ■

Q: I'm worried that ordinary, rambunctious little boys are getting labeled with a disease: attention deficit disorder. I mean, how would Tom Sawyer be diagnosed today, ADD or conduct disorder? Please comment.

A: You make an excellent point. We must be extremely careful not to pathologize normal, little-boy behavior. And you're right, it is usually the boys who get called down, because their aggressive behavior gets them into trouble.

Before one can entertain the diagnosis of ADD, the core symptoms—restlessness, distractibility, and impulsivity—must be present to such an intense degree that they are causing major problems in the child's life at home and at school.

If we are conservative and careful in how we make the diagnosis, then we will not diagnose young Tom Sawyers. Instead, we will only diagnose children who are suffering in their frustration at not being able to control their own behavior or focus their own minds, and with the correct diagnosis we will relieve their pain.

.2.

To Be Here and There
and Everywhere

ADD IN CHILDREN

■ ■ ■

Parents' Questions

■ ■ ■

Q: My son is a first-grader who was recently diagnosed with ADD. I am finding it very difficult to live with this diagnosis. I am embarrassed to say this, but I just can't accept that he has something like this wrong with him. Do you have any advice?

A: My hat is off to you for being so honest. First grade is the age when most parents have to come to terms with their children's imperfections; this leads most parents to have secret thoughts like the one you just acknowledged.

It can be traumatic for a parent to learn that his or her child has ADD or any learning disability. It might be the first evidence that the child isn't perfect. As parents, we all like to imagine our children are perfect. We want for them to suffer none of the pain in life that we had to suffer. We want them to have all the good, none of the bad. We forget, all parents do, that no one is perfect. We forget that having a hard time now and then is a necessary part of being alive. We forget what we all know, at least in our heads—that mistakes are part of learning, that suffering can be formative, that learning how to deal with adversity is an essential part of growing up.

We parents forget these things. In our devotion to our children we sometimes champion them as if they were gods—immortal, perfect, beyond criticism. We take any hint that our child might have a problem as a direct attack on us, and the most precious part of us at that.

If a doctor tells us that our child has a problem such as a learning disability or ADD, we might fire the doctor. If several doctors tell us the same thing, we might go into mourning. Dr. Michael Jellinek, a child psychiatrist at the Massachusetts General Hospital in Boston, has described receiving this diagnosis of a child as a "near-death experience" for many parents. They take it almost as hard as if their child had died.

As a parent, don't be ashamed of such a reaction. A part of your child really has died. It is the part that dies usually about the first grade. For some unfortunate children it lives longer. For a lucky few it dies much younger. But for most, it dies at first grade. It is the unreal, perfect part. It is the version of the child that can do no wrong and have no flaws.

Once the perfect part dies, you can love your child as he or she really is. This is the love your child needs. Your child needs this love much more than your love of the illusion of the perfect child, the child that never was and never will be. It is a cause for celebration when you let the perfect child die and accept the child you have.

■ ■ ■

Q: At how early an age can ADD be diagnosed?

A: Theoretically, ADD can be diagnosed at any age. In practice, people differ as to when the earliest cutoff point is. I myself do not diagnose ADD in children younger than five. This is because I think it's so hard to differentiate ADD from normal toddler behavior. In children under five who present with symptoms suggestive of ADD, I recommend nonmedication treatments like increased structure, consistent limits, predictable schedules, plenty of play and exercise, and increased parental presence, if possible.

However, many responsible practitioners do diagnose ADD—and treat it with medication—in children younger than five, even as young as two. Their reasoning is that since the medication is safe, even in very young children, and since the behavior associated with severe ADD is often quite *unsafe*, then it makes good medical sense to give the medication a try. The choice of treatment ultimately is made by doctor and parent working together.

■ ■ ■

Q: How is ADD diagnosed in the very young?

A: The younger the child, the more the diagnosis rests upon physical behaviors. Even children who do not have ADD do not sustain attention very long. The younger the child, the shorter the attention span.

■ ■ ■

Q: Are there any risks to having a young child diagnosed and "labeled" by the school bureaucracy?

A: There are always risks, but I think the greater risk is in the school *not* knowing. Only if the school knows can it participate creatively in the child's treatment program.

Telling the school is usually not the hard part, though. Education is. I hope you live in an enlightened school district, but if you do not, you take on the sometimes gargantuan task of trying to educate the school about ADD. You cannot do this by yourself! You need the help of parent groups like CH.A.D.D., books, professionals—and a few guardian angels.

■ ■ ■

Q: Should the school *always* be told?

A: You should almost never say *always* to anything.

However, I can think of no instance when the school should not be told the child has ADD. If it is unsafe for the school to know, then the child should not be in that school.

Let's look at both sides of the question. What is to be gained in the school's not knowing? Avoidance of possible prejudice, I suppose. Since some schools do not understand ADD, they may mistreat children who have it, or worse, discriminate against these children once they are informed they do have it.

However, the best way to put an end to this poor treatment is to inform the school the child has ADD, and not to stop there but to continue to inform, educate, and work with the school—and other authorities and professionals—until proper treatment is secured. This may take months. It may take years. I know some parents who have had to fight a battle every single year of their child's academic career, up to and including college.

The process is often difficult. Schools sometimes resist; other parents sometimes make trouble; school consultants and even judges sometimes gum up the works. Trying to get help from a school for a child with ADD can become an ordeal—expensive, exhausting, frustrating, and, sadly, ineffective.

However, the best way to get full support is to be honest. To get the protection the law affords, you must be open about the diagnosis. To get the help from the members of the school community who understand ADD and would be sympathetic to your case, you must be open about the diagnosis. To show your child—and your family, and your child's friends, and their families, and the teachers and the administrators, and yourself—that there is nothing to be ashamed of in having ADD, nothing necessitating secrecy, you must be open about the diagnosis.

At first, it may be difficult to be honest. But over the long haul honesty is definitely the best policy. Once you get in the habit of being honest about ADD, *with everybody,* you'll be amazed at how much better you feel within yourself, and how much better your child feels, too. The air gets cleared. The message gets out: it is OK to be yourself. It is OK to have ADD. We don't have to be ashamed any more.

■ ■ ■

Q: What would be your advice to parents of ADD students in highly stressed, low-wealth urban school districts?

A: Many urban areas are near teaching hospitals. These are hospitals associated with a medical school. And you can get the biggest bang for your medical buck these days by getting a doctor in training—a "resident"—at a teaching hospital to take on your case, whether in pediatrics, neurology, or child psychiatry. These young doctors tend to be very idealistic, highly motivated, and indefatigable. They are also closely supervised, and they discuss and study every case with great care. They take on cases with determination and enthusiasm and they can become just the sort of staunch ally an ADD parent absolutely needs.

■ ■ ■

Q: What attributes should I look for in my child's teachers?

A: Flexibility, a sense of humor, and a willingness to learn are the three main ingredients to look for. You cannot expect your teacher to be an expert in ADD, but you can hope that he or she wants to learn as much as possible about it.

Flexibility is key for obvious reasons. And a sense of humor saves the ADD day more times than any of us can count. Beware of teachers who tell you that they already know everything about ADD (because no one does), and beware of teachers who never laugh.

■ ■ ■

Q: My school's consultants don't believe my son has ADD. What can I do?

A: This is a common situation. First of all, try to avoid getting into a struggle. Struggles almost invariably devolve into personal hostilities, with the child caught in the middle. However, you do need to take action. It makes sense to get a second opinion. That way you will have another professional's viewpoint to support you.

■ ■ ■

Q: What do you recommend for a child taking Ritalin who has trouble sleeping?

A: Let me make a couple of points about sleep. In answer to the specific question asked, if a child is taking Ritalin and is having trouble getting to sleep at night, then the dose of Ritalin should be lowered, or the time he takes the Ritalin should be earlier in the day, or the Ritalin should be changed to another medication.

If these steps do not work, another medication may be added. Joseph Biederman's group at the Massachusetts General Hospital has reported good luck with a low dose of clonidine at bedtime. Clonidine is good for both sleep and ADD. Or a traditional sleeping medication for children, such as Benadryl, may be used.

I would like to make a more general point about sleep and ADD, particularly in adolescents and young adults. There is a pattern I have seen so often that I call it the "ADD sleep pattern." Here the individual—usually a teenager or young adult—has trouble getting to sleep at night, and tremendous trouble waking up in the morning. In other words, he or she has problems with deactivation and activation of the brain. Usually, medication significantly ameliorates this problem. However, when it does not, the problem can be disabling, particularly for college students who need to get up for their classes.

The worst-case scenario, which is not uncommon in college-age individuals, finds a student partying, working on his computer, listening to music, talking to friends, playing poker, making telephone calls, watching TV, or all of these until the wee hours of the morning. He then does not get out of bed until noon or later. He misses his classes. He sleeps through exams and other obligations. His problems around sleep cause him to flunk out of school.

It can be said without exaggeration that this problem with getting to sleep at night and waking up in the morning can ruin the academic career of a college student and carry over into job-related problems as well. It is imperative that the student, his parents, and the treating physician take it *very* seriously. Comical as it may sound, it can lead to disaster.

■ ■ ■

Q: What if the treatment doesn't work, or is incomplete? My son was diagnosed with ADD at college. Medication has helped, but he still lacks motivation and is doing very little. What can I do?

A: It is not uncommon to see in young men this pattern of being unmotivated, and at sea. I know it is not peculiar to young men with ADD; many others are in the same predicament.

I think a coach can help a great deal, whether the young man has ADD or not. Working with someone outside the immediate family to help him set goals and to work toward them can be of enormous benefit.

You also want to *make sure* there is not some other problem you're unaware of, a medical problem or another psychiatric problem, most likely substance abuse or hidden depression, or both. So an evaluation by a professional is essential. Over time, most young men like your son find themselves; the hope is to minimize the time that takes and the mistakes that are made along the way.

■ ■ ■

Q: Please tell me more about what a coach does. I've read what you've written about it, and I've heard you talk, but I'd like to hear more specifics on how to prepare a coach for what he—or she—is supposed to do.

A: When I started working with children, and later with adults, who had ADD, I discovered that most of these people needed a special kind of assistance. This assistance most closely resembled what a football coach does, so I coined the term "coach" for this very valuable part of the treatment of ADD.

Since I began to talk and write about coaching, I have had many requests like yours for further elaboration. There are several key principles.

First of all, a coach is just what the name implies. A coach is a person who stands on the sidelines of your life barking out instructions, reminders, and encouragement. The coach gets on you when you stray from your game plan. The coach reminds you where the goal line is. The coach picks you up when you are down. The coach snarls at outsiders who try to interfere with your practice schedule, and the coach sticks up for you when you need an ally. The coach is a teacher. The coach is a watchdog. The coach is a parent figure. The coach is a friend.

The coach becomes a major figure in the life of the person he or she works with. The coach should always be there, with the player, either physically or mentally. The coach must work a heavy schedule to establish this presence. In coaching a child or an adult with ADD, the coach should meet with the individual three or four times a week for about twenty minutes each time. The meeting should follow the acronym H.O.P.E.:

H—Hello. Start the meeting by saying hello. Wave your hands and arms if you must. You need to get your client's attention. Make sure you have his attention completely before going any further.

O—Obligations. Ask your client what his obligations are. For the day, for the week, for the month, for the year. Once in a while, ask about longer-term goals. But make sure you focus on short-term obligations. Be dogged. Your client will often be evasive.

P—Plans. Ask your client what his plans are for meeting his obligations. Remember, he will be evasive. When he says something vague like "I have that covered," ask for specifics; the chances are, he doesn't have it covered at all and he's just bluffing because talking about it makes him anxious. Persist. Pry. Press.

E—Encouragement. Having grilled your client regarding his obligations and plans, you now end the meeting by giving him a big dose of encouragement. We all need encouragement, but people with ADD need lots of it. They need to head off into their work feeling hopeful.

If the coach follows that sequence regularly, and if the client cooperates, it will be difficult to get off track.

I have suggested three or four sessions a week for twenty minutes, but they can be longer and/or more frequent. They probably should not be shorter or less frequent, particularly in the beginning. The client, or the client's parents, should pay the coach a fee.

The question often arises, Who should be the coach? It is best if the coach comes from outside the immediate family. Sometimes a sibling can be a good coach, if the sibling is mature enough that competitive issues don't interfere. Sometimes a parent is pressed into service, but this should occur only as a last resort. It is almost impossible for a parent to be a successful coach. Part of what makes the coaching model such a good one is that the child can listen to a coach where he might be unable to listen to his parents. Similarly, it is difficult for a spouse to effectively coach his or her mate. The risk of coming across like a nag is too great.

Other family members can make good coaches. For children, uncles and grandparents are particularly good coaches. Ideally, they should live in-house or nearby, but if there is great distance, the coaching can be done over the telephone.

The coach need not have an advanced degree in mental health or any other field. Ancillary school personnel can make good coaches. One of the best coaches I ever worked with was a custodian at a private school. Each morning he and my patient took out the garbage barrels and had their coaching session while they worked. The fee was the physical labor the boy put in. Both the custodian and the boy loved their routine, as did the boy's parents, who didn't object in the least to driving him to school a half hour early so he could "do the garbage," as the boy put it. He had his best year ever in school, and we all attribute his success in part to the custodian, who feels like a proud teacher.

Other good coaching candidates are family friends, former teachers, tutors (but coaching must be distinguished from tutoring), and other parents. Sometimes it can work well for two families to trade children for the purpose of coaching. In this model you become your child's friend's coach, and your child's friend's parent becomes your child's coach.

Once you find your coach, or your child's coach, it is important that the coach understand what ADD is. You might give the coach a book to read. A few visits with a professional can be very educational. The coach and coachee can go to the professional together. That way they will both hear the same description of ADD, and they can plan out their coaching routine with the professional's help. It will be useful for the coach to know the professional is available when questions or frustrations arise.

Encourage the coach to take on his or her work with gusto. The best coaching relationships teem with enthusiasm. The coach gets psyched for the job. This pumped-up attitude is infectious. Pretty soon the person getting coached is psyched, too, and the pair tackles life's issues with growing confidence. Confidence leads to success, which in turn leads to greater confidence; a positive cycle supplants the cycle of negativity so many with ADD have struggled with.

■ ■ ■

Q: Do ADD children have trouble determining what is wrong and what is right?

A: Yes, they do. But then again, so do all children, and all adults, at one time or another. Still, I would have to say that ADD children have an even harder time than most of their peers in making these moral determinations. Do not take this to mean that they are bad children, or bad people. Children (and adults) with ADD are poor self-observers. They often need to be *told* that what they are doing is inappropriate, or unacceptable, or strange, or just plain bad, because they often are unaware of that fact.

Also, the impulsivity of ADD is lightning quick, and can outrun the slower deliberations of morality. In other words, by the time your brain can tell you it's wrong to do it, you may already have taken a cookie from the cookie jar.

■ ■ ■

Q: What specific advice would you give to a student with ADD who is about to enter college?

A: The key to managing ADD in college is to set up a good plan in advance. College sets a student free—from parents, from hovering teachers, from bedtimes and schedules and all sorts of routine structures that most kids can't wait to be free of. The problem is that for the student with ADD the sudden jolt of freedom may be *too* liberating. If he is not careful, he may forget to go to college altogether.

I had one patient, a very bright young man named Hank whom I diagnosed with ADD when he was in the tenth grade. After getting diagnosed, and with some help from his parents, teachers, a good tutor, and the right medication, Hank turned around his academic career during his tenth-grade year from barely passing to maintaining a B+/A- average.

He had had to work hard to make this advance. Much of his progress depended upon the schedule he and his tutor set up. What he did not anticipate when he got to college was how much he had come to rely on his tutor, who had fit the role of what I call a coach, and how much he had relied upon the schedule his parents lived by at home. Without these supports, without someone to stay on him to go to class and get his work done, he discovered the life of the party animal.

He had a lot of fun his first year of college, but his grade point average at the end of the year was 0.00.

It is understandable that his parents were irate. However, as I told them and Hank, it was not as much Hank's failure as it was a system's failure, my failure, if a finger need be pointed, to set up an adequate treatment plan before college began.

Hank's magnificent grade-point average taught me a lesson I have never forgotten. In sending a student with ADD off to college, no matter how well he has done in high school, never underestimate the shock to his system of the total freedom college usually affords and the massive influx of high stimulation he will find—sex, drugs, and rock 'n' roll. Bear in mind that he, more than most students, will need help in staying on task.

This is not to say he should be sequestered in a locked cell or sent to a college designed like a prison farm. However, he will need help in learning how to balance the many pleasures college life serves up with the duties of scholarly pursuit college should also require.

To pull off this balancing act, one should plan in advance. Whatever plan you make—and the plans will vary according to what college your child is attending and what flavor ADD your child has—all treatment plans for college students should include the following:

1. A coach—the key. Find a person at your son's or daughter's college who can coach. A coach meets with the student three or four times a week and goes over obligations, and plans to meet those obligations, and also offers encouragement. A coach keeps abreast, so the student can never fall hopelessly behind.

2. An arrangement with the college to make whatever specific accommodations the student needs, such as untimed tests or a waiver of the foreign-language requirement. A physician's letter may be needed for this.

3. A realistic course selection. Many of us with ADD like to bite off more than we can chew. It doesn't make sense in your first semester of college to take four laboratory science courses, or five humanities courses, all of which require two forty-page papers, or three courses on the novel, each course requiring ten books to be read, averaging four hundred pages per book, so that the student must read some 12,000 pages during the semester just to satisfy the minimum requirement. (Don't think this sort of thing doesn't happen—I've had patients who have signed up for all of the above.) Encourage your child to sign up for a challenging academic load, but one that he or she can handle. It is easier to add on later, rather than frantically dropping courses that are burying you.

4. Some means of monitoring medication. If your child has been on medication while at home, make sure there is a doctor at college who will continue to prescribe it and make sure it is working and not creating untoward side effects. Above all, make sure there is a doctor around who will make sure that the medication is being taken. College students, particularly male college students, like to discontinue their medication as a means of demonstrating that they do not need it. What usually happens is some kind of unexplained academic collapse. The student tries to hide that he has stopped the medication because he doesn't want to need it. Confusion reigns.

Better to have an ongoing relationship with a physician at college who understands ADD.

All this advice can be summed up by quoting the Boy Scouts' motto: "Be prepared."

■ ■ ■

Q: Can you recommend a good, *short* book for an ADD student entering college?

A: Yes. *ADD and the College Student: A Guide for High School and College Students with Attention Deficit Disorder,* edited by Patricia O. Quinn, M.D. (Magination Press, New York, 1994). This short paperback is an excellent, up-to-date reference for students and parents alike. It gives advice on selecting colleges that are "ADD-friendly;" it summarizes what students' legal rights are; and it details what accommodations students can reasonably ask for.

■ ■ ■

Q: Should recovering alcohol-and-drug-abusing parents be concerned about treating their eight-year-old with Ritalin?

A: Yes, they should be *concerned.* Any parent should be concerned about treating their child with any medication. A parent with a history of substance abuse should be even more concerned because of the genetic chance that the child will be carrying a predisposition toward substance abuse him- or herself. But is it still OK to do it? By all means. Ritalin, in the doses we give to treat ADD, is in no way addicting. And it does not set the child up to want something "stronger." If anything, it does the opposite. By treating the child's ADD, it scratches that itch the child may be tempted to try to scratch with an illicit substance at a later age. The parent's history of substance abuse should not deny their child's getting the treatment he or she needs.

■ ■ ■

Q: I have read your book and wept for myself and for my sons who have been "blessed" with ADD. The school years are so tough! Is there an effect on personality from so much humiliation? I was shy and tongue-tied in front of people until I was forty or so years old.

A: Yes, there is a corrosive effect of ongoing humiliation on a child's psyche. The worst consequence of having undiagnosed ADD throughout one's school years is not attributable to the ADD directly, but to the indirect emotional damage that occurs. The child takes in all the bad things that are said about him and, over time, begins to believe them.

■ ■ ■

Q: I have a daughter, diagnosed with ADD, who exhibits hostility in an impulsive way. I understand from the reading I've done that this is not uncommon with the condition, but I don't understand why or how it works.

A: One way of conceptualizing ADD is as a basic failure of the inhibitory systems in the brain. The ability to behave properly in everyday life depends in part upon our ability to inhibit certain impulses, particularly hostile impulses. During the course of an average day we all have the impulse now and then to lash out at someone, either physically or verbally. Most people are able to inhibit that impulse. Their brains give them a millisecond of reflection before putting the impulse into action. If during that time to reflect the brain decides, "No, I had better not punch out this policeman who is giving me a ticket," then the average brain will inhibit the impulse to punch. However, ADD often wipes out that millisecond of time to reflect. As the policeman reaches into his hip pocket to get his pad of tickets, the ADD fist hits his nose, and what had been a quiet day in Mudville becomes a catastrophe in the life of at least one of its citizens.

So it is with your daughter. She doesn't hate you, nor is she a bad person. However, due to her ADD, she does lack, on a biological basis, the complete set of brain wirings that would enable her to inhibit her aggressive impulses more successfully. This is not altogether a bad thing. She will probably go through life not taking much guff from anyone, being quite spunky, taking chances, calling out when the king has no clothes. She will not let opportunity pass her by. On the other hand, she will have to take care not to punch too many policemen in the nose.

■ ■ ■

Q: My child shows no interest in competitive sports. I was told this is normal with ADD. Is this true?

A: No. Children with ADD tend to be quite playful and competitive. If they have been beaten down by repeated humiliations, they may shy away from competitive situations. This is not due to their ADD, but due to the humiliations they have suffered. All efforts should be directed at restoring their sense of confidence and willingness to participate and compete. Since children with ADD tend to be resilient and plucky, it should not be difficult to bring them back into the fray once the correct diagnosis has been made.

■ ■ ■

Q: Do children with ADD have a harder time with reading, writing, and spelling than a child without ADD?

A: At times yes and at times no. As much as I hate to give wishy-washy answers, that is the truest answer to this question. One of the hallmarks of ADD is variability. Indeed, I think the word "deficit" in ADD should be changed to "variability." The child's attention varies tremendously depending upon a number of factors, chief among them the degree of motivation, structure, and novelty present in any given task or activity.

Thus, if a child is reading a book he really wants to read, he may read better than any of his classmates. On the other hand, if he is reading simply because he is required to do so, his reading ability may drop to the bottom of the class.

Attention does indeed influence one's ability to read, write, and spell. During those moments when one's attention flags, these abilities diminish. During those moments when one's attention hyperfocuses, these abilities soar. Since, in ADD, attention flags at times and hyperfocuses at other times, it is fair to say that ADD sometimes improves and sometimes worsens one's ability to read, write, and spell.

■ ■ ■

Q: What is the difference between a learning disability and ADD?

A: ADD affects learning globally; it can compromise all cognitive functions. ADD turns down all the lights in the room; it can make it difficult to see anything. A learning disability, on the other hand, compromises one specific cognitive function, for example, doing math. It turns down the lighting in one part of the room, but the rest of the room remains well lit.

Another way to think of the difference between ADD and a learning disability is to think of an athlete. When the athlete is extremely tired, it is difficult for him to perform any athletic feat, from running to jumping to throwing a ball. This is like ADD. On the other hand, if he has a pulled muscle in his arm, he may not be able to throw a ball with that arm, but he may be fully able to run or jump or even throw a ball with the other arm. This is like a learning disability.

■ ■ ■

Q: Do you place a fifteen-year-old in the category of child or adult in regard to treatment and diagnosis?

A: It doesn't really matter. The diagnostic criteria and treatment modalities are basically the same in children and adults. They differ only in the context. For example, as part of the diagnostic interview, one asks a child if he has trouble sitting still in class, whereas one asks an adult if he has trouble staying put at a business meeting. Or one asks a child if he tends to blurt out answers in class without first raising his hand, whereas one asks an adult if he's prone to speak impulsively during meetings. The core symptoms one is looking for are the same. They manifest somewhat differently depending upon the context in which they occur.

■ ■ ■

Q: Can you offer advice to a parent of an ADD child who is trying to manage chaos? When is medication the answer as opposed to "discussion," "negotiation," or "compromise"?

A: I can see your frustration in the quotation marks you put around those last three terms. Don't feel alone. *Every* parent of a child with ADD has felt at some time extreme rage, frustration, or hopelessness. ADD is a syndrome that brings all parents to their knees at one time or another.

It is a mistake to think of medication, however, as an alternative to the "talking" measures you mentioned. Medication should be used in conjunction with discussion, not as an alternative to it.

■ ■ ■

Q: What are the odds of having an ADD child if one of the parents has ADD?

A: We don't really know. The genetic data, which is growing fast, suggests, according to Russell Barkley, an authority in the field, that ADD is the most inheritable of all psychiatric conditions. What that means statistically we do not know exactly. It is safe to say that the chances are greater than if neither parent had ADD and smaller than if both parents had ADD. But the inheritability pattern is not that of a straightforward Mendelian dominant or recessive gene. Other factors come into play.

The other question this question brings up is, Who cares? Does it matter what the odds are of having an ADD child? Would one choose not to have a child if it were likely that that child would have ADD? Of course, this is a personal decision, but we strongly believe that if the parents fully understood what ADD was and how it could be treated, they would decide to have the child, regardless of the odds.

■ ■ ■

Q: Before children are diagnosed with ADD and treated, is it true they have no control over their behavior?

A: No. A hallmark of ADD is inconsistency. One hour the child with ADD may be quiet and serene and the next hour be rambunctious and disruptive. The child's control waxes and wanes throughout the day.

■ ■ ■

Q: How should I explain to my child that he has ADD? Should I tell his brothers and sisters? How about my own parents? And the school?

A: The basic answer to the question of how to explain ADD to others is, *be honest.* ADD should never be a secret. Secrets imply there is something to hide, something to be ashamed of. ADD is nothing to be ashamed of, any more than wearing eyeglasses is something to be ashamed of. Siblings, grandparents, aunts, uncles, cousins, and pets smart enough to understand should all know about ADD. The key here is education. You, the parent, should learn enough about ADD to be able to explain it to your child and his siblings, to your spouse, and to your extended family.

Then you need to explain it to your child's school. You may need some help here from a professional as schools can sometimes be quite obstinate. At other times schools are remarkably knowledgeable and understanding. Obstinate or understanding, it is imperative that schools be informed of what is going on, as they need to know that the child has ADD in order to treat the condition properly. Parents sometimes are tempted to keep the ADD secret from the school, or to keep the fact that the child is on medication secret. This is a big mistake. It hamstrings the school and denies the parents full feedback. It also sends a message of mistrust to the school, should the school ever find out, and it usually does. Parents and school need to be working as a cooperative team, not as cagey adversaries.

■ ■ ■

Q: I have a son with ADD in high school and another in college. What kind of accommodations can I reasonably expect from a high school or a college?

A: I have adapted the following list of accommodations from Elizabeth Leimkuhler, an outstanding neuropsychologist in Providence, Rhode Island. These measures apply to students both in college and high school.

1. Extended time on all examinations and quizzes, including standardized testing

2. Testing in a separate room to eliminate distractions, if the student desires

3. Use of a word processor during all written assignments, including essay tests and note-taking, with spell and grammar checks

4. Use of a calculator during math tests

5. Use of a dictionary, thesaurus, or Franklin Speller during tests

6. Permission to tape classroom lectures

7. Preferential seating to enhance attention or assist taping

8. Access to notes from another student or the professor

9. Tutoring in specific course content when needed

10. Academic advising to reduce the number of courses in a semester that stress weak areas, such as heavy reading courses, foreign languages, or highly theoretical courses

11. Reduction in required number of courses per semester

12. Access to textbooks—and other literature—on tape

13. Regular conferences with professors to review progress

14. Willingness on the part of the teacher or professor to hear advice from a professional regarding student's ADD should this be deemed necessary

■ ■ ■

Q: Do you have any tips on how to deal with an impossible teacher?

A: Some of my best teachers were "impossible." The very qualities that can make a teacher seem impossible may serve your child well in the long run. These are qualities of skepticism, strong (if not rigid) beliefs, honesty to the point of bluntness, insistence upon hard work, high expectations, and a no-nonsense attitude. Put these qualities together with a disbelief that ADD exists and you have an impossible teacher.

However, take that same teacher and convince him or her that ADD is a bona fide syndrome and you will have the best teacher imaginable for your child. I have witnessed such a transformation more than a few times, often enough for me to be convinced that you *can* teach an old dog new tricks (although age knows no bias when it comes to these teachers; the young ones just out of graduate school are usually more stern and stubborn than their experienced elders).

So my main tip for dealing with an "impossible" teacher is this: Don't give up. Stay out of a struggle. Bring in reinforcements. Deluge the teacher with information, consultants, superiors, peers, whomever and whatever you can find. Do this persistently, but politely, always with an attitude of persuasion, not intimidation. Don't try to intimidate teachers; that only makes them dig in, as it does most people. Persuade, educate, converse. Don't try to do it alone.

Remember, knowledge is power. Acquire the knowledge yourself, or find someone who has it, and you will wield influence. Avoid the great mistake of getting into a struggle too soon.

Sometimes, however, the struggle seems unavoidable. As an absolutely last resort, you may feel you must fight the teacher and the school to get your child the treatment he or she needs. You may find yourself wanting the services of a lawyer, but try to resist such an adversarial process if at all possible. It usually ends up with everyone feeling bad. To stay out of this situation, negotiate until you are blue in the face and then negotiate some more. Go into the principal's office and stay there until you have a solution you both are happy with. Bring your doctor or psychologist with you, and make sure both you and your spouse are present. Bring information and knowledge. Bring a friendly but determined attitude. Don't get mad, but be assertive. Stand up for your child and what he or she needs. Persist, and leave the lawyers out of it. Sweat, get dirty, but keep at it, and you'll usually find a solution.

■ ■ ■

Q: I have weekly twenty-minute meetings with my daughter's teacher, and sometimes we talk on the phone at night, but I get the feeling she doesn't want to talk to me. What should I do?

A: I am going to say something you may not want to hear. Try to see this from the teacher's point of view. Weekly twenty-minute meetings plus the availability of after-hours phone time is a lot! It may be that you get the feeling that she doesn't want to talk to you because she doesn't! She may feel that your needs are greater than she can handle.

What you should do in this situation is examine your own feelings instead of blaming the teacher. Perhaps you are feeling panicked about your daughter and need to talk to a professional, or to the head of the school. Perhaps you are bothered by some other fear that you aren't aware of; you might be able to talk this out with your spouse. Or maybe you are carrying such a heavy burden with your daughter's ADD plus life's other demands that you simply need more support. You have been looking to the teacher, because she's there, but you might also do well to look elsewhere before you tap out the teacher.

Don't feel guilty. Almost every parent of a child with ADD needs more support than he or she gets. The question is not whether you need the support but where to find it. You can't find it all in one place. The logical sources of support include your spouse, your child's teacher, the rest of the school—such as its resource room, learning specialist, department head, or principal—your pediatrician, a counselor for your child or for you or for both, or a support group for parents of children with ADD such as those run by CH.A.D.D. (a national ADD support and education organization, the acronym standing for Children and Adults with Attention Deficit Disorder).

■ ■ ■

Q: Do you have any suggestions for parents as to how to remain supportive and calm while giving the same instructions for the umpteenth time to their children who have ADD?

A: This can be very taxing. You may feel like screaming. If you really are losing your temper, walk away. Do something else for a little while. Speak to your spouse and have him or her take over where you were.

In general, rely upon your sense of humor and also your knowledge of ADD to keep your own feelings in perspective. It is simply part of the condition that children with ADD need repetition. Don't punish your child for having ADD.

■ ■ ■

Q: Do too many activities in one week, too many stimuli, cause children with ADD to burn out? Sometimes even one program can send them into orbit, and yet they need the structured activities.

A: You can have too much stimulus and you can have too little. The trick is finding the right amount. This is like finding the right height for the flame under the soup you are cooking. Too hot and it boils over. Too little and it never cooks.

Unfortunately, there is no cookbook for the ADD child (although this book tries to be one!). Like a good chef, the parent of a child with ADD must experiment. Vary the amount of activity you give your child until you discover the right amount. This will change from day to day, even from season to season, but if you watch closely, you will be able to recognize your child's tendencies. You will be able to sense when he is about to boil over, so you will turn down the heat. You will sense when he is getting bored, so you will add more action. Such adjustments are key in a child (or adult) with ADD.

■ ■ ■

Q: What is the most common mistake parents make in dealing with their child who has ADD? What is the most harmful mistake? What is the most overlooked mistake?

A: It is of course impossible to rank these mistakes accurately, as we do not have any controlled studies to provide us with answers, but I will hazard some guesses, based upon my experience.

Most common mistake: Forgetting that the child has ADD. Actually, the most common mistake is not getting the diagnosis in the first place, but I am assuming this question refers to cases where the ADD has already been diagnosed. In those cases the most common mistake is forgetting the child has ADD. It is also the most common mistake made by classroom teachers. Parents and teachers can spend an hour or two putting together a comprehensive treatment plan for the ADD child and then go home or return to the classroom and start making demands on the child as if he did not have ADD at all.

Once the diagnosis has been made, it is important to *remember* the diagnosis.

Most harmful mistake: Disregarding the diagnosis, knowing of it but either not believing it or willfully ignoring it. "I don't care if he has ADD or XYZ," one teacher said to me. "He is going to get his homework in on time and he is going to pay attention in my classroom or he is not going to pass. It is as simple as that." It would be nice, and it would be convenient for the teacher, if it were that simple. All the teacher would have to do to teach would be to demand that his students learn.

But this is cruel folly. It is comparable to a psychiatrist insisting that all his patients get happy if they want to continue in therapy. Should I say to my patients, "Look, just cheer up. If you want to continue to come to see me, I'm afraid I'll have to insist that you be happy"? And should I say that without any regard for obstacles in their way? It is striking how many teachers—and parents—behave like this toward children with ADD. "Look," they say to these kids, "shape up. I don't care what lame excuse you've got, I expect you to pay attention and get your work done." It is a strong attitude borne out of a weak position. The weak position is one of ignorance and helplessness. The parent or teacher doesn't know how else to get results from the child, so they try force. As my uncle (who had ADD) used to say, "When all else fails, ignorant people try wielding a bigger sledgehammer."

Most overlooked mistake: Thinking that the medication can do it all. Particularly when the child gets a good response to, say, Ritalin, parents, teachers, and professionals alike tend to heave a sigh of relief and move on to the next problem. But the problem of ADD does not end with a good response to medication. There are issues that will persist through the individual's whole school career—and whole life, in all likelihood—that require ongoing attention. These include practical issues of planning and structuring one's day, emotional issues of staying motivated, and interpersonal issues of getting along with others. Medication is not the whole treatment for ADD. Never was. Never will be.

■ ■ ■

Q: As a parent, how much can I reasonably expect my child's teacher to know about ADD?

A: The safest assumption is that the teacher knows nothing. You should not expect the teacher to know anything about ADD. ADD is not yet common knowledge, nor is it knowledge that every teacher will have. Keep this in mind. Do not react with shock if you discover the teacher knows little about ADD. The teacher will feel embarrassed, and you will feel tongue-tied if you are not prepared for a situation in which the teacher knows less than you'd like.

However, you *can* expect your child's teacher to be willing to learn. Almost every teacher is willing to learn, if you approach him or her with respect and trust. You don't want to come across like some reforming zealot who is on an ADD crusade. Just provide information and work out a plan that will serve your child through the school year.

In the unlikely event that the teacher is unwilling to learn, don't get into a struggle. Simply take the matter up with the teacher's superior.

■ ■ ■

Q: What if the teacher has an "attitude" about ADD?

A: Many teachers do. Again, my advice is to try to work with the teacher or the school. Getting into a struggle only deepens the problem. Once the struggle begins, then constructive dialogue ceases.

So try to empathize with the teacher. Put yourself in his or her position. Over the past few years the diagnosis of ADD has started popping up all over the place. As a teacher, you don't know that much about it, but you have seen the diagnosis misapplied, and you are concerned that every child who has a behavioral problem will have a parent who ascribes that problem to ADD, instead of taking responsibility for it. You are pestered by parents with so many references to ADD that you begin to resent the diagnosis itself. You have tried to read about and attend conferences on the subject, only to come away more confused than ever. You have looked for help from your school, but you find that superiors and consultants are confused as well. You have read the piece in the *New York Times* about the private school in New York where they did a study and found learning disorders were outrageously overdiagnosed. You are beginning to think every diagnosis of ADD is a potential misdiagnosis. You wish the whole thing would just go away.

That is how many teachers—and professionals and administrators—think. It is quite understandable. We in the medical field have not done enough to clarify the diagnosis and to educate teachers and parents. It is best just to acknowledge the confusion, on both sides of the school yard, and try to learn together. Most teachers want to do right by their students. As a parent, help them by trying to understand what teachers are up against.

■ ■ ■

Q: Where can a parent get support in dealing with a child who has ADD?

A: There are a number of books, articles, and journals that deal with ADD and LD. Some of these are listed in appendix IV at the back of the book. There is also the national educational and support organization CH.A.D.D., which has local chapters all around the country; the addresses of many of these are given in appendix IV.

Other parents make a great source of both information and support. If there is not a group in your area, contact CH.A.D.D. or simply start one on your own. Not only do groups provide information to members, they offer the important intangible of emotional support. Raising children who have ADD can be harrowing at times. Without emotional support, a parent can be in crisis all the time.

Finally, be sure to consult often with professionals. Sometimes parents don't want to "bother" their doctor. As a parent myself, I understand that feeling well. But as a doctor, let me reassure you that doctors would much rather hear from their patients before disaster strikes than after.

■ ■ ■

Q: How do you tell ODD from ADD? Can one child have them both?

A: First, let's explain what all the initials mean. ODD refers to oppositional defiant disorder. This is classified in DSM-IV among the so-called "disruptive behavior disorders." It is defined as follows:

A. A pattern of negativistic, hostile, and defiant behavior lasting at least six months, during which four (or more) of the following are present:

1. often loses temper
2. often argues with adults
3. often actively defies or refuses to comply with adults' requests or rules
4. often deliberately annoys people
5. often blames others for his or her mistakes or misbehavior
6. is often touchy or easily annoyed by others
7. is often angry or resentful
8. is often spiteful or vindictive
    NOTE: Consider a criterion met only if the behavior occurs more frequently than is typically observed in individuals of comparable age and developmental level.

B. The disturbance in behavior causes clinically significant impairment in social, academic, or occupational functioning.

C. The behaviors do not occur exclusively during the course of a psychotic or mood disorder.

D. Criteria are not met for conduct disorder, and, if the individual is age eighteen or older, criteria are not met for antisocial personality disorder.

Many people upon reading that definition respond that it describes *all* children. In fact, there was a review lambasting DSM-IV in the *New York Times* not long ago, and it used the definition of ODD as exhibit "A" of the fuzzy-minded, vague, overly inclusive thinking it claimed pervaded that book. However, if you read the definition carefully, you will see there are important qualifiers that help separate ODD from most children. The behaviors must last six *months* or more, they must occur *often,* they must be *more intense than found in peers,* and they must cause *significant impairment* in functioning.

ODD is indeed quite common. But I do not think that means the definition of ODD is flawed. Rather, I think, it means what we all know: that there are a lot of children out there who need help and guidance. Estimates of the prevalence rates of ODD range from 2 percent to 16 percent of children. A comparison of the diagnostic criteria for ODD with the criteria for ADD listed in chapter 1 shows that, while there is some similarity, the two syndromes are distinct.

They may indeed coexist. When a child has both ADD and ODD, treatment is of course more difficult than if the child had either by itself.

■ ■ ■

Q: Please comment on the behavioral syndromes that oftentimes go along with ADD, such as conduct disorder.

A: Conduct disorder is an official diagnostic entity, listed in DSM-IV as the other "disruptive behavior disorder," along with ODD. Like ODD, it is quite common, prevalence rates in boys ranging from 6 percent to 16 percent and in girls from 2 percent to 9 percent. Conduct disorder is more severe than ODD. As with ODD, a child may have both the diagnosis of conduct disorder and ADD.

DSM-IV defines conduct disorder as follows:

A. A repetitive and persistent pattern of behavior in which the basic rights of others or major age-appropriate societal norms or rules are violated, as manifested by the presence of three (or more) of the following criteria in the past twelve months, with at least one criterion present in the last six months:

AGGRESSION TO PEOPLE AND ANIMALS

1. often bullies, threatens, or intimidates others
2. often initiates physical fights
3. has used a weapon that can cause serious physical harm to others (e.g., a bat, brick, broken bottle, knife, gun)
4. has been physically cruel to people
5. has been physically cruel to animals
6. has stolen while confronting a victim (e.g., mugging, purse-snatching, extortion, armed robbery)
7. has forced someone into sexual activity

DESTRUCTION OF PROPERTY

8. has deliberately engaged in fire-setting with the intention of causing serious damage
9. has deliberately destroyed others' property (other than by fire-setting)

DECEITFULNESS OR THEFT

10. has broken into someone else's house, building, or car
11. often lies to obtain goods or favors or to avoid obligations (i.e., "cons" others)
12. has stolen items of nontrivial value without confronting a victim (e.g., shoplifting, but without breaking and entering; forgery)

SERIOUS VIOLATIONS OF RULES

13. often stays out at night despite parental prohibitions, beginning before age thirteen years

14. has run away from home overnight at least twice while living in parental or parental surrogate home (or once without returning for a lengthy period)

15. is often truant from school, beginning before age thirteen years

B. The disturbance in behavior causes clinically significant impairment in social, academic, or occupational functioning.

C. If the individual is eighteen years or older, criteria are not met for antisocial personality disorder.

If a child meets the criteria for *both* conduct disorder and ODD, he or she is assigned the diagnosis of conduct disorder, since it is regarded as the more severe.

The main differentiating factors between ADD and both conduct disorder and oppositional defiant disorder are:

1. The symptoms of ADD usually do not by themselves violate age-appropriate societal norms.

2. The symptoms of ADD are under much less volitional control than the symptoms of ODD or conduct disorder.

3. There is a much greater pattern of variability of symptoms in ADD than there is in ODD or conduct disorder. The child with ODD or conduct disorder is usually equally disruptive from day to day, while in ADD the child is really tuned in and focused in one class and then completely tunes out in the next.

■ ■ ■

Q: What do you do when conduct disorder and ADD occur in the same child? My son has both.

A: A child with both ADD and conduct disorder usually requires intensive intervention. As a parent, you probably already know that he needs more help than you alone can provide. Do not think that it is your fault or that you are doing something wrong if you find that you're at the end of your rope most of the time.

These kids are at great risk for serious trouble later in life unless they get sufficient help now. They are the kids who later commit crimes, get into selling and using drugs, serve time in jail for felonies, and in general leave the treatment system for the legal system, and leave the family for the street.

James Satterfield in California has studied the treatment of these children who have the diagnosis of ADD plus delinquency or conduct disorder. He suggests a treatment that combines medication and psychotherapeutic interventions, what he calls multimodality treatment, or MMT.

MMT includes the full range of therapies available with children and adolescents. Knowing that one size does not fit all, Dr. Satterfield selects his therapies to fit his patients' needs.

These high-risk children, after an initial diagnostic-assessment and treatment-planning phase, all enter fifty-minute individual therapy and ninety-minute group therapy. They are also seen on a regular basis by a psychiatrist, for medication. In addition, depending upon the needs of the family and child, other modes of therapy are used, including child educational therapy, parent individual therapy, parent group therapy, parent educational therapy, and family therapy.

He also employs variations on these basic modalities. In one particularly interesting innovation, he sets up a parent-child group therapy, where the parents are paired with children other than their own. This allows the parents a certain distance on the children, and allows the children a different look at their "parents."

Through these techniques, Satterfield and his team work to increase the child's and the family's repertoire of coping skills. They learn new methods of dealing with strong feelings, methods other than tantrums or assaults.

Satterfield's methods achieve excellent results. What he advocates requires much time and expertise, but it is well worth the expense, as these children are at high risk indeed.

■ ■ ■

Q: I'm concerned that all these diagnoses for children risk labeling good-natured boys as bad. Conduct disorder, oppositional disorder, attention deficit disorder? Find me one boy who does not have any of those and I'll show you a boy who is asleep. It is just about impossible for a child not to meet the criteria for one of those "disorders" and still be alive! What do you think?

A: I think you are right that we must use extreme caution in making these diagnoses. We absolutely do not want to fall into the trap of using psychiatric diagnosis as a form of punishment or control.

An earlier question asked what would Tom Sawyer's diagnosis be today, and the question makes a good point. If we are not careful, we will pathologize much of what is special about childhood—the chance to be rambunctious, carefree, irreverent, and playful without thought of dire consequences. We do not want to sterilize childhood and we do not want to put leg irons on little boys.

How much do we all owe to childhood, to that time of life when we could spread our wings and fly, or try to? How much do we owe to the chances we were given to make mistakes, and to be forgiven, to explore unknown regions and take risks, to play jokes and maybe get punished, but not be condemned or "diagnosed"? We owe more than we know. I think we adults forget how much we owe to those years. I think we forget, just as we forget how much of our energy comes from the sun, how much of today draws energy from our youth. We all took shape in those early years. How important even the pain of that time is to us now. How fraudulent to call it a disease!

On the other hand, science has advanced since we were children, and one of the great blessings in the field of mental health is that we now know that some childhood problems that in our youth would have been ascribed to bad parenting or simply being a bad child can now be approached as treatable syndromes. This is not to pathologize Tom Sawyer. It is to treat humanely and adroitly the suffering of many parents and children.

■ ■ ■

Q: Running our family, with five children, two of whom have ADD, is totally draining. Any advice for my husband and me on how to keep *us* together?

A: ADD in children puts a big strain on any marriage. If I had one piece of advice to give you, it would be to make sure, at all costs, that you have time set aside for each other. You need two blocks of time, one for planning and one for fun. Without time set aside for planning, you will always plan on the run or in the midst of a crisis. This makes for haphazard work. Breakdowns in communication become epidemic. A set time, after the kids are in bed, for example, even just fifteen minutes, is invaluable.

Also, *make time for yourselves.* Somehow, someway, get yourselves off together for at least an hour or two a week just to have fun. If you cannot afford a sitter, ask a friend or a relative. You absolutely, positively must have time alone together when you can blow off steam.

■ ■ ■

Q: A friend told me I should read Russell Barkley's "Eight Principles" on managing ADD at home or in the classroom. Are you familiar with these?

A: Russell Barkley, Ph.D., Professor at the University of Massachusetts Medical School in Worcester, has contributed as much to the research on ADD as any person alive today. His "Eight Principles" are as follows:

1. Use more immediate consequences.
2. Use a greater frequency of consequences.

3. Employ more salient consequences.
4. Start incentives before punishments.
5. Strive for consistency.
6. Plan for problem situations and transitions.
7. Keep a disability perspective.
8. Practice forgiveness.

Of principle number 8, Dr. Barkley writes, "This is the most important but often the most difficult guideline to implement consistently in daily life." For a discussion of these principles by Dr. Barkley, see *The ADHD Report,* vol. 1, no. 2 (April 1993). (This report, along with other selected publications, organizations, and support groups, is referenced with instructions on how to find them in appendix IV.)

■ ■ ■

Q: My high-school–age son was diagnosed last year with ADD. Now he uses it as an excuse for mistakes, forgetting, not being organized, etc. How can we help get him over this negativity and into second gear?

A: The answer is contained in your question. Using ADD as an excuse is, as you suggest, a form of negativity. It is just another fancy way of saying, "I can't do that." For many adolescents this is first gear. ADD comes to them as if from heaven—a ready-made doctor's excuse! They can take it everywhere and produce it whenever it is needed. They can feel justified in not being able to achieve. They feel excused.

But this is only first gear. You'll do better if you do not attack it as a moral failing or a discipline issue but instead see it as a camouflage for pain. Young people do not want to feel incompetent. They do not want to have to make excuses. They may dance for joy at being given an excuse, but it is false joy. They would much rather not need to make an excuse at all. They would much rather achieve and succeed.

You, and whoever is treating your son, need to work with him to start risking failure. You need to work with him to put aside all excuses and go for success. Give him encouragement. Give him positive goals. Show him he can do it. After a while, he'll forget about excuses and start looking for ways to succeed.

■ ■ ■

Q: How do we assure that schools do not use Ritalin as a disciplinary measure?

A: Ritalin is not prescribed by a school; it is prescribed by a doctor. If you think the prescribing doctor is influenced by the school, get a second opinion. No one should take medication of any sort unless it is being used properly. Ritalin should never be used as a tool of discipline, but only as a medical treatment for ADD.

Young Children's Questions

All the questions in this section come from young children, ages four to ten. The answers are written for young children. It is intended that the answers be read to the child, or that the child read them himself or herself with an adult, so that an adult is available to answer any questions immediately.

■ ■ ■

Q: What is ADD?

A: The letters ADD stand for "attention deficit disorder." Having attention deficit disorder is like needing to wear glasses. It means you have trouble seeing life clearly. You have trouble paying attention. You may like to move around a lot, and this also makes it hard to pay attention to what is going on. Just as it can be annoying for people who wear glasses to have to put on their glasses, it can be annoying to have ADD. But there is nothing wrong with it. It doesn't mean you are stupid or dumb. Not at all. In fact, lots of really smart kids have ADD, just as lots of really smart kids wear glasses.

■ ■ ■

Q: Does ADD mean you're stupid?

A: No. Absolutely not. Lots of very smart people have ADD. The man who invented the light bulb, Thomas Edison, had ADD. He invented many other amazing things besides the light bulb. He's the greatest inventor in American history.

■ ■ ■

Q: My friend said if you have ADD, you're a retard. Is he right?

A: No, he is not right. Having ADD has nothing to do with being smart or stupid. Many very smart people have ADD. Your mom or dad may have ADD. Your teacher may have ADD. The principal of your school may have ADD. Both people who wrote this book have ADD (and one of them has dyslexia, too). Your doctor may have ADD. So may a fireman or a police officer or the person who brings the mail or an airplane pilot or an astronaut. Anyone may have ADD.

■ ■ ■

Q: I have a friend who takes Ritalin and I don't like him. If I take Ritalin, will I become just like him?

A: No. Ritalin will not change the basic way you already are. It's like if you take an aspirin, you don't necessarily become just like everyone else who has ever taken an aspirin. I'll bet, in fact, that you and the friend you don't like have both taken an aspirin at some time. The aspirin didn't turn you into someone like him, did it? Neither will the Ritalin.

■ ■ ■

Q: I don't want to take the medicine. Why do I have to?

A: I don't think you should *have* to take it. I think you and your mom and dad and your doctor should talk to each other until you reach some kind of agreement so nobody is doing anything against their will. Tell your mom the medicine will work better if you take it without being forced to.

But just because I don't think you should *have* to take the medicine doesn't mean I don't think the medicine can't help you. Lots of kids have been helped by medicine for ADD. It is very safe, and when it works, it really helps a lot.

■ ■ ■

Q: What good does the medicine do?

A: When it works, the medicine helps you pay attention better than you can now. It helps you focus better, like a pair of eyeglasses. It can make it easier for you to pay attention in school and at home. It can make reading easier. It can make homework go better. It can make school less boring. It can make it easier to get along with your brother or sister, if you have one. It can help you remember things. This is the good the medicine does when it works. If it doesn't work, you just stop taking it.

■ ■ ■

Q: Does the medicine do bad things?

A: Sometimes, but the bad things are not very bad, and they go away as soon as you stop taking the medicine.

Sometimes the medicine takes away your appetite, so you have to be careful to eat plenty. Sometimes the medicine makes it hard to sleep, so you have to be sure not to take it too close to bedtime. Sometimes the medicine just makes you feel funny. If that happens, you simply stop taking it, and the funny feeling goes away.

Once in a great while (that means almost never), the medicine slows down your growth. This scares many kids. But they do not need to be scared. If the medicine slows your growth, you just stop taking the medicine and you grow as big as you would have grown if you'd never taken the medicine.

Most of the time the medicine does not do anything bad, and it does a lot that is good.

■ ■ ■

Q: Will taking the medicine mean I'm crazy?

A: No, not at all. No more than taking an aspirin for a headache means you're crazy.

■ ■ ■

Q: My friend says I should be able to do OK on my own without taking medicine and if I take medicine it means I'm a wimp. Is he right?

A: No. He is not right. I'll bet he's had shots to keep him from getting serious illnesses. Does that mean he's a wimp to have had those shots? Of course not. And I'll bet if your friend had blurry vision he'd wear glasses. That wouldn't mean he was a wimp, just that he needed glasses. And it does not mean you are a wimp to get treatment for your ADD, anymore than wearing glasses means you're a wimp or taking vitamins means you're a wimp.

■ ■ ■

Q: If I take the medicine, how long do I have to take it?

A: We don't know. What your doctor will do is tell you to stop taking it once or twice a year to see if you still need it. Sometimes kids take it for years. Sometimes just for months. The only way to find out is to stop it now and then and see if you still need it.

■ ■ ■

Q: I just found out I have ADD. How can I keep this secret from my brother?

A: It is a hard secret to keep. If you really want to, you probably can, with your parents' help, but it will take a lot of work. Instead, why don't you and your mom and dad figure out a way for you to tell your brother. I understand the problem is to figure out a way to tell him so he won't tease you and use it against you and make you feel dumb. But I'll bet your parents can help you with this. Life will be a lot easier if your brother knows. Believe it or not, he might even help you out.

■ ■ ■

Q: I heard ADD means you're weird. Is that right?

A: No. That is not right. ADD does not mean you are weird any more than needing to wear glasses means you are weird.

Also, I'd be careful of that word "weird." Lots of really nice people get called "weird" just because they are a little different from somebody else who doesn't like them. Being called "weird" really hurts their feelings. Nobody likes being called "weird," so why hurt people's feelings?

■ ■ ■

Q: Is it true that if you have ADD you can think faster than other people?

A: Sometimes. And sometimes you think slower. It probably evens out in the long run. But it's true that sometimes people with ADD think *really* fast. So fast they lose track of their own thoughts. It's sort of like watching a train go by so fast that you can't see the individual cars, just a blur.

■ ■ ■

Q: Sometimes I want to take the medicine, and sometimes I don't. Is that OK?

A: It is usually better to take the medicine regularly than once in a while. If you find you want to take it sometimes, but don't others, why don't you talk to your parents or your doctor about it? Maybe you have some questions that need to be answered about the medicine. Or maybe the dose is wrong or the time you take it is wrong.

■ ■ ■

Q: Is there anything bad the medicine will do to me that they don't know about now?

A: The answer is almost a definite no.

Ritalin, which is the main medicine we use to treat ADD, has been around for a long time. We have found it to be very safe. Can I tell you absolutely, 100 percent for sure, without a doubt, that there is no problem? No, I can't. But pretty close.

■ ■ ■

Q: Why does the school nurse have to give me my medication instead of me taking it myself in school?

A: Because that is the school rule. Why is that the school rule? So you'll remember to take the pill. So the school will know you took it, in case you forget whether you did or not. So you won't lose it and some other kid pick it up and take it. So if you get sick the nurse will know what medicine you're taking. These are all good reasons.

■ ■ ■

Q: Will the medicine make me smarter?

A: No. But it might make you get better grades because you might be able to pay attention better and do homework better. But the medicine won't make you any smarter, just better able to use the brain you've got.

Adolescents' Questions

The questions in this section are from adolescents, ages eleven to eighteen. The answers are written for individuals in that age range. The answers are meant to be read with an adult or some professional available for comment.

■ ■ ■

Q: What is ADD?

A: ADD stands for "attention deficit disorder." It is a neurological syndrome characterized by distractibility, impulsivity, and restlessness. "Neurological" means having to do with the brain and nervous system. ADD is a label for how the brain and nervous system of people with ADD works. People with ADD tend to think quickly and creatively. They are usually smart, intuitive, and full of new ideas and plans. They like to try out new things and they like to have fun. Sometimes they procrastinate, have trouble staying on task, completing projects, or following through on ideas. Sometimes they are hot-tempered, tactless, or loud. Sometimes they underachieve in school or unintentionally disrupt social occasions. All these problems relate to their brain having trouble focusing attention and regulating impulses. The problems do *not* relate to their being lazy, stubborn, stupid, or subversive. In other words, ADD is not their fault; it is just how their brains are wired. Furthermore, there is nothing wrong with having ADD. A lot of great people in history have had ADD, like Benjamin Franklin and Thomas Edison, and many highly successful adults have ADD.

For a young person to have the best chances of success in dealing with ADD, the trick is to get the diagnosis and treatment as soon as possible. It is never too late to treat ADD, however. And with treatment the negative aspects of ADD can usually be contained. This allows the many positive aspects to really flourish. There is no limit to the amount of success an individual with ADD can achieve.

■ ■ ■

Q: How can I believe this diagnosis is real and not just another way to try to get me to do what my parents want?

A: Look at the scientific evidence. Satisfy yourself. Question your doctor as to how you were diagnosed. Pin him or her down aggressively. Say that you are worried this is all a put-up job. The only way the treatment will ever work is for you to get behind it, and you will never get behind it if you think you are being duped.

■ ■ ■

Q: I don't like having to rely on a drug to do my homework. It just doesn't seem right. Either I can do the work, or I can't. But to take a pill for it? It almost seems like cheating.

A: Does wearing eyeglasses seem like cheating? There's really no difference except that in one case you swallow a pill and in the other you wear eyeglasses. Does taking a vitamin seem like cheating? All a vitamin does is replace a chemical that is missing or deficient; that's exactly what the medication for ADD does.

■ ■ ■

Q: Some days I take the medicine and feel fine about it. Other days I just want to do it on my own. Problem is, that's when I screw up. Any advice?

A: Keep taking the medicine as long as it works. Talk with your doctor and your parents about these feelings you have of wanting to do it on your own, but don't stop the medicine because of them.

Don't feel alone. Most young people feel as you do, especially young men. It becomes an issue of self-reliance. What you have to understand is that *you* are still doing the work, not the medicine.

The medicine won't read the book for you or write the paper, anymore than another person's eyeglasses will. The medicine simply makes it possible for you to read the book or write the paper as well as you can. It evens the playing field.

■ ■ ■

Q: How do you know the medicine isn't dangerous?

A: Because medical research has given us much information about it, if you're referring to Ritalin, which is the most common medicine used to treat ADD. But don't just take my word for it. Ritalin has been studied by hundreds of scientists over decades. It is one of the most thoroughly studied medications we use. What side effects there are—agitation, appetite suppression, sleep loss—are easily controlled most of the time. The most annoying side effect is that Ritalin wears off in a few hours, and so you have to remember to take another. Of ominous side effects, growth suppression is probably the worst, and this is reversible by stopping the medicine. It is also very rare. On the whole, Ritalin is an extremely safe, well-investigated medication. Of course, it, like all prescription drugs, should be used only under a doctor's supervision.

■ ■ ■

Q: Does the medicine interfere with sex?

A: Stimulant medication can make getting an erection more difficult. For females, there is no interference. If you plan to have sex, you may plan not to take your medication that evening. The other medications used may, but usually do not, interfere with sexual function. If you have any problem in this sensitive domain, be sure to talk it over with your doctor. If you feel too embarrassed to bring it up, perhaps one of your parents could broach the subject with your doctor for you. Above all, do not rely on rumor and hearsay. There is a lot of damaging misinformation out there about what these medications can do to you. The misinformation I have heard would almost be funny if it weren't that some kids believe it. So, get professional, informed advice, then make up your own mind.

■ ■ ■

Q: Should I tell my friends I have ADD or keep it a secret?

A: That is entirely up to you. It is your business. However, my advice is to be open about it if you can. There is nothing to be ashamed of. I myself have announced on national television that I have ADD, and no one has given me a hard time about it.

Believe it or not, the biggest barrier is your own feelings, not other people's. Once *you* feel OK about having ADD (or any sort of learning disorder), you will find it much easier to tell others. So what's the big deal? So you have ADD? So what? So did Thomas Edison and Benjamin Franklin. So does Dustin Hoffman. John Irving has various severe learning disabilities. Not bad company. There is nothing to be ashamed of. Keeping it secret only perpetuates a feeling of shame within yourself.

■ ■ ■

Q: Any advice on how to deal with the fact that I feel like a reject because I have ADD?

A: Remember the good side of ADD. Keep in mind the pluses. High energy, creativity, warmth, openness, spontaneity, intuitiveness, resilience, persistence, and a good sense of humor are some of the positive qualities often associated with ADD. Keep those in mind, because you need them.

The biggest negative that goes with ADD is not the ADD itself but the negative thoughts that churn up in the wake of it. The ADD symptoms themselves—distractibility, impulsivity, restlessness, and so on—can be dealt with. But negative thinking defeats you. Sometimes you probably get into a mood when you think one bad thought after another about yourself. You sit there hammering away at yourself, for minutes and hours, until you practically have to be pulled up off the floor, you feel so bad.

Don't do this. The moment you feel one of those moods coming on, take action. Go for a run. Call a friend. Do something to get you out of the negative cycle before it gets you into its clutches and you can't escape.

It's good if you have a coach, too. Someone you can talk to. Someone who can help pull you out of the bad thoughts and get you back on track. It is hard to do this alone. A coach or a therapist or a friend can really help.

■ ■ ■

Q: How long am I going to have ADD? (I'm sixteen now, and I've had ADD since I was in the first grade.)

A: You'll probably have it for the rest of your life, if you have it now. Kids who are going to grow out of it do so before they reach your age, usually. But that is not such a bad thing. Sure, you may need to take medication indefinitely, but once you get used to that, it's OK. And many kids learn certain techniques or tricks while on the medication that carry over to when they're not taking it. If this is the case for you, then you'll be able to stop taking the medication.

The nonmedication approaches to treatment last longer than medication anyway. Practice these (they're outlined in chapter 7, "Making Up Your Mind"). In the course of a lifetime, ADD need not be disabling; indeed, it can be a definite benefit.

■ ■ ■

Q: Can I take the medicine just once in a while?

A: In general, it is best to take the medication regularly. On the other hand, it may be that your target symptoms appear irregularly.

If that is the case, you may need the medicine only intermittently. This is OK. There is no danger or harm in taking the medication on an intermittent basis. The reason I say it is better to take it regularly is that, for most people, the symptoms are present most of the time. Therefore, by taking the medication on a regular schedule they get maximum benefit, and they also get into a dosing routine that decreases the likelihood of their forgetting a dose.

■ ■ ■

Q: I just read *Brave New World*. In that book there's this drug everyone takes to keep them happy called *soma*. The government basically uses it to keep the people quiet. That made me nervous because I just started on Ritalin for ADD. How do I know Ritalin isn't like *soma*?

A: Just ask yourself. Does your Ritalin make you serene and happy, as *soma* does in *Brave New World*, oblivious to the problems around you? If it does, you should stop taking it right away.

I doubt, however, that you find Ritalin does that, because Ritalin is not a medicine that induces oblivious or "happy" feelings. All Ritalin should do is help you focus better. That means you can focus on problems better, as well as on pleasant topics.

■ ■ ■

Q: What is the best way to deal with my mom, who is constantly reminding me about *everything*, as if I had brain damage instead of ADD?

A: Ask her to back off. Explain to her that you think you can handle the details of everyday life on your own. Tell her you want to set it up as an experiment. If the experiment works, and you handle things successfully, then she will stay backed off. However, if you start dropping the ball, then she will have your permission to reinvolve herself.

If you would like *someone's* help with daily details, just not your mom's, then talk over with her the possibility of another person's getting involved. Tell her, "No offense, Mom. I love you, but you push my buttons when you remind me to do things, and it makes me not want to do them." I think she'll understand; she probably felt that way once about her mom as well.

■ ■ ■

Q: Ever since I got the diagnosis of ADD, I have this feeling in my gut I'll never be successful. My mom and dad tell me it doesn't matter, but they used to tell my brother it didn't matter he had zits, and I knew it did. Tell me the truth. Just how bad is ADD?

A: It all depends. How bad is it to be nearsighted? If you never get treatment for your nearsightedness, it can be really bad to be nearsighted. You could flunk out of school because of it. Same thing with ADD. If you don't know you have it, it can cripple you. But if you do know, as you do, it can actually prove to be an asset.

First of all, you have to get treatment to take care of the bad aspects of ADD—the distractibility, the impulsivity, the restlessness, the forgetfulness, the procrastination, the disorganization, and the mood problems. Once you get a handle on these, you can start benefiting from the positive—the high energy, the creativity, the openheartedness, the resilience, the willingness to work hard, and the ingenuity.

Not only can you be a success, you can be a great success. Many highly successful people have ADD. I have treated multimillionaire businesspeople, professional athletes, actors and actresses, doctors, lawyers, university professors, authors, real estate developers, racecar drivers, airline pilots, and many others.

■ ■ ■

Q: I'm really burned out from school, and I feel I need time off to recharge my batteries. I feel guilty, though, that I'm taking the easy way out. What do you think?

A: There is a difference between taking the easy way out and *finding the right way in*. If you are going nowhere in school, it may make a great deal of sense for you to take time off.

I have treated a large number of high-school and college students who came to me feeling the same way you do. Some of them wanted to leave school. I did not think it was a good idea for all of them to do so. Some of them needed a little encouragement and some redirection to get more out of school.

However, some of them really needed a break. They were lost where they were. They were not keeping up, they were getting more and more depressed, their self-esteem was plummeting, and I was worried they were at risk for more intense depression, or substance abuse, or simply a miserable educational experience.

By leaving school these young people were able to step back and regroup. I was able to set up a thorough neuropsychological evaluation for them, so that we knew exactly what we were dealing with from that standpoint. They were able to sit and talk with me for a while without the pressure of school impinging upon them, so we could begin to sort out what was going on in their emotional lives. I urged them all to get jobs, which they did. This gave them a regular daily activity that brought them both income and the satisfaction of doing work. Some of them found interesting jobs, and some of them found menial jobs, but they all reported they were happier having a job than not. I also required that they pay for a fraction of my bill, rather than letting their parents carry it all. I required they pay a sizable enough fraction that they approached our sessions seriously, wanting to get their money's worth.

Some also worked on an academic program set up through their school or college in preparation for returning. This was not pressured—just a short reading list or one session a week with a tutor—but it was enough to keep their scholastic hand in, so to speak.

Others took trips. Some were vacations, some were unstructured roaming, some were adventures, some were work-related, but all were liberating. These kids needed to stretch their wings and fly. They needed to be free for a while.

For most, the time away from school was about one academic year. Typically, they left school in October or November and returned the following September. Some planned the year off in advance, so they left from June of one year to September of the next. But most had not planned to take a year off. When they arrived in my office exhausted and burned out, as you describe, we decided then that a leave of absence made sense.

These young people returned to school in much better shape than they had left. Some had ADD; some did not. Of those that had ADD, we were able to get treatment stabilized during the year away and set up a good coaching relationship with a person at their school so the next year could be more productive.

A year away from school that is wasted makes no sense. But if the time is wisely spent, under some guidance, it makes all the sense in the world. In fact, it takes courage to leave your friends and leave the mainstream and go off on a program of your own design. It takes courage and creativity. In a subtle way you increase your visibility in your family and your community because you are doing things differently, and this always causes people to look twice. With increased visibility comes increased accountability. So this is no easy way out.

Instead, it can be the right way in. You may need a year to learn about yourself, your learning style, your emotional life, and your long-term goals. You may need some perspective on school. By leaving for a while, you may return in much better shape to make the best use of your time in school.

■ ■ ■

Q: The shrink I see makes me pay for part of my sessions even though my parents would be willing to pay the whole bill. Why does he do that?

A: I alluded to your question in my previous answer. It makes sense for you to pay as much as you can because you are the one using the services. If you pay, there is a natural human tendency to take the services more seriously, no matter what they are. If your parents pay, you can just show up and pass the time. But if you pay, you'll be more likely to go into your therapist's office with an attitude of "I want my money's worth." That's good. It makes for better therapy.

Sometimes young people don't know that there is a fee associated with therapy. I remember a twelve-year-old I was seeing eight or nine years ago. Let's call him Tommy. One day Tommy said to me, "Does it cost money for me to come here?"

"Yes, it does," I replied.

"How much?" he asked.

"Seventy-five dollars," I replied. I'll never forget his response to that.

"Wow!" Tommy said, wide-eyed. "I could buy *two* skateboards for that much money."

Tommy would be shocked to know that my fee has risen to $125 per session today. But so has the price of skateboards, so it is still probably about a two-skateboard transaction.

I urge all my patients to share Tommy's reaction. For an adult, one session amounts maybe to their monthly telephone bill or the cost of an evening out. For an adolescent, it's a dozen CD's or four rock concert tickets. For Tommy, as I'll always remember, it's two skateboards. Whatever your age, if you consider the money that is going to your therapist and then imagine where else you could spend it, that will help induce you to make as much of the sessions as you can. Particularly if you have to work to earn the money, and you then have to part with the money for something as apparently trivial as talking to a therapist, you will try very hard to make that therapist work to earn his money. That is good.

■ ■ ■

Q: I want to join the Navy Seals, but I can't continue to take Ritalin in the military. Do you think I would still have a chance of success without medication?

A: Absolutely, yes. It may be more difficult without medication, especially at first, but would you have a chance? Yes, indeed. There are many tips on the nonmedication treatment of ADD outlined in this book. See which ones seem relevant to you, then try to follow them. Work closely with someone who understands ADD before you join the Navy, so when you go in, you will be ready.

■ ■ ■

Q: Why do teachers sometimes think you're not paying attention if you ask a question about something they just finished explaining and you don't understand it?

A: Because they cannot imagine that their explanation wasn't clear. If you were paying attention, say so, then add, "I just don't understand. Would you explain it again, please?" It is important that you let the teacher know that you *want* to understand. Otherwise the teacher may assume that you don't care. This is a big trap lots of students with ADD fall into. Stay out of that trap by telling your teacher you do want to understand. Don't assume that is obvious, because sometimes it isn't.

■ ■ ■

Q: I am a high-school sophomore with ADD without hyperactivity. My history teacher doesn't believe in ADD and tells the whole class that I am fat and lazy. How can I convince him that ADD exists and that it affects my performance?

A: Maybe you can't. If this teacher is so backward that he openly insults his students, as you describe, then he may be one of those teachers you simply have to work around.

But before you do anything else, talk to him one-on-one. Give yourselves the chance to solve the problem simply and directly. You'd be amazed how many year-long struggles with a teacher could have been avoided with a direct conversation early in the year.

So ask your teacher for an appointment. Don't talk to him on the fly, between classes. Get an appointment, just the two of you. Tell him you want to work with him, not against him. Tell him you feel hurt when he calls you fat and lazy. Tell him you've been diagnosed with ADD and you'd be happy to have your parents and/or a professional meet with him to explain the diagnosis. Be open, honest, and straightforward.

If he does not respond favorably to that, then I would suggest the following. First of all, make sure someone in authority knows what this teacher is saying to you. I'm sure you do not want to "tell on" your teacher; on the other hand, the people in charge can't control this person's behavior unless they know it is going on. Perhaps your parents could intervene.

Second, try to change teachers. Again, your parents will need to help. Unless there is no other teacher available, I think you have clear grounds to change teachers.

Third, get together with your parents and a school consultant or other professional to put together a plan for dealing with this person if you are stuck with him. Your parents may need to be quite aggressive in dealing with the school. You are protected under various statutes and laws. The school knows this. Your parents need to make sure the school knows that you and your parents know this. If your teacher wants to play hardball, you and your parents need to put together a team that is ready to take on the teacher—and the school.

I learned a valuable lesson about this kind of situation when I was working with psychotically violent patients at the Massachusetts Mental Health Center in Boston. When a patient got really crazy and violent, the best way for us to intervene was to surround him with a team of large young men. If we did that, rarely did we have to rush the patient and tackle him. Rarely did anyone get hurt. The patient quieted down at the sight of a force he knew could contain him. The key was in preparation, in quickly gathering the needed resources, in this case at least four large young men.

In your case, you need to put together a team that can bring this teacher under control. For him to be denying your diagnosis and calling you fat and lazy is the teacher's equivalent of psychosis. This teacher needs to be brought under control. The school should help you and your parents do this. If the school refuses, put together a team that can contain the teacher *and* the school.

You cannot do this by yourself. Don't try. It is good for you—and other students with ADD—to be able to act as your own advocate, but you must know your limits. In an extreme situation like this, you need the help of people in authority.

Before the confrontations begin, though, try to work it out one-on-one, if you can.

.3.

Making or Breaking the Spirit of the Child

TEACHERS AND ADD

■ ■ ■

Q: Should a teacher ever diagnose ADD?

A: No. A teacher should never take responsibility for making a medical diagnosis. Sometimes parents will look to teachers to make diagnoses; when this happens, teachers should feel comfortable making a referral to a pediatrician or child psychiatrist.

However, while teachers should never be the official diagnosticians, often they can be the diagnosticians *ex officio*. Teachers can call attention to symptoms and recommend evaluations. I have consulted extensively at schools, and I have found that teachers know children better than any other professionals. Teachers live with children day in and day out. They *know* what a fifth-grader is like and they *know* what a fourth-grader is like. They usually know when to be alarmed. Teachers should trust their instincts; if they feel a child has some kind of a learning disability or ADD, they should relay this to parents right away. This is not making a diagnosis. This is doing what all teachers should do; relay their concerns about children to parents.

■ ■ ■

Q: What do you do as a teacher if a parent disregards your suggestions that a child needs an evaluation for ADD?

A: I have three solutions to this predicament: persist, persist, and persist. The first no is usually the parents' own denial borne out of guilt. The second no is usually an "ouch." The third no usually means "I want to say yes if only you can show me how." So persist. Get support. Don't give up. And give yourself and the parents time. It takes most people a while to change their minds.

Furthermore, if you get the parents' cooperation, don't expect their admiration. If you bring them news they do not want to hear, don't expect them to say thank you. All you need is for them to work with you. I once treated for three years a little boy whose mother would bring a paper cup into our once-a-month meetings to use as a spittoon. From time to time—it seemed related to how aggressive I was being—she would rumble like a cement mixer as she cleared her nose and throat and lungs of everything she could summon, and then she would spit into her cup. She had no medical condition that warranted such expectoration. No, she was sending me a clear message: I spit on you for needing you. That was fine. All I needed was her cooperation. Admiration she could save for her son. The important thing was to make the connection and get the work done. This can be very difficult. For a teacher, the most realistic goal may be just getting professional help.

■ ■ ■

Q: I have heard you talk about yourself having ADD and dyslexia. As a reading teacher, I am curious to know how your teachers handled your dyslexia.

A: I am glad you asked that question because it gives me the chance to tell you about Mrs. Eldredge.

I have dyslexia, diagnosed in the first grade. I also have attention deficit disorder, diagnosed during my fellowship in child psychiatry, after four years of Exeter, four years of Harvard (B.A. magna cum laude in English), four years of Tulane Medical School, and four years of residency in psychiatry as well as an internship in medicine.

What worked for me?

First, I should say that nothing has worked completely in that the treatment is not finished. I am not "cured," and I never will be, except, perhaps, in the way a ham is cured. I age, and with age I seem to improve in certain ways, while deteriorating in others. Every day brings its own struggles, and every day I feel the pain of being different, of missing what others get, and of getting what others miss.

But I also feel the joy of making headway.

I got my start against the odds from my first-grade teacher in Chatham, Massachusetts, then (the 1950s) a little fishing town on Cape Cod. Her name was Mrs. Eldredge, and she did more to help me overcome my learning problems than any single person.

What did she do? Most of all, she liked me. While other teachers, especially in unsophisticated towns like Chatham, might have greeted my halting attempts to read with impatience or derision, and in so doing encouraged the other students to follow suit in teasing me, Mrs. Eldredge took me under her wing—literally. She had me sit next to her during Reading, and she put her arm around me. This was no ordinary arm, as Mrs. Eldredge was, how shall I say, a *big* woman. Wherever she put her arm, that was protected territory for sure. I can see her now, wearing a dress with apples on it—she always seemed to wear white dresses with red apples, or at least that is how I remember her—supporting my shoulders with her large arm as I tried, clumsily, to sound out words.

I was a bad reader, no doubt about that. I had dyslexia. My father looked skeptically at me and told me I had a mirror in my brain that made me see some things backward. But Mrs. Eldredge didn't seem to mind, and so neither did I. Not only did I not mind, I loved reading period. Mrs. Eldredge made it fun. The other kids didn't giggle when I read, although I'm sure they wanted to, because they would have Mrs. Eldredge to answer to. And they didn't get after me for being teacher's pet, because Mrs. Eldredge had just the right technique; she knew how to help me without favoring me too much.

She had no special training, but she liked children a lot, and she liked teaching them to read. After school I imagine she got in her car and drove home and cooked fish and took no more credit for what she had done that day than anyone else in the little town.

But I would like to give her some credit now, because what she did has made all the difference to me in my life. She introduced me to the world of reading in such a way that not only did I not suffer, I played. I had fun. Reading became my favorite pastime, even though I was the worst reader in the class, if not the whole school. Mrs. Eldredge gave me the gift of reading and of words. I can think of only a few gifts I value more.

I think this is what works above all in treating the dyslexias, and ADD, and all the rest: You must give it your heart. You must take your student and put your arm around his or her shoulders and say, "Let's have some fun!" Know of the pain, know of the struggle, know of the fears of humiliation, but work right past them into the special kingdom reserved for those who take the chance of leaping beyond where they know they can land. Ruffle the hair of your students and say, "You can do it."

■ ■ ■

Q: I am a teacher. I don't like to think I ever make mistakes, but of course I do. What do you think are the most common mistakes teachers make in the classroom with children who have ADD?

A: It's brave of you to ask. But, if I may say so, typical of a teacher. I think most teachers are devoted to their work and to their students.

The worst mistake you can make is to treat a student with disrespect. This will shatter his respect for himself, his respect for you, his respect for school, and his respect for learning. It happens all too often to students with ADD.

How can this be if, as I said, most teachers are devoted to their students?

It happens because of the nature of ADD. It happens for the same reason loving parents can become abusive to their ADD child.

It happens for the same reason an adult with ADD can make people who love him hate him at times. Anyone who has ADD can be extremely difficult at times.

Because of their distractibility they can seem not to listen or not to care. Because of their impulsivity they can seem to be willfully disruptive. Because of their restlessness they can stir up a whole classroom. These symptoms obviously can perturb even the most even-tempered teacher.

But the overt expression of annoyance is not the insidious kind of disrespect I am referring to. It makes sense for a teacher to express irritation when a student behaves in an irritating fashion. What does not make sense, however, and what is most damaging is for a teacher to express annoyance when the student is not doing anything wrong, when the student is in repose, so to speak. These are the times when the covert hostility of the teacher can dart out, like a viper's tongue, if the teacher is not careful and aware.

Take, for example, this exchange between a teacher and a student with ADD I observed one day in a small private school:

STUDENT: Mr. Hinkle, may I be excused to go to the bathroom?

TEACHER: How long do you plan to be gone, Donny?

STUDENT: Well, I don't know, as long as it takes.

TEACHER: Now don't get smart with me, young man.

STUDENT: I wasn't, sir. I just want to go to the bathroom.

TEACHER: And I asked you a simple question. You are able to answer simple questions, are you not, Donny?

STUDENT: Yes, sir, I believe I am. I believe the answer I gave you was a simple answer.

TEACHER: It was a simple, *smart* answer. I would like to know if your trip to the bathroom is likely to take you into the next county before you remember where you are going and decide to return to this classroom. You do have to learn some history today before today becomes history, you know.

STUDENT: (*upset and embarrassed at the smirking reaction of the other students*): I just would like permission to go to the bathroom. I'll be back as soon as I can.

TEACHER: Very well, be gone. I'll be timing you. You have three minutes.
(Student exits hurriedly, crouched over and embarrassed.)

That is not an unrepresentative example of the kind of sarcasm that can sneak into a teacher's attitude toward a certain student, particularly a student who is a chronic problem for the teacher. We can surmise that Donny has gotten lost before, that he probably gets lost in class as well, and that this teacher feels annoyed with Donny. We all, however, would agree that public humiliation is not the most useful corrective step to take. In fact, it is the most corrosive. Shame and humiliation burn away the fabric of self-esteem like acid. Young people remember these moments for years. These moments close down open minds, sometimes forever. They build mistrust, paranoia, rage, and fear into the psychic system.

Where a teacher must be most careful is in his or her unguarded remarks. This is where the covert or unconscious hostility, scorn, and derision appear. How can a teacher, or anyone, take care with what is unguarded, with what is, by definition, carefree? The best approach to this problem is to be clear within yourself what you really do feel toward a given student. If you really do feel antipathy, then take care not to express it. Talk it over with a colleague or a supervisor. By airing these feelings away from the student, you greatly reduce the likelihood that you will unwittingly express them directly, or covertly, to the student, and you also give yourself a chance to work on these feelings. You give yourself a chance to understand what buttons the student may be pushing within you, and you give yourself a chance to recast your attitude toward the student.

It is inevitable that as a teacher you will have a student who irritates you or who gets to you in ways you don't understand. It is inevitable you will have a student you don't like or you don't respect. It does not mean you are a bad teacher if you have these feelings; it simply means you are human.

What you do with those feelings is crucial. If you ignore them or try to bury them, they will probably come out in the nasty, petty ways I have described. However, if you acknowledge them and talk about them with an appropriate colleague, you will probably be able to understand and redirect the feelings so they do not hurt the student or you.

■ ■ ■

Q: As a teacher, I am often frustrated with checklists to monitor students' behavior. Wouldn't descriptive narratives (even a few lines) help more?

A: I agree with you. In evaluating a child I would much rather read a few sentences in English than look down columns of check marks. I worry that we are all becoming slaves to checklists and forms that don't allow us to say what we really mean.

The advantages of checklists are that they save time and they are standardized. You gather the same data on every student. This gives at least the illusion of a scientific basis for decision-making.

However, what checklists cannot do is allow the teacher to say what he or she really wants to. All the "Mild/Moderate/Severe" or "Never/Rarely/Sometimes/Often/Always" boxes in the world can't say those special words that defy categorization. The checklists and boxes are necessarily too general; by design they lack specificity.

And yet what I want to know about a child, and what teachers can tell me so well, are the specifics. What does she look like? What does she enjoy? What does she hate? How does she dress? What does she do when she gets frustrated? What does she like for lunch? Are Tuesdays better than Mondays? Does she have pets? What are their names? Does she have a song in her heart?

I haven't seen a checklist yet that had a box for "song in her heart." And the names of pets, what relevance there? I don't know. But I know I want to know those names. Think about it. How much more do you know about a child if you know she has two pets, a dog named Queenie and a cat named Pickle?

My colleagues who write the checklists would laugh at me. But I would say Queenie and Pickle, the names, are of great significance. Certainly, it will help me in talking to the little girl to be able to call her pets by name. She will be impressed that I cared enough to learn the names of her pets.

And why will she be impressed? Because *she* cares about those names. Those names take the pets off the checklist— "Pets: ___Yes___No"—and place them into real life, where little girls live. That's why I want to know their names. That's why I would rather have two narrative sentences than all the checklists you can throw at me.

■ ■ ■

Q: Is it unfair to other students if ADD kids get more time on tests?

A: Is it unfair to normally sighted children if nearsighted children wear eyeglasses? All you're doing is evening the playing field. Unless you believe that remediation is cheating, then it is not unfair.

Furthermore, I think it would be fine if *all* children were allowed to take tests on an untimed basis. I can think of no pedagogically sound reason for giving timed tests to anybody. Timed tests reward a special skill—performing speedily under pressure—while not allowing students who lack this skill to demonstrate how much they know.

My teachers always told me that tests should give me the chance to show how much I knew. If that is still the case, then why not give all students as much time as they need to complete a test? If you want to have a special test to see who is fastest, then give a timed test separately. But don't make the mistake, which virtually every school now makes, of combining the two.

Don't combine the test of speed with the test of knowledge. They are not the same.

■ ■ ■

Q: Does it cost too much to provide a better environment for ADD children in school?

A: It costs too much not to. The longer the school delays dealing with ADD, the more expensive the ultimate intervention will be. In fact, it is inexpensive to equip a classroom so that it can be ADD-friendly. The main investment should be in teacher education.

Schools often shy away from setting up programs to deal with LD and ADD because they think they will cost too much. Then the schools end up spending huge amounts of money paying for students they cannot deal with to go to special schools. Many of those students whose education the school board now subsidizes could have been handled effectively in the home school if only it had been prepared.

Without pricing it out, the main expenses would be as follows:

Consultant's fee. Find someone who has been there before, who really knows schools, who has set up this kind of program in another school and seen it work. Take the time to find such a person; there are charlatans in this field just as there are in any field.

Teacher education. Your teachers will need to learn the simple, practical means of handling ADD and LD in a mainstream classroom. These methods are not disruptive to other children; in fact, they *help* other children. Everyone benefits.

Materials. You will need to invest some money in special equipment, but not much. How much depends upon what you and your consultant decide you want to use. However, the best programs are low-tech, high-personal-attention. "Tech" costs a lot more than "attention." Fortunately, or unfortunately, human warmth, skill, and energy are still relatively cheap in education. We need to use them freely, because they are the best "remedial tools" we have.

Backup resources. These are in-house programs for children who need more help than the mainstream classroom can provide. You will still need to refer some children to other schools, but not as many as before. How much backup you want to provide in-house before you make a referral is a question of school policy and philosophy as well as resources.

Continuing education. You must include money in your budget for ongoing education. This field is advancing rapidly.

Administrative costs. You should have a person in charge. That person will need secretarial and other kinds of help. These salaries should pay for themselves many times over.

I'm not a businessperson nor a school administrator, but I have seen schools in both the public and private sectors do an excellent job in setting up these kinds of programs. I have also seen, too often

I fear, schools waste vast sums of money and vaster sums of human energy running away from the problem.

■ ■ ■

Q: As a college professor, I find that not only are some students disabled, so are our schools. Are there written guidelines for minimum services for ADD and LD in high school and college?

A: The "standard of care," to borrow a term from the medical field, is constantly being redefined.

When I went to high school, the standard of care was summed up by a teacher of mine at the Phillips Exeter Academy who was asked in class one day what a learning disability was. Knowing I had dyslexia at the time, I listened up for the teacher's response, which I have never forgotten. He said, "There are two kinds of learning disabilities, one treatable, the other not. The treatable one is laziness, and the untreatable one is stupidity."

To be fair to the teacher, I'm sure he didn't know I had dyslexia. I imagine he thought no one at Exeter had any sort of learning disability. The dean at the time said the school "screened them out." You had to be smart to go to Exeter. That meant no LD. Or so they thought.

That was the standard then. My teacher was not being cruel. He was speaking what most people thought, and many people still think today, if they will admit it. There is smart and there is stupid. And there is hard work and there is slacking off. And that's pretty much all you need to know.

Well, there is more to it than that. Happily, neuroscience has given us much more understanding than we had when I was in high school some twenty-five years ago.

But a single standard for schools and colleges to follow has not been codified since it is changing so fast. We do, however, have guidelines. The Orton Dyslexia Society can provide you with guidelines, as can the Learning Disabilities Association of America, the National Center for Learning Disabilities, and the National Information Center for Children and Youth with Disabilities (see appendix IV for addresses).

In addition, certain laws protect students with LD and/or ADD. There is the Individuals with Disabilities Education Act and the Americans with Disabilities Act. Both of these provide guidelines, as well as redress if the guidelines are violated.

■ ■ ■

Q: What is "borderline ADD"? It shows up on many evaluations of my students.

A: It is a dodge. It means the evaluator doesn't want to commit to a diagnosis.

To be fair to the evaluator, many cases fall in the borderline area and are hard to call one way or the other. The evaluator finds some evidence of ADD, but not enough to make the diagnosis for sure.

Many authorities in the field would disagree with me on this point, but in my opinion, the ambiguous cases should be signed out as not having ADD. If there is doubt, then I think the diagnosis is *not* ADD. This is because you can make a case that just about everybody in the United States has ADD if you try to. I think for the diagnosis to make sense we have to rigorously exclude the "borderline" cases and reserve the diagnosis for only those people we are sure have true ADD.

■ ■ ■

Q: What percentage of children with ADD do you think can be taught in a mainstream classroom as opposed to a resource room or a special school?

A: It all depends upon the classroom teacher and the size of the class. If the teacher knows the simple techniques of managing ADD in the classroom, and if the size of the class is reasonable, then most children with ADD can be managed in a mainstream classroom.

Some children definitely cannot, however, and these children must receive special services.

■ ■ ■

Q: What techniques can a teacher use to manage children with ADD in a regular classroom?

A: The following tips on classroom management of ADD were presented in *Driven to Distraction*. They are revised, updated, and reprinted here because we have heard from many teachers that they have found them to be very helpful. These techniques will assist all students, whether they have ADD or not, but they are especially helpful for students who have ADD.

Fifty Tips on the Classroom Management of ADD

These suggestions are intended for teachers of children of all ages. Some suggestions will be obviously more appropriate for younger children, others for older, but the unifying themes of structure, education, and encouragement pertain to all. With the *persistent* and *consistent* application of the techniques contained in these tips, and with the cooperation of the rest of the school faculty, the parents, and the student, you can see frustration evolve, step-by-step, into mastery and success.

1. First of all, make sure what you are dealing with really is ADD. It is definitely not up to the teacher to diagnose ADD, but you can and should raise questions. Specifically, ask if someone has tested the child's hearing and vision recently, and ask if other medical problems have been ruled out. Keep questioning until you are convinced an adequate evaluation has been done. The responsibility for seeing to all of this is the parents', not the teacher's, but the teacher can support the process.

2. Build your support. Make sure there is a knowledgeable person with whom you can consult when you have a problem. (Learn-

ing specialist, child psychiatrist, social worker, school psychologist, pediatrician—the person's degree doesn't really matter. What matters is that he or she knows a lot about ADD, has seen lots of kids with ADD, knows his or her way around a classroom, and can speak plainly.)

3. Know your limits. Don't be afraid to ask for help. You, as a teacher, cannot be expected to be an expert on ADD. You should feel comfortable in asking for help when you feel you need it.

4. Ask the child what will help. This obvious step is almost always overlooked. We adults are usually so busy trying to figure out by ourselves what is best for these children, what we should do to or for them, that we forget to ask them what they think will help. These kids are often very intuitive. They can tell you how they can learn best if you ask them. They are often too embarrassed to volunteer the information because it can be rather eccentric. But try to sit down with the child individually and ask how he or she learns best. By far the best "expert" on how the child learns best is the child himself or herself.

5. Remember the emotional part of learning. Priscilla Vail has written a wonderful book stressing this point called *Emotion: The On/Off Switch for Learning*. These children need special help in finding enjoyment in the classroom, mastery instead of failure and frustration, excitement instead of boredom or fear.

6. Remember that ADD kids need structure. They need their environment to structure externally what they can't structure internally on their own. They need reminders. They need previews. They need repetition. They need direction. They need limits. They need structure.

7. Post rules. Have them written down and in full view. The children will be reassured by knowing what is expected of them.

8. Repeat directions. Write down directions. Speak directions. Repeat directions. People with ADD need to hear things more than once.

9. Make frequent eye contact. You can "bring back" an ADD child with eye contact. Do it often. A glance can retrieve a child from a daydream or give permission to ask a question or just give silent reassurance.

10. Seat the ADD child near your desk or wherever you are most of the time. This helps stave off the drifting away that so bedevils these children.

11. Set limits, boundaries. This is containing and soothing, not punitive. Do it consistently, predictably, promptly, and plainly. *Don't* get into complicated, lawyerlike discussions of fairness. These long discussions are just a diversion.

12. Have as predictable a schedule as possible. Post it on the blackboard or the child's desk. Refer to it often. If you are going to vary it, as most interesting teachers do, give lots of warning and preparation. Transitions and unannounced changes are very difficult for these children. They become discombobulated around them. Take special care to prepare for transitions well in advance. Announce what is going to happen, then give repeat reminders as the time approaches.

13. Try to help the children make their own schedules for after school in an effort to avoid one of the snares of ADD: procrastination.

14. Eliminate or reduce frequency of timed tests. There is not great educational value to timed tests, and they definitely do not allow many children with ADD to show what they know.

15. Allow for escape-valve outlets such as leaving class for a moment. If this can be built into the rules of the classroom, it will allow the child to leave the room rather than "lose it," and in so doing begin to learn important tools of self-observation and self modulation.

16. Go for quality rather than quantity of homework. Children with ADD often need a reduced load. As long as they are learning the concepts, they should be allowed this. They will put in the same

amount of study time, just not get buried under more than they can handle.

17. Monitor progress often. Children with ADD benefit greatly from frequent feedback. It helps keep them on track, lets them know what is expected of them and if they are meeting their goals, and can be very encouraging.

18. Break down large tasks into small tasks. This is one of the best teaching techniques for children with ADD. Large tasks quickly overwhelm the child, and he recoils with an emotional "I'll *never* be able to do *that*" kind of response. By breaking the task down into manageable parts, each component looking small enough to be doable, the child can sidestep the emotion of being overwhelmed. In general, these kids can do a lot more than they think they can. By breaking tasks down, the teacher can let the child prove this to himself or herself. With small children this can be extremely helpful in avoiding tantrums born of anticipatory frustration. With older children it can help them avoid the defeatist attitude that so often gets in their way.

19. Let yourself be playful, have fun, be unconventional, be flamboyant. People with ADD love play. They respond to it with enthusiasm. It helps focus attention—the kids' attention and yours as well. These children are full of life—they love adventure. And above all they hate being bored. So much of their "treatment" involves boring-sounding stuff like structure, schedules, lists, and rules, that you want to show them that those things do not have to go hand in hand with being a boring person, a boring teacher, or running a boring classroom.

Every once in a while, if you can let yourself be a little bit silly, that will help a lot.

20. Still again, watch out for overstimulation. Like a pot on the fire, ADD can boil over. You need to be able to reduce the heat in a hurry. Use techniques like falling silent yourself, or sitting down, or putting your fingers to your lips to say "Hush," or even turning down the lights to reduce the stimulation in the classroom. There is always a fire underneath the pot of the classroom. You, as the

teacher, need to be expert at regulating the intensity of that flame. Turn it up when the class is flat. Turn it down when the class is bubbling over.

21. Seek out and underscore success as much as possible. These kids live with so much failure, they need all the positive handling they can get. This point cannot be overemphasized: these children need and benefit from praise. They love encouragement. They drink it up and grow from it. And without it, they shrink and wither. Often the most devastating aspect of ADD is not the ADD itself, but the secondary damage done to self-esteem. So water these children well with encouragement and praise.

22. Memory is often a problem with these kids. Teach them little tricks like mnemonics, flashcards, etc. They often have problems with what Dr. Mel Levine, a developmental pediatrician and one of the great figures in the field of learning problems, calls "active working memory," the space available on your mind's worktable, so to speak. Any little tricks you can devise—cues, rhymes, codes, and the like—can help a great deal to enhance memory.

23. Use outlines. Teach outlining. Teach underlining. These techniques do not come easily to children with ADD, but once they learn them, the techniques can help a great deal in that they structure and shape what is being learned as it is being learned. This helps give the child a sense of mastery *during the learning process,* when he or she needs it most, rather than the dim sense of futility that is so often the defining emotion of these kids' learning.

24. Announce what you are going to say before you say it. Say it. Then repeat what you have said. Since many ADD children learn better visually than by voice, if you can write what you're going to say as well as say it, that can be most helpful. This kind of structuring glues the ideas in place.

25. Simplify instructions. Simplify choices. Simplify scheduling. The simpler the verbiage, the more likely it will be comprehended. And use colorful language. Like color coding, colorful language keeps attention.

26. Use feedback that helps the child become self-observant. Children with ADD tend to be poor self-observers. They often have no idea how they come across or how they have been behaving. Try to give them this information in a constructive way. Ask questions like, "Do you know what you just did?" or "How do you think you might have said that differently?" or "Why do you think that other girl looked sad when you said what you said?" Ask questions that promote self-observation.

27. Make expectations explicit.

28. A point system can help as part of behavioral modification or a reward system for younger children. Children with ADD respond well to incentives. Many are born entrepreneurs.

29. If the child has trouble reading social cues—body language, tone of voice, timing, and the like—try discreetly to offer specific and explicit advice as social coaching. For example, say "Before you tell your story, ask to hear the other person's first," or "Look at the other person when he's talking." Many children with ADD are viewed as indifferent or selfish, when in fact they just haven't *learned how* to interact in a way that will make others like them. This skill does not come naturally to all children, but it can be taught or coached.

30. Teach test-taking skills. The following five are particularly important for students with ADD:

    a. Show up on time for the test.
    b. *Always* read the directions first.
    c. Look over the whole test before starting on it.
    d. Budget your time (unless, obviously, the test is untimed, as it should be for students with ADD).
    e. On multiple-choice tests with a separate answer sheet, take great care to put your answer in the correct box or circle.

31. Occasionally, make a game out of learning. Use other ploys to increase motivation, particularly with dry topics like grammar or

vocabulary. Motivation and novelty tend to overcome the symptoms of ADD.

32. Separate pairs and trios of children, whole clusters even, that don't do well together. You might have to try many arrangements until you find the one that works best.

33. Pay attention to connectedness. These kids need to feel engaged, connected. As long as they are engaged, they will feel motivated and be less likely to tune out.

34. Give responsibility back to the child whenever possible. Let him devise his own method for remembering what to put into his book bag, or let him ask you for help rather than your telling him he needs it.

35. Try a home-to-school-to-home notebook. This can help with day-to-day parent-teacher communication and help avoid crisis meetings. It also gives the frequent feedback these kids need.

36. Try to use daily progress reports. These may be given to the child to hand on to his parents or, if the child is older, read directly to the child. These are not intended as disciplinary, but rather informative, and encouraging.

37. Physical devices such as timers and buzzers can help with self-monitoring. For example, if a child cannot remember when to take his or her medication, a wrist alarm can help, rather than transferring responsibility to the teacher. Or during study time, a timer placed on his desk can help the child know exactly where the time is going.

38. Prepare for unstructured time. These kids need to know in advance what is going to happen so they can get ready for it internally. If they suddenly are given unstructured time, it can be overstimulating.

39. Praise, stroke, approve, encourage, nourish.

40. With older children, suggest they write little notes to themselves to remind them of their questions.

41. Handwriting is difficult for many of these children. Consider developing alternatives, like learning how to type or taking some tests orally.

42. Be like the conductor of a symphony. Get the orchestra's attention before beginning. (You may use silence, or the tapping of your baton, to do this.) Keep the class "in time," pointing to different parts of the room as you need their help.

43. When possible, arrange for students to have a "study buddy" in each subject, with phone number (adapted from Gary Smith, who has written an excellent series of suggestions on classroom management).

44. Explain to the rest of the class any special treatment the child receives in order to normalize it and avoid stigma. It is a common mistake to think that pretending there is no problem or trying to hide the special treatment will prevent the other children from noticing it and making fun of the child. The opposite is true. Avoidance and secrecy only heighten the mystery and make the ADD child seem stranger. An honest, straightforward approach works best.

45. Meet with parents often. Avoid the pattern of meeting only when there are problems or crises.

46. Encourage reading aloud at home. Read aloud in class as much as possible. Use storytelling. Help the child build the skill of staying on one topic.

47. Repeat, repeat, repeat.

48. Encourage physical exercise. One of the best treatments for ADD, in both children and adults, is exercise, preferably vigorous

exercise. Exercise helps work off excess energy, it helps focus attention, it stimulates certain hormones and neurochemicals that are beneficial.

You may also use exercise when the child is acting up or seems overstimulated in the classroom. Instead of sending him to the principal's office, tell him to go out and run around the building a few times, not as a punishment, but as a means of letting off excess energy. (This works well at home, too.)

49. With older children, stress preparation prior to coming into class. The better idea the child has of what will be discussed on any given day, the more likely the material will be mastered in class.

50. Always be on the lookout for sparkling moments. These kids are far more talented and gifted than they often seem. They are full of creativity, play, spontaneity, and good cheer. They tend to be resilient, always bouncing back. They tend to be generous of spirit, and glad to help out. They usually have a "special something" that enhances whatever setting they're in. Remember, there is a melody inside that cacophony, a symphony yet to be written.

.4.

The Pleasures (and Pains) of Sudden Wonder

ADD IN ADULTS

■ ■ ■

The pleasures of sudden wonder are soon exhausted, and the mind
can only repose upon the stability of truth.
—*Samuel Johnson*

Q: It was a relief to find a medical explanation for my frustrations with my lack of finesse and sensitivity, my impulsive and gauche behavior. But I still feel ashamed. Is there anything positive about ADD?

A: Let me give you the words of Mary Alice King, a clinical social worker from New York, who wrote me a letter, excerpted below, after reading *Driven to Distraction:*

> I was diagnosed with ADD two years ago, and I've begun to see now how my life was impacted from day one by this disorder. I've brought what I've learned into my work, and I hope to run a group soon and do some public speaking myself.
>
> I'm *so* happy that you destigmatized the syndrome in your book!!! We [people with ADD] *do* add spice to the world! We *are* different, and vive la différence!
>
> Thanks to my ADD energy and outlook, my clinic has a beautiful garden in the entry area that used to house decrepit yews. Same with my local library—it now has 1,000

sq. ft. of gardens I initiated and designed and maintain (including a wonderful fragrance garden that has two seating areas within it). And on and on. I've transformed every institution or organization or family I've been involved with—infused vitality, generosity of spirit and hopefulness.

It's time to claim our fair share of self-esteem that was stolen from us by people who were threatened by our abilities.

Please let me know if there's anything I can do to help your efforts. I'd like to help you because it's *important* and I get jazzed just thinking about getting the word out.

Thanks again!

Mary Alice King

P.S. I chose this stamp [a Cherokee Strip Land Run 29-cent stamp] because my paternal great-grandfather was a participant in the Oklahoma Land Run—and my father was a Top Gun–type Air Force pilot—that's the ADD link.

That is one of my all-time personal favorite letters. I like it so much not only because of the spunk of this woman, this descendant of wild ADD stock, although I like that a lot. I like it also because it speaks straight to the heart of the experiences of so many people who have ADD.

She comes right out and says what many feel: "I've transformed every institution or organization or family I've been involved with—infused vitality, generosity of spirit and hopefulness." Without shame, indeed with pride, she lays claim to what she has done. Many adults with ADD can say the same as Ms. King, that they invigorate whatever environment they're in, adding humor, taking risks, being open, being willing to be wrong or foolish, giving their heart without thinking twice about being safe.

Often the person with ADD is so ashamed over some missed deadline or forgotten obligation or inappropriate remark that he takes no credit—and receives none either—for the jovial, relaxed atmosphere he's created around him. That relaxed atmosphere, which fosters creativity, humor, and productivity, is worth a ton of dotted *i*'s and crossed *t*'s, and makes up for more inappropriate remarks than Mrs. Malaprop herself could dream up.

■ ■ ■

Q: Is it more difficult for people with ADD to incorporate positive feedback or believe praise than it is for other people?

A: Yes! I do not know why this is, but I have seen it often, both in my work with individuals and with groups. The paradox is that people with ADD need and want reassurance, and yet they have great difficulty accepting praise. They seem to be more of the Groucho Marx mind-set that they wouldn't want to join any club that would have them as a member.

Part of the reason is that criticism is more stimulating than praise. In general, most people remember a critical comment from years ago but forget yesterday's praise.

Additionally, in ADD the individual has built such a wall of negativity around himself that it is almost impossible for positive remarks to find their way to his core. They strike his outer wall and glance off, like rubber-tipped arrows, barely even noticed by the inner being. Criticism, however, pierces the wall and finds its way right to the center of the self, where it joins all the other arrows sticking there. Worst of all is that the critical arrows are often shot by the individual himself.

How to put a sharp point on praise and blunt the criticism? This is one of the most important tasks in the treatment of ADD: to open your heart and mind to feeling good about yourself.

It is so difficult. We often feel more comfortable in paralytic states of self-criticism. Samuel Johnson said he could waste a whole morning lying in bed watching drops of water fall from a faucet as he heaped criticism upon himself for lying in bed. Why do we obsess upon the negative?

In its extreme form this may be obsessive-compulsive disorder, which is sometimes seen with ADD. But more often it is simply a drift of mind most people with ADD have, which is counter to the upbeat message they usually give out.

What to do about compulsive self-criticism? Psychotherapy can help. Coaching can help. Reassurance can help. Prayer can help. Physical exercise can help. Medication can help.

But above all, I think the best antidote to the negativity that can permeate the ADD mind is love. This may be the love of a person, of a family, of a job, of a place, or of a mission in life. Wherever it is, find it. Join groups where you are appreciated. Take jobs where you're wanted, and leave jobs where you aren't. Stop trying to persuade the world that you're OK. Instead, love someone who loves you back, for who you are, not someone who is always correcting you or criticizing you for how they think you ought to be.

■ ■ ■

Q: What are the similarities, if any, between codependent behavior and ADD behavior?

A: First of all, let's try to make a working definition of "codependency," since it has become an almost meaningless piece of psychobabble because of overuse.

Codependency refers to people's endorsing other people's pathologically dependent behavior by excessively taking care of them, worrying about them, rescuing them, and/or putting the other people's needs before their own. Codependent behavior is common in people in the helping professions and in adult children of alcoholic parents. It is also common, it should be noted, in good-hearted people.

The distinction between being good-hearted and being codependent rests upon the intensity, motivation, and covert destructiveness of the behavior. It might be summed up in jokes such as "Tell a codependent he has a minute to live and your life will flash before his eyes," or "Watch out for codependents when you hire them; they're always trying to squeeze a lower salary out of you."

If the "being nice" is so intense as to seem self-negating, if the motivation is fundamentally to allay one's own anxiety rather than to take care of another person, and if the caretaking is covertly destructive in that it perpetuates immature or maladaptive behavior on the part of the other person, then we may call it codependent.

ADD people are usually good-hearted, in the best sense of that phrase. They tend to be generous, tolerant, and forgiving. When they are not distracted, they are very attentive and intuitive. They usually have a "special sense" about them for other people, an unusually acute empathic meter. While this may look like codependency at times, unless it meets the criteria noted above, it is not.

Furthermore, we had better be careful of pathologizing what friendly behavior there is in this world. We have precious little of it.

■ ■ ■

Q: Please talk about driving. I have to navigate the freeway on a regular basis, and the only way I have been able to master this is by visual landmarks. "Near this building I need to be in this lane," etc. My distractibility when I drive is so significant, and my ability to process choices, read signs, and make informed decisions is *so* slowed down, that I can't think fast enough to make the appropriate turn.

A: You're not alone. People with ADD have a much higher rate of accidents than the average driver. In some ways, driving creates ADD heaven. You're moving at a high speed, listening to music or maybe a book on tape, lost in your own thoughts, being your own boss, and in control of where you're going. On the other hand, for the reasons you pointed out, driving can be ADD hell.

What to do about it? The first and most important step is to *be careful.* Know that you are at great risk in a car, and drive accordingly.

Second, use the usual treatments for ADD. Structure your trip. You are already doing this by your creative use of landmarks. However, the landmarks are rushing by you before you've had a chance to notice them. You may want to look for a landmark that comes before the key landmark, a premonitory landmark. You may want to write down your route in big block letters so you can easily refer to it as you are driving. If your car has a tape deck, you may want to dictate your directions onto a cassette and play it as you drive. Best of all, take a passenger to act as navigator along with you whenever you can. Also, make sure you are on the right dose of the right medication.

■ ■ ■

Q: How can you tell when a mistake is a result of ADD and when it is just being a normal human?

A: You can't. That is because "normal people" make the same mistakes ADD people do. What distinguishes the two groups is not the quality of the mistakes but the quantity, the frequency. In ADD life mistakes occur all the time, and they cause big problems. In non-ADD life, they occur much less frequently, and are often the source of humor rather than irritation.

■ ■ ■

Q: I was diagnosed with ADD eight months ago. I am thirty-eight. After I started on medication, I noticed signs of dyslexia. My questions are (1) Can you get dyslexia at my age? or (2) Is it because I am taking medication for ADD that my ADD symptoms are being controlled and are in the background so the dyslexic symptoms are more noticeable and brought to the fore?

A: You can't suddenly acquire dyslexia at your age. The explanation you offer is correct. It often happens that treatment for ADD unmasks other conditions, much as turning up the lights in a darkened room may reveal what had gone unnoticed.

■ ■ ■

Q: Do you find that ADD people respond to rhythm? Can hearing music with a strong beat help one become more focused, able to think better, even make one more punctual?

A: Oddly enough, the answer is yes on all counts. While music may distract most people, it will often help the person with ADD focus on a task. One theory says this is because the music engages that part of the brain that would otherwise be sending distracting signals to the part of the brain that is trying to focus.

It is not just music that can have this effect. Many people with ADD find that having a TV set on where they are working helps them focus, even though they are only barely aware the TV is on. Others find that working in a commotion helps focus, say, working in the city room of a large newspaper or working on the subway.

Perhaps the oddest example of this phenomenon I have ever encountered was a patient of mine who said he did his best thinking by walking around his office balancing a four-foot dowel rod on his right index finger. An amusing sight to imagine, but, according to my patient, a most effective focusing device.

■ ■ ■

Q: As a builder, I've noticed melancholia sets in as a job is completed. A paralysis follows this and I need a real kick in the pants to jump-start me again. Is this common in ADD?

A: Yes, extremely. As you finish a job, you lose a source of stimulation. We normally think of completing a task as a time for celebration. However, in ADD it is often a time for the blues. The task gives us not only stimulation but structure and a goal. We need these. When we do not have them, we get depressed. The time for celebration and rest can expand, if we are not careful, into months of inertia, months of lethargy and limp unhappiness. When others think we should be exulting in our successes, we are often fighting to put up a happy face to cover the emptiness we feel inside.

This is not a fear of success in the classic psychoanalytic sense. Rather it is a reaction to a loss of stimulus and structure. The best way to deal with this reaction is to see it coming, know it for what it is, give yourself a little time off to recharge your batteries, but get back to work as soon as possible after that. Often a person on the outside needs to intervene—a coach, a therapist, a friend or a spouse—to help bring you out of your doldrums.

■ ■ ■

Q: How do you cope with boredom when it drives you berserk, without getting into trouble?

A: Don't let yourself reach the point of explosion. In other words, know your brain. Recognize your own feelings and reactions. When you feel boredom setting in, and when you feel yourself bracing against it, getting tense, about to go berserk, do something to relieve the tension before you explode and do something you'll regret.

For example, if you are sitting in a lecture and you are getting bored, get up and go to the rest room rather than force yourself to stay put and risk blurting out some inappropriate remark. The same advice holds for a conversation you can't stand, a movie you can't abide, a task you hate, or a project you can't focus on. Pull away before you stay too long and get into trouble.

■ ■ ■

Q: All of my life I had learning disabilities. The first eight years of my life everybody thought it was just my hand-eye coordination. But when it came to learning classwork, I had no clue. So they tested me and said she is badly disabled in every sense. Could it be more than that?

A: This question was handed to me exactly as it appears above except that it was written in longhand. It is the kind of question that makes me glad I am writing about LD and ADD, and sad that more people don't know the field.

If you read the question carefully, there is evidence, even in the few sentences provided, that this woman is smarter than she thinks. First of all, she writes in complete, correct sentences. She progresses logically from one thought to the next and packs emotion into the short paragraph without becoming disorganized. She can spell words many people misspell, like "coordination" and "disabilities." She is able to use the hyphen in "hand-eye" appropriately. She uses clear, but not rudimentary, diction and syntax, as in ". . . she is badly disabled in every sense. Could it be more than that?" Her question can even be set to read almost like a poem:

> All of my life
> I had learning disabilities.
> The first eight years
> Everybody thought it was just
> My hand-eye coordination.
> But when it came to learning classwork
> I had no clue.
> So they tested me and said
> She is badly disabled in every sense.
> Could it be
> More than that?

My answer to your question is yes, yes, a thousand times yes. It certainly could be more than that; it could be so much better than that. You are living in misunderstanding. You are living with a misconception of who you are. You probably think you're dumb. You're not. You are smarter than you know. You are more talented than you think. I can tell you there is more to your case than meets your eye, or the eye of the people who tested you.

You are most certainly not "badly disabled in every sense." It is a crime that those words were ever applied to you. I hope, wherever you are, you and the thousands like you out there who have been misunderstood and misdiagnosed, that you go get proper assistance. Get the right diagnosis and get the right kind of help. Don't believe the people who tell you that you are less than you know yourselves to be.

It is very hard to argue with someone who has tested you and told you you aren't smart, let alone that you're badly disabled in every sense. It's amazing you have the courage even to write me a question. When we undergo psychological testing or intelligence testing, we all tend to take it as scientifically sound and indisputable.

That is because most of us do not know just how variable and unreliable the testing can be. It depends on who is doing the testing, what tests are given, what condition you are in when you take the tests, and assorted other factors as well. I can tell more from the short, one-paragraph question you wrote to me than the person who tested you could tell from the whole battery of tests you took.

Don't believe those tests. They are wrong. Listen to yourself. Go with what you know is right. All of you.

■ ■ ■

Q: How do you handle the balance between personal responsibility and a tendency to "blame the ADD"?

A: ADD is not an excuse for anything and it should never be used as one. It may be an explanation for certain behavior, but it cannot excuse any behavior. If you tell a traffic cop who stops you for speeding that you have ADD, he will still give you the speeding ticket. If you tell the IRS you have ADD, you will still have to pay your taxes. If you tell your boss you have ADD, you will still be expected to do your work. If you tell your wife you have ADD, she will still expect you to pay attention to her. The demands of everyday life do not yield to the diagnosis of ADD. It is up to the individual with ADD to adjust to the demands of everyday life.

However, you can and should use your knowledge of ADD to make your life go more smoothly. Avoid getting the speeding ticket by using your knowledge that you have a taste for high speed and deliberately drive more slowly. Stave off the IRS by using your knowledge that you procrastinate: hire a tax person to prepare your taxes every year. Talk to your boss about your ADD and work out a plan so you adapt better to your workplace. Come to an understanding with your wife so she can use hand signals or verbal cues to bring you back when you tune out or involuntarily cease paying attention. These are examples of using your knowledge of ADD not as an excuse but proactively, to prevent problems before they occur.

■ ■ ■

Q: Why does structure come so hard for ADD-ers?

A: For the same reason that running comes so hard for fish. They don't have the equipment. The ADD brain lacks the internal organization that naturally leads most people to structure their lives. People with ADD must make a conscious, deliberate effort to build structure into their lives.

■ ■ ■

Q: Is there a connection between a seizure disorder, manic-depressive illness, and ADD all in the same person? It seems like it *can't* be a coincidence.

A: There is the basic connection that all three are neurological conditions originating in the brain. Beyond that, it is tempting to speculate, but we don't really know.

■ ■ ■

Q: I get mad or annoyed extremely easily over little things. Is anger a particular problem for adults with ADD, or just for me?

A: Don't feel alone. The management of anger is a major problem for most adults with ADD.

Over the past few years I have run several long-term psychotherapy groups for adults with ADD. I keep track of the themes that repeatedly come up in those groups as a way of studying adult ADD. The management of anger ranks near the top of the list of recurring topics (along with the management of time, money, medication, intimacy, and children).

The big problem is that people with ADD get angry easily. Knowing this, they usually behave in one of two ways: either they sit on their anger too tightly and risk never expressing it—which can lead to depression—or they can't control it at all and offend people by popping off.

Eddie presents the latter problem vividly. "I don't know where it comes from. I'll be sitting at the kitchen table reading the paper, having my morning cup of coffee, and my wife will walk in and say, 'Hi, honey,' and I'll tell her to leave me alone. She'll ask what's wrong, and I'll yell at her to get out of my face, can't she see I'm reading the damn morning paper and doesn't she know by now I damn well like to do that in peace? So she'll leave hurt and angry, and we'll start the whole day off on the wrong foot. I have no idea where that reaction comes from in me. Why can't I just say 'Good morning, honey' and go back to reading my paper? Instead, I bite her head off. I do it before I have a chance to think about it. It's as if her interrupting me is a physical attack. It's like she's jabbed me in the ribs or something. I snap at her, 'Get away from me,' when all she's done is walk by me and said hello. I don't like this part of me at all."

Eddie's problem is typical. Many people with ADD, particularly men, have a problem with what I call "snap attacks." These are impulsive verbal assaults, nasty little jabs at another person, usually precipitated by an interruption or by the other person's not responding as wanted or not *immediately* understanding what is meant, as in the following example:

Martha, who has ADD, is talking to her husband, Joe, at a restaurant. "Joe, can you believe that woman?"

"Which woman, honey?"

"Marion, my secretary, the woman I told you about."

"Oh, Marion. I thought maybe you were referring to the woman who just walked past the table."

"Why, what was wrong with her?" Martha demands.

"Nothing was *wrong,* per se, I just thought she might have caught your eye."

"Why?" Martha's voice has an edge now.

"Don't get annoyed, honey. It's just not every day a woman walks by with green and purple streaks in her hair."

"Yes, it is every day, Joe, unless you haven't been alive for the past ten years. I mean, haven't you noticed, there's this new look, called *punk,* and you see it every day, unless, of course, like you, all you do is sit at home and watch TV, which even then surprises me because I would think you'd see it on TV, unless, of course, how could I forget, you fall asleep."

"Geez, Martha, what did I do?"

"I was *trying* to tell you about *Marion,* and all you can do is talk about some stupid teeny-bopper with a punk hairdo who happens to walk by."

"I just happened to notice her, that's all. I didn't mean any harm or neglect." Joe feels hurt.

"You just didn't *get it* when I wanted you to, Joe. You never do. You're *slow.*"

There's the key. Martha has a snap attack because she feels Joe is slow. Joe doesn't get it *when Martha wants him to,* so she becomes momentarily hasty. The ADD mind does not want to have to explain. It wants to plug in and connect immediately. It does not want to recapitulate events or explain what's going on. It wants the other person to know. Since this is often impossible, conflict is inevitable, and snap attacks persist.

■ ■ ■

Q: You stress the importance of developing friendships as part of the ideal treatment for ADD. And yet I have a hard time making plans to see people. I always feel that I need to have an escape route available to me. I like people, but I hate feeling trapped. Advice?

A: You could do what one of my friends does, and leave me a half dozen messages on my answering machine during the twenty-four hours preceding the time we're supposed to get together, altering plans or warning me of his possible need to alter plans. I used to find this abysmally annoying until I finally resigned myself to the idea that that is just how he is, and I can't change him. The friendship is worth the price, so I pay it. Now I chuckle as I listen to the messages I get before we get together, and I always check my answering machine just before going to meet him, hoping to arrive in the right place at the right time.

This friend of mine has ADD, but he doesn't know it. When I used to point out to him how frequently he changes plans, or warns me he might need to, he would defensively deny the tendency. He has a hard time acknowledging what you acknowledged in your question, that he hates feeling fenced in.

Since you were able to acknowledge it, you should be able to counter the tendency, while my friend cannot. When it happens, when you feel the minipanic at having a date or a meeting time, reassure yourself that you are still an independent agent, that you *could* change plans if you needed to, but you don't need to. Nor do you need to tell your friend, as mine tells me, that you might change your plans. Try to recognize what you're feeling as a form of claustrophobia and deal with it by reassuring yourself, not by tormenting your friends.

■ ■ ■

Q: I have ADD, recently diagnosed. I also have, well, a mood problem of sorts. I'm not really depressed. It's just that I have trouble taking pleasure in much of anything some of the time. It's more like boredom than depression. Although it isn't quite boredom either. I have trouble getting my interest in gear, getting my good mood started. I guess it is how coffee drinkers feel before their first cup of coffee. Have you seen people like me?

A: I have seen people like you. Your question makes me wonder if the diagnosis of ADD is sufficient in your case. You say you're not depressed, but it may be that what you're experiencing is depression without your knowing it. How can this be? If you're depressed, you know it, right? Not necessarily. Children who are depressed, for example, often do not know it. And so, too, adults with ADD. That is because adults with ADD are not skilled at recognizing their own feelings. They may be angry and not know it. They may be afraid and not know it. And they may be sad or depressed, and not know it.

■ ■ ■

Q: Is there an upper age limit to being diagnosed and treated for ADD?

A: No. In fact, the oldest patient I have diagnosed—and treated, quite successfully—was eighty-six years old when the diagnosis was made. She is now eighty-nine and doing well. Her treatment included medication, a very low dose of Norpramin (desipramine), as well as insight, coaching, and structure. She told me, "After all these years of thinking I was just a scatterbrain, it's really quite wonderful to be able to think straight."

To play devil's advocate, it might be argued that her diagnosis actually was depression, instead of ADD, since her main symptom, distractibility, may accompany depression, especially in the elderly, and she responded to desipramine, which is an antidepressant (also used to treat ADD). However, her childhood history was classic for ADD, replete with stories from school of daydreaming, forgetting everything all the time, being called "Lost Lucy," and her never having any patience at all. The symptoms of impulsivity and restlessness followed her all her adult life, so I think the diagnosis of ADD is justified by her history. But her case does point up the importance of looking into early history, even in old people.

■ ■ ■

Q: I am so addicted to shopping that I have almost bankrupted my family. I have run up over a hundred thousand dollars' debt on credit cards. My husband loves me, but our marriage is in jeopardy because of my compulsive spending. All my efforts to curtail this have failed. I have a friend who says I have many of the symptoms of ADD. Could my spending problem be related?

A: In fact, compulsive shopping, like compulsive gambling, can indeed accompany ADD. Of course, not every compulsive shopper, nor every compulsive gambler, has ADD. We do not have studies to know for sure what percentage do, but I think a fair estimate would be around 15 percent. It is important to recognize, because if the ADD is treated, there is a good chance the shopping or gambling can be controlled.

The shopper, like the gambler, is self-medicating with their activity. The gambler uses the "action" of gambling to medicate himself, while the shopper uses the thrill of perusal and purchase to medicate himself.

I have treated severe individuals like you, who came to me on the brink of financial ruin and divorce. One woman I recall brought her shopping habit under control in a most imaginative way. She didn't want to give up her credit cards completely, in case one day she really needed them. At the same time, she didn't want them to ruin her. So she took her cards and put them in a bowl of water and put the bowl in the freezer so the cards would freeze into a chunk of ice. That way she would have to wait for the ice to melt if she wanted to use the cards, and by then the impulse to shop would have passed (she didn't own a microwave).

The best way to find out if your spending is related to ADD is to get an evaluation by a psychiatrist who understands ADD. You don't want to jump to the conclusion that you have it, as there are other psychiatric diagnoses that can manifest in overspending, most notably agitated depression and bipolar, or manic-depressive, illness. However, you also do not want to overlook the possibility of ADD as a potentially treatable cause of your shopping compulsion.

■ ■ ■

Q: After being diagnosed as an adult, I have extensively educated myself about my disorder, but I am having problems educating those close to me who don't understand the complexities of the syndrome. They feel they understand—"It's just a focusing problem"—and they get angry or irritated when I try to discuss it further. I express how much more there is to learn, and they resist and say they've given enough. Is there anything I can do to get through?

A: This is a common and frustrating situation. It is frustrating for both sides. You want to be understood; the people close to you think you are making too much out of what they think is a simple diagnosis. Both sides think they are right, which is always dangerous, no matter what the topic may be.

If they won't *listen* to you, you might try giving them something to read, some articles or a book. Or give them something to *watch*. Russell Barkley has two excellent videos on ADD. Or, if they won't listen to *you*, you might try bringing in an expert, a therapist or a friend with special credentials. Failing these steps, you might try backing off for a while. Give the subject a rest. Perhaps then they will be able to take a fresh look at what you're trying to put across.

Also, try to understand their objections. Try to see it from their point of view. If you can let them know that you understand why they feel as they do, instead of leaving them feeling you think they are ignoramuses, they might be more inclined to listen to you.

Sometimes you simply have to agree to disagree. One of my best friends in all the world, the best man at my wedding, thinks that ADD is a totally bogus diagnosis, the latest excuse people use to get out of their responsibilities. Try as I might to convince him otherwise, I can't. He remains obdurate, a paragon of committed inconvincibility. The great irony is, at least in my opinion, he has one of the most flagrant cases of ADD I've ever seen. Rather than snarling at each other (which we do now and then), we chuckle at what each of us takes to be the other's folly, and leave it at that.

■ ■ ■

Q: Having ADD, I am a bottom-line person. During discussion I often get overwhelmed by the amount of detail I am forced to use trying to get my point across. What is the easiest way to get a point across without having to go into too much detail?

A: This is a common problem. Sometimes a person will avoid telling his or her spouse what kind of day he or she had so as not to have to go into any detail describing the day's events. It almost hurts, physically, to slow down and go over a series of events you have already experienced. You want to be able to give headlines and have the story automatically fill itself in. For example, you would like to recount your day as follows: "Jerry Bunyon, got pissed, found alarm receipt, little stain on cuff, idiot in elevator, saw Penny, sweet rolls in store window made me want to go back to Paris, whadya think?, incredible relief, never go near him again, phoned Alex, damn headlight, had martini with Hank, thought of you driving home and here I am!"

But human communication depends upon more details than that. For the bottom-line person, providing those details can cause pain, what one of my patients calls, "the agony of recapitulation."

Although you can't avoid the pain altogether, you can minimize it by first of all letting your spouse know you feel it, and then working together on ways of making these recapitulations less painful, even enjoyable. They should not be arduous recitations like some old-fashioned schoolboy declining his Latin verbs. What really hurts you in these conversations? Why do you get so aggravated? The answer probably relates to the mental effort it takes to recreate a scene. It takes so much work it hurts. So, don't work so hard! You don't have to get every detail right. These are not Latin verbs. Be impressionistic. Just give the gist of the story. Elaborate, fabricate, invent. Have fun! You don't have to tell the truth, the whole truth, and nothing but the truth. Your spouse is interested in more than "just the facts." Give the feelings, too. Give what you want. It's OK. Relax.

■ ■ ■

Q: My handwriting is terrible. It hasn't improved since fifth grade. I find that I can print much more legibly. Is there a connection with ADD?

A: Yes. Many people with ADD—and other learning disabilities—have illegible handwriting. They often write with a clawlike grip on the pen or pencil. Printing or using a keyboard can be good solutions.

■ ■ ■

Q: How do we educate doctors about the treatment for ADD?

A: Doctors, like the rest of us, are trying to learn. There is so much new in medicine that it is impossible for any doctor to keep up with every new development in every field. If your doctor does not know about ADD, help him or her by supplying articles, books, or other references. Doctors want to learn, too.

If you find it difficult to talk to your doctor, get a second opinion. Sometimes it is easier for another doctor to talk to your doctor, physician-to-physician. This can save time.

■ ■ ■

Q: There is a lot of emotion inside me that I want to express, but I can't seem to learn how. It is as if I'm congenitally stoic. I know men tend to be this way, but it feels different than what I think holds back most men. I was treated really badly as a child. Lots of physical abuse. It wasn't called abuse back then, but my dad beat me up pretty much every day I can remember before he left home. I have a lot of anger about that, but it never comes out, except in my dreams. I have many really violent dreams.

Recently, I was diagnosed with ADD. Treatment with Ritalin has helped me pay attention to my work. It's been pretty amazing. My boss can't believe the change. My wife is happy with the "new me" also. But I'm still upset inside. Is this part of it? What can I do?

A: What you describe may be partly due to ADD, but it is more likely secondary to what is called posttraumatic stress disorder. You were treated badly as a child. A part of you went into hiding at that time, and that part hasn't been able to come out yet. I would advise you to find a therapist experienced in dealing with adults who suffer from posttraumatic stress disorder and talk through these issues.

■ ■ ■

Q: I've heard you mention that ADD and problem gambling are sometimes linked. I've always thought of serious gambling as a backroom activity, sort of a low-life pastime I didn't need to concern myself about. Am I wrong?

A: Yes, you're wrong. Consider this from the *New York Times Magazine* of July 17, 1994:

> Gambling is now bigger than baseball, more powerful than a platoon of Schwarzeneggers, Spielbergs, Madonnas and Oprahs. More Americans went to casinos than to major league ballparks in 1993. *Ninety-two million visits!* [Italics in original] Legal gambling revenues reached $30 billion, which is more than the combined take for movies, books, recorded music and park and arcade attractions. Thirty-seven states have lotteries; 23 have sanctioned casinos. More than 60 Indian tribes have gaming compacts with 19 states. As this century turns, it's expected that virtually all Americans will live within a four-hour drive of a casino . . . *Gaming & Wagering Business* magazine, in its most recent survey, figured the aggregate illegal take for horses and sports betting books, cards and numbers to be $43 billion.

As these statistics make clear, gambling is a huge business, hardly restricted to any one group or socioeconomic class. Sadly, gambling remains tarnished with the stigma of immorality, thus leading many people who need help with their gambling to feel too ashamed to ask for it. Gambling can become a dangerous addiction, as potentially ruinous as any addiction.

It is beyond the scope of this book to probe into the psychology of the gambler, but it is worth mentioning here one of the greatest psychological works of fiction ever written. Fyodor Dostoyevsky's short novel *The Gambler* enters the mind of a gambler like no other piece of writing I know of. It is brilliantly compelling in its depiction of the rush and excitement of the "action," and of the desperation of the fall.

Pathological gamblers usually do not get treatment. If they get treatment at all, it is often too little, too late. One of the reasons for this is a general lack of knowledge about the treatment of gambling. That, coupled with the gambler's own denial, seals the fate of most pathological gamblers.

One of the treatable underlying causes of pathological gambling is ADD. Certainly, not every problem gambler has ADD. We do not have reliable statistics, but a fair estimate would be at least 15 percent of problem gamblers have undiagnosed ADD. If they could get treatment for their ADD, it would become much easier for them to quit gambling and thereby avoid the emotionally and financially disastrous consequences that befall most pathological gamblers.

.5.

Work Smarter, Not Just Harder

ADD AND WORK*

■ ■ ■

Q: What professions or jobs should someone with ADD consider and which ones should we avoid?

A: Above all, do something you like. Motivation overrides ADD, so if you're doing something you like, chances are your ADD will not get in your way too much, regardless of what job you have.

The reverse of this is also true. If you hate a job, leave it if at all possible. This advice may seem obvious, but you'd be surprised how many individuals with ADD get into jobs they hate and feel they are obliged to stay there. It is the workplace equivalent of marrying a punishing spouse and feeling that he or she is what you need and deserve. Some folks with ADD simply feel that they are morally obliged to show up every day in a job they loathe—even though they have been offered other, more appealing jobs.

As to which kinds of jobs or careers suit adults who have ADD, it depends: Some individuals with ADD need a great deal of structure in the job in order to do productive work. Others thrive in an at-

---

*Many of the answers to questions in this chapter were composed with the help of Nancy Ratey.

mosphere of independence. One type is not "better" than the other, but it's important to determine which type you are.

Those who find structure supportive should also look for the following in a job:

- *Mission.* A company, or line of work, that has a mission, something you really believe in and can get psyched about.
- *Hierarchy.* Clear lines of command and definition of duties. But it should be a hierarchy you believe in, with goals and values you embrace.
- *Supervision.* Make sure, though, that the supervisor is thoughtful and responsive to the employees' strengths and needs.

Those who find formal structures more often frustrating than enabling should seek an occupation that offers the following:

- *Independence.* Ideally, be your own boss.
- *Flexibility.* IBM is probably not the place for you.
- *Variety.* You definitely do not want to do the same thing every day.

Both types seem happiest when the job offers a significant outlet for creativity.

Many jobs and careers have these qualities, and many others can be made to have them. On the other hand, some jobs advertise as if they did, then when you get inside, you find it isn't so. Get out fast!

Good fits between a job and an adult with ADD might include the following:

- Starting your own small business
- Medicine, especially the surgical specialties and emergency-room medicine
- Cabdriver
- Computer software and programming
- Airline pilot (Don't worry, they're focused when they're flying.)
- Trial lawyer
- Physical-education teacher or athlete such as golf pro

- Politics
- Journalism
- Entertainment
- Chef (preferably at your own restaurant)
- Teacher, academic, professor

I can't compile a list of jobs that are bad for people with ADD because almost any job can be turned into one that is good for someone with ADD if the employer is flexible. However, there are a few jobs I cannot imagine a person with ADD ever liking or doing well at. Chief among them would be working at the registry of motor vehicles. No independence, no creativity, no mission, no variety, and no flexibility.

■ ■ ■

Q: Can you give me some examples of people who changed their careers or adapted their current jobs because of their ADD?

A: I can use coming to terms with my own ADD as an example. When I finished my training in 1983, I intended to stay in hospital-based, academic jobs for at least part of my day because I liked to teach and I liked the esprit and activity of a hospital.

However, as time moved on, I found the bureaucracy ever more distasteful, the paperwork ever more onerous, and the lack of independence ever more irritating. I tried changing positions within the hospital several times, but all the positions carried with them these unpleasant aspects. I loved most of the work, but the part I didn't love I was starting to hate, and I thought I should leave while I still had pleasant memories.

I decided to try to go with my strengths. I wanted to set up a work situation that would take advantage of my abilities—a modicum of creativity, an ability to use words, a knack for doing psychotherapy well, a willingness to work hard—while minimizing my weaknesses—politics, paperwork, and "procedure." I realized I would be better off on my own, if I could make it in solo private practice, which is a dying model in medicine these days.

So I took the risk of setting up my own practice, without any built-in benefits or guarantees of work or income. I also committed a fraction of my time to writing, hoping that if I worked hard at it, I could earn enough to make writing financially feasible. These were big risks. I had two small children and neither my wife nor I have money backing us up.

It was one of the best decisions I ever made. I found that I missed teaching the residents and medical students, but I made up for that by donating a little teaching time at a nearby hospital, and by giving lectures to the general public in the Boston area and around the country. I found that I liked speaking to a nonmedical audience, and the feedback I got suggested I was good at it. So I became a teacher not just of medical and academic people, but of people in all walks of life. I still find this greatly rewarding.

I also got lucky with my writing. I set aside time for it every week. This seemed a dangerously luxurious indulgence at first. But as my writing improved, I wrote more and more talks, and I began to find an audience. I was lucky enough to sell a few books, and now I spend about a quarter of my work week writing.

I'm my own boss. I'm not a part of any institutional bureaucracy. I treat patients, I write, I lecture, and I serve as a consultant for schools. I love the variety and flexibility of my work. I love the mission, the independence, and the chance to be creative each day.

The changes I made were based upon trying to use my strengths to full advantage while not putting myself in a position where my weaknesses would be overtaxed. Having ADD, I did not do well with details, with paperwork, with schedules, with "procedure," with miscellaneous memos from unnecessary bureaucrats demanding inconsequential but time-consuming work, with academic politics, with rules and regulations I couldn't make sense of, with changing administrators, and with the insecurity one finds in institutions everywhere these days. Although a part of me wanted to belong to an institution, another part of me bristled being there. So I left.

The general principle I used comes up often in the work I do with adults with ADD. "Is this job the right job for me?" they ask. And I go through with them what I went through with myself.

How can we change your job in such a way that you can spend most of your time doing what you are good at, and as little as possible of your time doing what you are not good at? I was able to change my job description without totally changing careers. Most people can do this as well.

Ask yourself, "What five things would I change about my job if I could?" Then think creatively about how to do this. With a little nerve, and a little luck, you can change more than you may think.

I had one patient who could not work in an office. The distractions there kept him constantly off task. Since he was talented, his company did not want to let him go. So they worked out an arrangement where he does almost all his work from his computer terminal at home. I had another patient who kept getting fired from jobs because he would make suggestions to his bosses that sounded like belligerent criticisms. We worked out a plan whereby he would put all his suggestions into writing. When he wrote them down, somehow he did not add the acerbic edge that always crept into his verbal remarks.

Other patients have made more drastic changes. One woman, a doctor, went from practicing pediatrics to running a school. It turned out what she was really good at was administration, and she did not like the emotional drain of a pediatric practice. She needed more support than she could find in medicine. She loves her work at her school. It happens to be a school for children with learning disabilities.

Another patient found that all that was keeping him going was the feeling that if he didn't work frantically he would drown. When he cut back, he realized he hated his work. So he quit. He got a menial job. But during those two years he went to night school, took some business courses, and now runs a successful store specializing in one of his great loves: sports memorabilia.

Another patient worked as a bookkeeper for a long time until he got up his nerve to do what he wanted to do: go into the restaurant business. In his case, what he was good at—number-crunching—bored him but was a valuable commodity. He knew it was his most marketable asset. He was able to sell this ability to someone who was doing what he himself wanted to do: own a restaurant. Now he is still number-crunching, but he is loving it because he is number-crunching as part owner of a successful new restaurant.

Other adaptations might include hiring a good secretary, finding the right schedule for your mental rhythms, explaining how you work best to your boss, cutting back on tasks that you repeatedly foul up, delegating appropriately, asking for help when you need it, or transferring to another department.

Whatever you do, try to put yourself in a position where you can work not to cover up weakness but to deal from strength.

■ ■ ■

Q: I'm the best salesman my company has ever seen. My boss can't believe all the accounts I've developed, yet she's ready to fire me because I never get my paperwork done. Should I tell her that I have ADD?

A: Yes. Your value to the company is clearly recognized by her. Once both of you address your deficits together, you will be able to develop a good plan of action. You can, for example, promise even further sales if you can get the administrative support you need. You could offer more work time in exchange.

It is often very profitable for an employer to enhance your attributes. ADD people can make stellar employees despite their deficits, since the energy, creativity, resilience, and charisma they bring to the job often overshadow their lack of patience, lack of facility with paperwork, and tendency toward procrastination.

■ ■ ■

Q: My boss and I have a good relationship, but I haven't had a raise in four years. He doesn't bother with the performance reviews anymore because nothing changes—including my performance. I usually start off every year with firm plans for improvement, yet I always lose my focus. What can I do?

A: You should consider telling your boss that you have ADD and would like his or her assistance in improving your performance. You may need to request frequent and thorough evaluations to help structure your goals and bolster your resolve.

Breaking up large tasks into small chunks can help you manage your ADD symptoms. Getting frequent and smaller changes in your work-related goals could help you maintain your focus. And more frequent communication can lead to a clearer set of expectations. You may even get genuine and heartfelt encouragement from your boss as you begin to succeed.

■ ■ ■

Q: I'm a project leader at work. I'm always coming up with brilliant solutions to new problems, and can easily grasp the overall scheme of things, but I can't seem to take the steps necessary to get things started. Is there any hope for a fifty-year-old who still hasn't lived up to his potential?

A: Yes! You've hit the snag that many ADD-ers get stuck in: they see the whole game played out in front of them and, in the thrill of it all, fail to see the significance of developing a strong lineup and getting everyone out on the field. Karl, a recovering alcoholic with ADD, described this problem aptly: "I lie to myself and say I can finish the initial tasks quickly and easily—and then I go about busying myself with everything else." Karl could see the initial steps that would be needed to make a project succeed, but trivialized them as unimportant and beneath him. He had the whole project mapped out in his head and got carried away imagining success. At one point he exclaimed, "I'd get so excited about getting it done that I immediately begin planning how to spend my bonus for doing such a great job."

When Karl did try to focus on the first concrete step he became overwhelmed by a sense of doom. As Karl described it: "I feel I am being pursued by doom. A nonspecific doom shaped by the legitimate awareness that I don't deliver. The doom causes me to run faster and faster, and sink into a familiar despair. I am a big-picture guy, so capable, and yet I don't please anyone. My confidence is eroded."

The suggestion that worked for him was to break down the project into smaller pieces and to recognize that he also could break down his feelings regarding the project into smaller pieces. This view allowed him to realize that the doom was really only related to taking the first step—a typical feeling for ADD-ers that underlies their procrastination. Isolating the sense of doom to the first step, instead of seeing it related to the whole project, made initiating the project less threatening. In addition, he was able to find a coach who helped him stay focused on the first step, thus preventing him from jumping to the end, running away, or getting lost in doom.

Interestingly enough, Karl was able to draw a parallel between this strategy and what he had learned from AA: the need to keep things simple, the need to put first things first, and the importance of getting a sponsor. He began to appreciate that the same concepts could help him manage his ADD.

■ ■ ■

Q: I always seem to work harder and longer, and take on more tasks than anyone else at work. I stay late and go in on weekends but never seem to get my work done. Now that I've started treatment, I'm getting better at prioritizing and realize I may be doing more work than I need to do. What should I do now?

A: Too often, ADD-ers act on everything; they intuit what needs to be done—and do it! Frequently this leads to overstepping boundaries in the workplace and alienating coworkers, while not doing what you were hired to do. After treatment many ADD-ers are able to actually increase their productivity and improve the quality of their work by focusing on one project at a time and seeing it all the way through. Now is a perfect time to have an open discussion with your supervisor, as she has undoubtedly noticed an improvement in your work performance. You should ask to review your job functions with her and ask to have your job defined as clearly as possible, explaining that this will help you to better understand what your primary job tasks are and to focus on them. This type of structure and clear definition of job duties will not only prevent you from falling back into old habits but should improve your relationship with your coworkers, improve job performance, and may even create some spare time for you to pursue outside interests!

■ ■ ■

Q: Help! I need advice on how to do the boring, tedious tasks that are part of my job. What can I do to motivate myself?

A: We all hate to do the tedious, boring parts of our jobs, but this resistance in some cases can cost people with LD/ADD their jobs. There are usually two factors that contribute to the difficulty in doing routine tasks: (1) if you are like the rest of us you probably have let the work pile up so far that it has become unmanageable, and (2) it doesn't excite you. However, I would suggest that you try to analyze whether there is anything else besides the two reasons mentioned above that is keeping you from the work. Ask yourself if you have a hard time doing this type of work because you can't concentrate at your desk. Is this because of outside noise and distractions? If so, ask for a partition to be placed around your desk or utilize earphones or white noise to cut down on outside noise. Chances are, if the distractions are preventing you from doing the mundane tasks, they are hindering the rest of your work, too. Or is it because these tasks involve working with graphs and numbers and you have a severe difficulty with them? In this case you may have a learning disability involving numbers. Get tested or ask for accommodations around performing these tasks, such as exchanging marginal duties with coworkers who are better at this type of work. However, if it truly is a matter of simple management and motivation, you should start to break the work down into small pieces. Put the different pieces into colored folders and work on only one folder at a time. This can help create a new "view" of the task and make it more exciting and manageable. Come in early or stay late when no one is there and it is quiet. You might also try taking the work to another space—use an empty room or office if possible. Sometimes simply changing the place or time in which you perform the tasks can create enough of a change and stimulating diversion to allow you to get the work done. Another suggestion is to stand or walk around while working—this should keep you awake and paying attention long enough to complete the work. Some people take ·the tedious tasks with them on plane or train trips when they know there will be little to do during the ride except the work they've brought along. The important thing is to schedule these tasks (put them in your appointment book) and make their completion a priority. Enlist help from others to keep you on task and to report back to on your progress. A fellow employee can function as an ad hoc coach. Just having a partner to whom you are responsible can organize and motivate you.

■ ■ ■

Q: I have a very difficult time getting along with my coworkers—mainly because they never like me! When I ask for feedback, people just tell me I'm too intense. I feel lonely and isolated. Please tell me what I can do.

A: Many ADD-ers have difficulty assessing the effect they're having on another person in any interaction. If you're having these problems at work, you probably are experiencing similar difficulties in other aspects of life—like with friends and other social relationships. Try to get a close friend or even a family member—someone you can trust to be brutally honest with you—to give you feedback on how you come across. Write a list of what you think your strengths and weaknesses are in relating to other people. Have your friend do the same, and compare the lists. You might be surprised at how some things seem to match and others not. Enlist the help of someone who seems to be very much at ease socially and ask how you might overcome your weaknesses. Improving social skills is by far the most difficult task an adult can tackle. It takes time, practice, desire, and constant self-monitoring. If possible, you might want to do some role-playing or have some one videotape you—this can provide you with instant feedback. Or have someone accompany you at work, perhaps a job coach to monitor your interactions. Joining a support group can be one of the most useful strategies to help you feel less isolated and to get ideas from others experiencing the same difficulties.

■ ■ ■

Q: My boss has recently told me that I don't make any sense when I speak during meetings and that my memos to her are incomprehensible. My boss has also told me that she has never seen anyone with as much commitment and enthusiasm as I have for my work. I do love my job and don't want to lose it, but I am confused because I thought my performance was great. Did I miss something?

A: Believe it or not, commitment and enthusiasm in today's workplace are rare commodities. *You are a valued employee!* Your boss is making a concerted effort to help you. Don't make what is a common mistake among ADD-ers: taking criticism personally. If you haven't disclosed your ADD to your boss, now might be a good time to do so. Let your boss know that the energy she values in you is one of the advantages of ADD, just as your tendency to ramble and not get to the point during meetings when you are called upon is one of the liabilities of ADD. Ask to have more frequent meetings with your boss and ask for more of the same kind of concrete feedback she gave you when she pointed out that your memos were incoherent. Take it a step further—ask for concrete suggestions to help you streamline your thoughts. For example, utilizing a simple form to help you collect your thoughts in an outline could help you stick to the main points and prevent tangents. These efforts will continue to make you an even more valued employee—one who is able to admit his weaknesses and to work on them.

■ ■ ■

Q: Does the Americans with Disabilities Act cover people who have ADD and learning disabilities? If so, what are my rights?

A: Yes, the ADA prohibits an employer from discriminating against an individual who has a physical disability, a learning disability, or any mental disability, including ADD. The ADA guarantees equal opportunity and prevents discrimination in private- and public-sector employment; places of public accommodation; state, county, and municipal services; public and private transportation services; and telecommunications services offered to the public.

In employment situations the ADA makes it unlawful for employers with fifteen or more employees to discriminate against qualified applicants and employees. "Qualified" means you have the necessary knowledge, skills, and abilities that the job requires and you are able to perform the essential functions of the job, with an accommodation if one is needed.

The ADA acknowledges that individuals with disabilities are just as capable and competent as other people if provided with the appropriate means to do their job, and requires that employers supply these means. So far, the ADA has influenced employers to be more accommodating to people with disabilities and may also prod organizational cultures to be more tolerant of people with noticeable or hidden disabilities. For more information about the ADA and your employment rights, you can contact the Equal Employment Opportunity Commission (EEOC), ADA Information, (800) 669-4000.

■ ■ ■

Q: What are work accommodations?

A: Accommodations are interventions, strategies, adjustments, modifications and/or techniques implemented in the workplace that enable a person with disabilities to perform his or her job at a level equal to others. They may include physical accommodations in the workplace, such as ramps and wheelchair access to elevators. They may include physical aids, such as braille keyboards for people who are blind or microcassette recorders for people who have auditory-processing problems. They may include the establishment of an environment that is free from distractions. In college settings they may even include providing extra time for completing exams or an extension of deadlines for papers. The specific accommodation, naturally, depends upon the disability.

In order to receive accommodations, you must ask for them. But because ADD is a hidden disability, your employer may request documentation of your disability—not only as proof that you have a disability, but to understand how to best accommodate you. Most employers don't know how to accommodate their employees with ADD and would welcome suggestions. A good starting point would be to provide your employer with some basic information about ADD and reasonable accommodations. The National Center for Law and Learning Disabilities puts out a wonderful pamphlet, *Attention Deficit in the Workplace: Employers and Employees in Progress*, which can be ordered by calling (301) 469-8308.

■ ■ ■

Q: How do I know what accommodations to ask for?

A: It depends on what kind of job you have and how your ADD affects your job performance. If you are experiencing difficulties on the job, you will need to analyze the situation and decide what hinders you at work. You should start by methodically going through a list of your job tasks, separating out essential job functions from marginal duties. For the essential tasks ask yourself: Do I have the knowledge or experience to perform this task? Am I performing this task well? Do I perform it with relative ease, or is it a real struggle for me? How much time do I spend on this task in relation to my overall job?

If your preliminary answers reveal that you are struggling and spending too much time on certain tasks you need to determine what could help you perform these tasks better, faster, and easier. This determination should lead you to effective interventions or strategies. If your analysis reveals that you are struggling with a marginal task, you might want to ask your employer to exchange this task with a fellow employee and take on more tasks that capitalize upon your strengths. For instance, Marilyn had a terrible time writing memos to the staff, one of her minor job functions. She would obsess over the construction of each simple memo and end up spending three times as long as it took on getting it right and making it understandable. She was a star at answering the phone and dealing with new customers, a duty she shared with Jim. She asked to trade by taking over all of the phone duties while Jim easily handled the memo writing. A better working environment was the result.

Many times ADD-ers realize through this job analysis process that they are in the wrong job. Even if they were given their "dream" accommodations, they still wouldn't be performing well. If this is so, it would be best for you to find another job where your strengths have a better match to your essential functions so you can excel. For more information on accommodations, you can contact the Job Accommodation Network (JAN), (800) 526-7234.

■ ■ ■

Q: I am interviewing for a new job. Should I tell my prospective employer that I have ADD?

A: It depends. Generally speaking, disclosure is done when and if an accommodation is needed. Usually, what governs the need to be accommodated is how severely your ADD affects your ability to perform your job. If an accommodation will help minimize the impact of your ADD and give you an equal opportunity at performing the job, then you should not let anything stand in the way of asking for what you need. Many ADD-ers forget they have difficulties and don't ask for accommodations until it is too late. The key here is knowing what you need and asking for it!

Disclosure is an individual choice and should be done on an individual basis. There is no law stating that because you have ADD you must tell your employer so. Many ADD-ers choose to wait until they have accepted a job offer before disclosing their ADD and asking for accommodations. In any case, you probably want to disclose only those aspects of your ADD that interfere with job performance. It is also to your advantage to offer solutions—for example, if you have difficulty concentrating at your desk because the phone is always ringing, ask to have the ringer turned off, or ask to have the phone moved to another location.

Whether you choose to disclose or not, it is imperative that you learn as much as possible about your employment rights as a person with a disability under the ADA (see resource list in appendix IV). An important thing to know is that all materials related to your disability are strictly confidential and must be kept in a file separate from your personnel file.

■ ■ ■

Q: I just started working at a company that has a drug-testing policy. I am taking Dexedrine for my ADD. Should I worry?

A: It would be best to tell your personnel office or employer that you are not taking an illegal drug but a controlled substance that is being medically prescribed for your ADD. Under the ADA, employers cannot exclude or dismiss persons rightfully using prescription drugs from their jobs. Information about the use of prescription drugs or any disability-related information obtained from such tests must be treated as a confidential medical record.

■ ■ ■

Q: Everyone at my office seems to have a social life except for me! My coworkers always have lunch together and go out after work. I never have time to join them because I'm always behind in my work. Is there something wrong with me?

A: First, I would like to stress how important it is for you to at least try to socialize occasionally with your coworkers. Socializing is part of the work culture in your office, and for you not to partake in these events may in the long run cause you more problems than being a little behind in your work. It is during these "social" times that important information and insights about the job, your co-workers, and yourself can be gained. Second, I would try to figure out why you are so behind in your work. Is it poor time management? Are you avoiding certain tasks? Is it the actual job? Are you doing too much? Should you be asking for an accommodation? In your situation possibly one of the best ways to figure out answers to some of these questions would be in a relaxed setting with a coworker.

■ ■ ■

Q: I've gotten fired from every job I've ever had. I know now that because of my ADD I am protected by the ADA in employment. Am I correct in assuming that I can't be fired anymore?

A: It is important to understand that the ADA is *not* an affirmative action legislation. In employment settings the ADA protects individuals with disabilities that are qualified for the position. The ADA is meant to give people with disabilities who have the necessary education, training and/or experience that the job requires an equal opportunity to obtain that job and not be disqualified solely by reason of their disability. You should take the opportunity that this law provides you with and ask for the accommodations that you probably have not been asking for.

■ ■ ■

Q: Sometimes after a long weekend or a vacation I become petrified thinking that I've forgotten how to do my job. What can I do to alleviate this anxiety so that I can enjoy myself more often?

A: This is common among ADD-ers. After taking breaks like long weekends or vacations it is normal for everyone to need extra time to reconnect with the work flow. However, for people with ADD the process of work reintegration requires more planning. Write yourself summary notes before you go on vacation for projects or tasks that you have left hanging or are in the middle of so you can review what was done. You can also use this technique for simple procedural things like accessing the computer files. Now that you are aware of the difficulties, planning will greatly help offset the jolt of reentry when you return.

■ ■ ■

Q: One of my coworkers who has ADD had to quit working in our office. It was simply too chaotic for her. There is little structure and little supervision and she felt lost. I also have ADD and I thrive on the job. Why should working in the same office be such a different experience for us?

A: ADD manifests itself differently in different people. That is why each individual needs to set his own goals and strategies. There is no one right job for ADD-ers; it is the match with your needs that is important. You obviously love the chaos and the challenge of setting your own directions while your colleague needs structure. Some ADD-ers need close supervision with frequent performance reviews while others resent the overly watchful eye and feel too confined. Many need to work in small spurts with segmented goals, while others do best on a mad dash from start to finish. For instance, Sarah was the head nurse of the busiest Intensive Care Unit in the city. She had ADD but had no trouble at work handling the multitude of everchanging demands on her brain. She found that taking her medicine at work was a waste and that it was best to use it when she was off-duty to help stimulate her to perform the less urgent, more mundane tasks at home.

If you are the hyperactive type you will need to walk and pace frequently if you have a desk job. Learn to build in a reward of a brisk walk to the coffee pot or a brief visit with a coworker after you've completed a boring task. Pay close attention to your need for movement, as without it you may do poorly and certainly enjoy work less. For instance, George complained that he just couldn't work in the afternoons but was a whiz in the morning. He ran three miles in the early morning before work and he burned through the morning's duties with ease and energy. After eating lunch every day with his coworkers he came back and found that he was exhausted and poorly focused despite adequate medication. We suggested a change in his routine: that he bring his lunch to work and use the time saved to walk two miles before returning for the afternoon's toils. His attitude and performance improved greatly.

If you are easily distracted by issues that may be interesting but are not relevant to your job, use visual reminders to call yourself back. James Carville's brilliant visual icon, "It's the economy stupid" serves as a wonderful, effective visual aid that kept the inevitable distractions from undermining the focus of Clinton's campaign.

Some ADD-ers work best in a team or with a partner while others need uninterrupted time and may feel bogged down by their slow-thinking, slow-moving coworkers. Still others feed off the personal contact and encouragement, using their colleagues as unappointed coaches or tacit accommodations. Others do best to work alone as they become too argumentative when offered any suggestion or observation.

The important issue is to consider what it is you need to succeed and plan it. Take a critical look at what worked or didn't work at school or at former jobs and make your plans accordingly.

.**6**.

Perchance to Dream

ADD IN WOMEN

■ ■ ■

Q: Are there differences in the way ADD affects women and men?

A: Women and men with ADD share many of the same symptoms. These include impulsivity, the inability to focus, temper problems, and subtle problems with memory and information processing.

It does seem, however, that fewer women than men suffer from ADD with hyperactivity. Women with ADD are often the daydreamers who didn't cause problems in school or at home as children, and who seem overly compliant as adults. Since they lack a history of conduct problems and restlessness, their ADD is usually not diagnosed as early as is the syndrome in males. This leads to many years of confusion, as the women can't understand why they fail to live up to other's expectations, can't seem to take charge of their lives, and generally feel as if they are being tossed around in life like a small raft in a storm.

In addition, ADD women seem to suffer from depression, shame, and guilt to a much greater degree than ADD men. Often the source of these feelings is their interpersonal relationships. Women tend to hold themselves accountable for the smooth functioning of relationships. This makes ADD women particularly vulnerable to feelings of failure, as the consistently inconsistent nature of ADD-ers' ways of relating to others often produces turmoil.

The shame and guilt generated by not being able to live up to role expectations takes a heavy toll on ADD women. The shame stems partly from their inability to be the gatekeeper in relationships, and partly from their chronic disorganization, which prevents them being the supermoms or wonder women they think they should be.

■ ■ ■

Q: Why don't girls with ADD come to the attention of schools, as boys do?

A: Many studies have confirmed what parents and clinicians suspected—ADD girls do not have as many behavioral problems as ADD boys, and usually it is behavioral problems that provoke parents or teachers to seek a diagnosis for the child. Research shows that ADD girls tend to internalize their frustrations instead of acting them out. Even if they are hyperactive, they are not as overtly hyperactive. In addition, early in their school years, ADD girls may show fewer problems with reading and math. This is significant because diagnosed learning disabilities frequently lead to the additional diagnosis of ADD.

■ ■ ■

Q: Why do girls with ADD have fewer learning difficulties than ADD boys?

A: The difference in boys' and girls' behavior and ability to learn might be due to early differences in the development of the brain. The presence in utero of testosterone in males slows the development of the left, language-side of the brain. Testosterone also slows the development of the frontal lobes, which are responsible for inhibiting our many impulses, whether they be impulses to move, to act, to speak out noisily, or to have tantrums.

In contrast, the lack of significant levels of testosterone in girls creates a more mature left hemisphere, and more robust frontal lobes. Indeed, the frontal lobes of girls are responsible for many more jobs than the frontal lobes of males. Speech, visual guidance skills, fine motor movements, and language skills appear localized in the frontal lobes of girls, whereas the same skills in men appear more dependent on posterior regions of the brain. It also appears that girls might have more connections between the left and right hemispheres of the brain, which allows the two hemispheres to communicate better.

These brain differences, including the more robust functioning of the frontal lobes in girls, possibly make the symptoms of ADD less overt, less debilitating, and more easily tolerated. The mature left hemisphere allows girls to use words and sentences easier and earlier than their male counterparts. And the more efficient communication between hemispheres might make girls with or without ADD better at regulating their behavior than boys.

■ ■ ■

Q: I am an ADD woman who is forgetful and quiet. I have an ADD male friend who is forgetful and sometimes dreamy like me. People say he's contemplative and complex, while my dreaminess is called spaciness. What can I do to change their perceptions?

A: It's the old story—behavior that would not be criticized in a man is, in a woman, held up to severe scrutiny. In the case of a woman who has ADD without hyperactivity, the forgetfulness, disorganization, and daydreaming causes her to be labeled a ditz or a bimbo. We know one ADD woman who recently described her resentment and sadness over this double standard. A successful businesswoman, she runs a leading advertising agency in a large city. Yet her ADD causes her to misplace things and sometimes to lose her way when travelling. As a result, she has heard herself described as an "airhead." She is convinced that a man of her status would not be described so pejoratively. As you've found, a man exhibiting similar behavior might, instead, be typecast as the endearing absent-minded professor.

Women who have ADD with hyperactivity are similarly slandered. Their hyperactive and aggressive behavior is seen as unladylike. As girls get older, they are more likely to be rejected by peers than are hyperactive boys because of their "deviant" or tomboyish behavior. In short, the personal and social pressures that plague many women also plague ADD women, but even more so, as the extremes of their behavior invite unfair criticism and impossible expectations. This causes the ADD woman's self-esteem to plummet, contributing to depression and a sense of failure.

How can the ADD woman fight these stereotypes? The best way to combat any type of prejudice is to educate others about the issue. Many people are not aware that they are looking at you through a fixed lens. By informing them that they are judging you using this double standard, you can often relieve the offense. Also, if treatment for ADD has afforded you newfound inner strength, you may want to share what you have learned about ADD with others, explaining its contribution to the way you are. Many adults report that this strategy helps both the ADD adult and the other person reach better levels of communication.

■ ■ ■

Q: My husband doesn't understand how I can function and be organized at work but can't seem to manage things at home. Sometimes I don't understand this myself. Should I feel guilty?

A: Many women with ADD feel much more successful at work than they do at home. Problems with attention, focusing, and organization seriously impair their ability to perform what they feel are instinctive and simple tasks: remembering to go grocery shopping, keeping a clean house, showering their loved ones with "quality time." At the same time, these ADD-ers shine in the office. It is helpful to realize that frequently the work setting offers exactly what the home situation does not: clear expectations, specific job duties, and structure. In contrast, family life can consist of needing to juggle a thousand things at once. At home one is subject to the many interruptions and demands of children, the phone, errands, neighbors, etc. An imposed structure and measurable goals are not easily available. All of these factors can contribute to the disparity between some women's managerial ability at home versus at the office.

Don't feel guilty. Explain to your husband that your ADD thrives in the unstructured home environment, and enlist his help in keeping home life organized and manageable. You'll both feel better.

■ ■ ■

Q: Does ADD make my PMS (premenstrual syndrome) worse? I am really out of control during these times. Is there anything I can do about it?

A: Although there hasn't been any research into this phenomenon, many women with ADD report that they experience moderate to severe PMS. They dread the monthly storm that seems to overtake them, the debilitating mood swings, depression, anxiety, and anger.

During the premenstrual phase, fluctuating hormones (prolactin and estrogen) affect the serotonin neurotransmitter system, which regulates mood and other brain activities. The ADD woman is already experiencing some dysregulation in the brain's neurochemical system, and it is safe to speculate that the hormonal activity preceding menstruation causes an already dysregulated system to become that much more out of balance. Because the serotonin system modulates mood, impulsivity, and the activity of other brain chemicals, this might account for the ADD woman's heightened PMS symptoms. Treating PMS symptoms with serotonin-active drugs such as Prozac, Paxil, Zoloft, and BuSpar has a good effect on PMS and subsequently on the ADD. We often use these drugs in combination with Ritalin, Cylert, or Dexedrine to treat ADD and PMS in the same woman, with very positive results.

■ ■ ■

Q: Is there a connection between ADD and eating disorders?

A: A number of ADD women recall being anorexic or bulimic during their adolescent and college years. Hans Huessy, one of the first psychiatrists to identify ADD in adults, observed a correlation between eating disorders and ADD women almost two decades ago.

We don't really know the nature of the connection, but women's reports suggest that the bodily starvation alleviates some of the ADD symptoms: anxiety decreases while attention and focus increase. Perhaps the deprivation of food and energy affects the brain's neurochemical system in a way that is advantageous to ADD-ers. Along with overeating, the eating disorders almost seem to represent the craving for stimulation, since starvation can result in a physiologically driven "high" and at the least throws the body and then the mind into a high-intensity state. Seeking high-intensity states is characteristic of the ADD syndrome.

Some research has indicated that Ritalin can be an effective treatment for anorexia—in which case the anorexic may be suffering from an underlying attention deficit—as can Prozac. For example, Jennifer, who had been successfully treated for her bulimia with Prozac, had other troubling symptoms that led her to seek additional help. Her life history was consistent with an ADD profile and it seemed that her bulimia followed a lifelong series of impulse-laden behaviors. She was a nonstop talker in grade school, intrusive in all her encounters with adults and peers, an early drug user, and a severe procrastinating "space shot." The Prozac helped curb the drive behind her bulimia and also helped many of the associated ADD symptoms. She still spaced out, but when treated with an added stimulant most of her symptoms disappeared and she began working to get her life on track.

■ ■ ■

Q: Can I take Ritalin during pregnancy, or should I wait and restart it after delivery? Will it affect breast-feeding?

A: Unfortunately, there are no adequate studies addressing either of these issues. It is recommended that pregnant and nursing women be off all medications if they can tolerate it. However, we have had a few patients who chose to stay on their stimulants while pregnant, though aware that the risk to the unborn was unknown. One mother restarted her Dexedrine after being pregnant for six months, and found that it not only calmed her down, but seemed to soothe her overactive baby as well. She had a normal delivery and birth and right now the baby appears to be fine.

Neither do we know whether the stimulants pass into breast milk. Perhaps the appropriate research has not been undertaken because the stimulants were not initially developed for use by adults. Generally speaking, as our knowledge increases about the effects of most medications on the fetus and the newborn, most mothers choose to discontinue any and all medication during these critical periods. As always, this issue warrants case-by-case analysis, and the effect of being off medicine for a prolonged period must be weighed against possible risks.

■ ■ ■

Q: What effect do birth-control pills have on my ADD?

A: Many women report that they feel more stable emotionally while they are taking birth-control pills. They do not have the monthly premenstrual endocrine storm and its accompanying affects such as depression, panic, and rage attacks. The absence of this mood fluctuation can add stability to the previously unstable emotional life of the ADD woman.

Also, women taking birth-control pills report that they can think clearer because they feel more balanced throughout the entire month. Others report that some birth-control preparations actually cloud their thinking and make it more difficult to focus. By changing the birth control used, there may be a positive change in the state of consciousness.

■ ■ ■

Q: What is the effect of pregnancy on ADD?

A: We have only begun to look at these issues, as we have only worried about ADD in adults for a short period of time and only recently have looked specifically at women. Pregnancy has a wide range of effects on all women. Some become less panicky, less anxious, and less depressed. Others note that they are more unstable.

With regard to ADD women, the reports so far are purely anecdotal, but it does seem that being pregnant has a mild beneficial effect on their ADD. Jane, now in her forties, remembered that the only time in her life that she could comfortably read literature was during her four pregnancies. This was not due to any kind of lethargy related to her pregnancy, but was attributed by her to being able to focus. Like many women, she was less anxious while pregnant, and she compared the effect of pregnancy on her attention to that of Ritalin. She was better able to sustain her attention, wasn't as fidgety and impatient, and generally felt able to finish pages and chapters. Although the general effect of pregnancy on ADD needs further study, Jane's report is similar to many others I've heard from ADD women.

■ ■ ■

Q: Does my ADD affect my ability to have orgasms? And how do the medications for ADD affect orgasms?

A: Many women with ADD are the envy of their friends in that they have frequent and intense orgasms. Others are less blessed. These are distractible types, who can't stop to focus on their own pleasure. While engaged in sexual activity they may be worrying about the children, their work, or about their last vacation. These women can be anorgasmic.

Our clinical experience shows that knowing about ADD's effects on concentration and focusing leads to an improved sex life for some women with ADD. The same medicine that helps keep a woman's focus on the page of a book while reading often allows her also to maintain her focus on her own pleasure. To quote from a letter in *Driven to Distraction:* "How could I feel so sexy, look sexy, be married to an incredible man, and yet think of tomorrow's shopping list as he's making love to me?" After being treated with a stimulant for ADD, this same woman commented: "What a difference! I have never read anywhere about how ADD affects sexuality, but in my case the change [due to the medication] was incredible! Now I could focus, now I could be there. After a while I didn't even need the medication. It was a matter of realizing that it was ADD, and not some inadequacy or hidden guilt on my part. Then it was a matter of taking steps to have sex at the right time, of providing soothing music to take over the daydreaming part of my mind, and of talking to my husband openly about it. Now I can have orgasms, but more than that, I approach sex with enthusiasm instead of dread."

Other medicines, such as Tofranil and Norpramin, can have negative effects on orgasmic potential. These antidepressants sometimes are used alone to treat ADD and may interfere with the sex drive per se, and the ability to have orgasms in particular. Another group of medicines that are frequently used as adjuncts in treating ADD are the SSRIs, the selective serotonin reuptake inhibitors. These medicines are notorious for decreasing sexual interest in both sexes and can have a negative effect on a woman's ability to have orgasms. A woman who starts having sexual problems after going on one of these medications should talk to her doctor about alternative medications.

■ ■ ■

Q: What effect do puberty and menopause have on ADD symptoms?

A: Any hormonal change can affect the brain and make it more or less dysregulated, throw it off, or change the state of consciousness. Puberty and menopause are times of tremendous hormonal changes and usually make ADD women more vulnerable to underlying core symptoms. In fact, some clinicians state that with the advent of puberty the gender ratio of boys to girls with ADD moves closer to parity. The idea advanced by some is that impulsivity and hyperactivity is kept in check in girls when they are prepubescent; but that during the upheaval of puberty's endocrine storm, they demon-

strate many of the classic ADD symptoms and then get the ADD diagnosis.

Many women with ADD have observed that most of their behavioral problems didn't begin until after puberty arrived. Before that
they were quietly frustrated but did not engage in attention-getting
behaviors. They just tried to live up to the image of a good little
girl. Then, with puberty, they got involved in a host of complicated
problems: early drug and alcohol use, teenage pregnancies, shoplifting, anorexia and bulimia, and other risk-taking, high-stimulus-
seeking activities. Perhaps the early daydreamers who turn into
"wild women" are those with ADD.

Menopause only recently has received wide attention for its effect
on a woman's life. Again, since we have only begun looking at ADD
in mature women, the information we have on the effect of
menopause is thin. We would guess that since increased distractibility, gloomy mood, irritability, restlessness, extreme fatigue, and even
memory problems can be a result of the change of life, these could
exacerbate the ADD symptoms. After all, menopause, like premenstrual syndrome, is driven by hormonal changes, and the same principles would seem to apply: the changing hormone levels in the
neuroendocrine system directly or indirectly influence levels of neurotransmitters. Because an ADD woman already suffers from a vulnerable neurotransmitter system, menopause can throw her whole
system—her mood, her memory, and her energy—out of balance.

This is, in fact, what we tend to see in our clinical practices. The
good news is that it appears treatment for menopause, such as hormone replacement therapy, can yield an improvement in ADD
symptoms.

.7.

Making Up Your Mind

NEW TIPS ON THE NONMEDICATION

TREATMENT OF ADULT ADD

■ ■ ■

Q: Can you please give us more tips like your "Fifty Tips on the Management of Adult ADD"?

A: Since the publication of *Driven to Distraction,* the one request we have received more than any other is for more tips on the non-medication management of adult ADD. This makes sense. While medication is usually effective, it is not the whole answer. And those people for whom medication does not work must rely entirely on nonmedication approaches. I am one of those people. I have tried all the medications used to treat ADD, and none of them is useful to me. I know, therefore, from personal experience how important and effective the nonmedication approaches to treatment can be.

In addition, sometimes the medication loses its effectiveness over time. However, whatever new habits you build into your life, whatever new strategies you may develop to deal with the business of everyday life, these last a lifetime. They are more durable than the effects of medication.

Therefore, we offer twenty-five new tips on the nonmedication management of adult ADD. We also include in appendix I at the end of the book an updated version of the original "Fifty Tips" from *Driven to Distraction.*

Twenty-Five New Tips on the Nonmedication Management of Adult ADD

1. Embrace your true nature. Be glad to be who you are. Don't practice being who others want you to be; let yourself be yourself. Remember these words from Ralph Waldo Emerson:

> Whoso would be a man, must be a nonconformist. . . . Nothing is at last sacred but the integrity of your own mind. . . . I am ashamed to think how easily we capitulate to badges and names, to large societies and dead institutions.
>
> What I must do is all that concerns me, not what the people think. This rule, equally arduous in actual and in intellectual life, may serve for the whole distinction between greatness and meanness. It is the harder because you will always find those who think they know what is your duty better than you know it. It is easy in the world to live after the world's opinion; it is easy in solitude to live after our own; but the great man is he who in the midst of the crowd keeps with perfect sweetness the independence of solitude.

2. Hire an organizational consultant. It is worth the money to hire someone to come into your home or office or both and spend a day or two going over your whole organizational system. These consultants have a great deal to offer those of us with ADD. They know us. They can save us lots of legwork. They know what we need.

3. Hire a financial advisor. Money management is often a big problem for people with ADD. We procrastinate, or we avoid it altogether. An independent financial advisor, a person with nothing to sell except advice, can pay for his services many times over by bringing some sense to your financial dealings.

If you doubt this, just imagine for a moment what a relief it would be to know that all those financial steps you've been *meaning* to take were now being taken care of. For example, do you have at present:

- A proper retirement plan?
- A will?
- Enough disability insurance?
- Enough life insurance?
- Proper health insurance at the best price?
- Enough liability insurance?
- A contingency plan for the early death of you or your spouse?
- A plan for your children's education?
- A nest egg of savings in case of an emergency?
- Proper monitoring of your investments?
- The best mortgage available?
- Someone to turn to when you have a financial question?

If you answered no to any of the above, or if reading down the list made you anxious, then consider getting a financial advisor. Rather than trying to do it yourself, this is one area where getting expert help makes a lot of sense.

If you don't really need a financial advisor, but you have big problems in the day-to-day management of money, consider delegating the responsibility for it to your spouse. Often the person with ADD agonizes at his or her desk every week or month paying bills and balancing the checkbook as a perfectly competent and willing spouse stands by. Let your spouse take over! There is no rule that says you have to handle the money yourself.

4. Never worry alone. People with ADD tend to worry and brood. When you find yourself doing this, talk to someone else. You don't have to talk about your worry; just talk to someone else. Otherwise, you're liable to fall into a paralytic state of rumination.

5. Learn how to give up. One of the more admirable traits associated with ADD is a tenacious, never-say-die attitude. However, sometimes it is best to jettison this approach; sometimes it is best to say die. For example, if you have dated five men all of a certain ilk, and they have all broken your heart, then you should consider giving up on that type of guy and trying another sort. Or, if you have been fired from six jobs in sales, it might be best to leave sales rather

than take a seventh sales job. In general, if you find yourself bailing out of a sinking rowboat, it might be better to swim away rather than go down with the ship.

6. When it comes to addictive substances or activities, the best advice is total abstinence. This is because the individual with ADD is at much greater risk than the average person for developing a problem with addiction. Whether it be alcohol, nicotine, cocaine, marijuana, or gambling, an addiction can ruin a life in a hurry. The most reliable way to avoid the problem is not to go near it at all.

7. Watch out for your trusting nature. Most adults with ADD are extremely open and trusting. They don't pause to calculate before they speak their minds or reveal their secrets. This is an appealing quality, but it can be dangerous. Others may take advantage of you and treat you cruelly if you are not careful.

8. Don't invest in too much hardware. A simple appointment book that you *use* is preferable to a computer system that lies dormant.

9. Find a physician. Like financial planning, taking care of one's medical needs often gets put off. Every adult should have his or her own physician, someone you can confide in about your medical worries, someone you can call when you're sick. Take the time to find a doctor. When was the last time you had your blood pressure checked? How about an EKG?

10. Delegate responsibility. Whenever possible, allow others to do what you cannot do well.

11. Develop strategies for dealing with anger in advance. Anger is a big problem for most adults with ADD. Instead of waiting for the situation to arise in which you get angry and perhaps become destructive, try to work on ways of reducing the anger and frustration you carry around with you. These methods might include:

- Frequent exercise to work off stress
- Control of substance use so that you do not lower your level of self-control with drugs like alcohol or cocaine

- Regular practice of meditation or prayer
- Getting a reasonable amount of sleep every night
- Psychotherapy or coaching to learn how to put feelings into words instead of actions

12. Don't be upset by your inconsistencies. Inconsistency is a hallmark of ADD, as much a part of ADD as change is part of the weather in New England. If it bothers you too much, take heart from these famous words, again from Emerson:

A foolish consistency is the hobgoblin of little minds, adored by little statesmen and philosophers and divines. With consistency a great soul has simply nothing to do. He may as well concern himself with his shadow on the wall. Speak what you think now in hard words and tomorrow speak what tomorrow thinks in hard words again, though it contradict everything you said today.—"Ah, so you shall be sure to be misunderstood."—Is it so bad then to be misunderstood? Pythagoras was misunderstood, and Socrates, and Jesus, and Luther, and Copernicus, and Galileo, and Newton, and every pure and wise spirit that ever took flesh. To be great is to be misunderstood.

13. If keeping track of keys is a problem for you, put a basket on a table next to your front door and *always* put your keys in that basket when you come home. Once you train yourself, your days of starting your morning off with a frantic search for your keys will be over.

14. If you have a secret sexual fantasy life, as many people with ADD do, go see a therapist and talk over the issues. You may be carrying around a huge amount of unwarranted shame and embarrassment. Once you talk it out, you will detoxify the topic so that it can become a source of pleasure rather than shame.

15. People with ADD are at much greater risk of getting into traffic accidents than the general population. This is due to their distractibility, their impulsivity, and their love of the high stimulation found in high speeds. Make it a point always to wear your seat belt

and never to exceed the speed limit by more than five miles per hour.

16. Try not to talk too much. When you do talk, try to get to the point quickly. People with ADD tend to talk at great length without stopping to listen. They can leave seemingly endless messages on message machines without ever getting to the point. They can ask questions that go on much longer than the answer. They can tell anecdotes that begin, but never end. This tendency is probably due to the way their brain's frontal lobes are wired. It can be countered with conscious effort, but you must be vigilant.

17. Listen actively. If you listen passively, you will tune out in a matter of seconds. Listen on the edge of your seat.

18. Ask for reassurance. Learn how to do this gracefully. You must coach your environment to teach it how to give you reassurance. Also give reassurance freely. Reassurance really helps patch the holes life blows in the fabric of each day.

19. Be free with praise. One of the assets of ADD is a big heart. Don't hide it out of fear or embarrassment.

20. Seek advice. Even if you do not heed it, you need the input of others. You are a born maverick; you want to do things your way. This is fine, but you are foolish not to consider the advice of other people, especially considering how many blind spots accompany ADD.

21. Don't *forget* you have ADD, especially when you get busy and you forget everything. It is surprising, but people often literally overlook the fact they have ADD as they berate themselves for being stupid, lazy, crazy, or bad. If you expect the rest of the world not to accuse you of those traits but instead to understand you have ADD, you must start by understanding and not forgetting this crucial fact yourself.

22. Schedule time for fun. This may sound ridiculous, but if you do not set aside time, even to have fun, the time will disappear. Reserve time in every week, or better, in every day, for having fun.

Make it real fun, not some activity you think ought to be fun. Whether it is watching TV, listening to a certain kind of music, attending a professional wrestling match, or playing poker, have fun regularly.

23. Do something you believe in. Get caught up in a cause. Be a person with a mission in life. Get excited about something and give it your all. Choose your cause wisely, but once you've chosen it, give it all you've got.

24. Get rid of firearms. People with ADD should not have guns around the house.

25. Eliminate one activity from your current schedule. People with ADD are good at adding on; they are not so good at cutting back. So pick one activity you no longer want or need to do and eliminate it. You'll love the feeling of getting rid of something that hampers you. You'll also free up some time. Who knows, you might take a nap!

.8.

You Are My Sunshine

ADD IN COUPLES

■ ■ ■

Q: Are people with ADD attracted to each other? Do they make good marriages?

A: Usually, people with ADD either love each other right away or run immediately in the opposite direction. It is as if an inner sensor informs them, in the first instance, that here at last is a kindred spirit, someone who finally *understands* in a world of misunderstanding. Here at last is someone who will know why I am always late or will know why I tune out in the middle of a conversation or will not mind that I keep two TVs on at the same time. Here is someone I can dance with through life without worrying whether I'm doing the right step.

Or, in the second instance, the inner sensor warns: "Watch out! This guy is as crazy as you are! Don't let him get within ten feet of you. Run for your life! All he'll do is charm you and disappoint you over and over again. Go while the going's good. He doesn't look like it, but he's impossible to live with. Trust me on this one. He is not for you."

As to whether ADD-ers make good matches, that depends on which sensors are at work. They can make wonderful matches, as the first voice anticipated, kindred spirits enjoying, forgiving, and romancing each other for a lifetime. Or they can make disastrous matches, as the second voice knew, tormenting each other with each other's problem.

How do you predict in advance? You can't be sure, of course, but the best advice is to do what all lovers should do, and listen to your voice within.

■ ■ ■

Q: Is there any kind of mate a person with ADD should watch out for? In other words, in your experience, is there one mistake you see people with ADD make over and over again in choosing a spouse?

A: Yes. They marry their fifth-grade teacher. Not literally, of course, but figuratively. They marry someone who is a caricature of a bad fifth-grade teacher. They marry someone who is critical, unforgiving, inflexible, taunting, petty, demanding, and clucking. They marry someone who anticipates their next mistake, not to help correct it, but to triumphantly point it out and to ruefully foretell that it will occur again. They marry someone who relentlessly hovers about, picking at this, picking at that, finding fault here, finding fault there, giving dour predictions of the future and grim assurances of your endless culpability. They marry a specialist in the fine art of killing self-esteem.

Why do they do this? Because they think they *need* such a person. They think that is what they deserve. They often actually believe they are *lucky* to have found this nitpicker of a mate. They buy into the notion, implanted since the fifth grade, that they are no good on their own, that they are crippled and need constant supervision and assistance, and that they should be grateful for anyone who has the patience to put up with them.

Needless to say, this is the wrong kind of marriage for both parties. And sadly, such marriages are not rare.

■ ■ ■

Q: What are the advantages—if any—to being married to someone with ADD?

A: Since I have ADD myself, I thought I would let my wife answer this question. She laughed when I read it to her, and said, "Just loving you is advantage enough." You can see I am very lucky. I did the opposite of what I cautioned about in the preceding question. I married someone who loved me for who I am. Why she loves me is another question.

But the best thing I ever did was marry Sue and have our children, and I like to think she feels the same way. When I titled this chapter, "You are my sunshine," I thought of her, and of our kids, Lucy and Jack. It is not a perfect marriage; it is not a perfect family. There are times Sue reminds me, "You know, it can be a pain in the ass to be married to someone with ADD," and there are times she can get on my nerves as well. But in the main we are each other's best friend, and we love our children, as parents tend to do, with crazy devotion.

Loving is probably the best medicine for almost any human emotional problem, so I do not mean to suggest its curative powers are restricted to individuals with ADD. However, I do offer my own example, and the examples of scores of others with ADD, as evidence that a good and loving union can stabilize a rocky ship. Before I met Sue, I was not in bad shape, but I lacked the feeling of centeredness and security I've found with her. My marriage has not cured my ADD, to be sure. I remain a nervous sort, worrying about this and that, fretting up a storm even when all is going well. I forget things often, and I have the hardest of times sitting through coffee at the end of a meal. My patients can tell you that I am late more often than I should be. But for all these issues—and they will dog me until I die, no doubt—I am much happier than I once was. Part of the credit for that should go to my psychotherapist, who for many years worked his common sense upon me and acted like a good coach, and part of the credit should go to my extended family, who were always there, come what may; but the bulk of the credit should go to Sue and Lucy and Jack, one grown-up and two children, who brought me out of the distempered state I'd lived in most of my life and into the clear-spring sphere where love rings us all. Love—old, reliable, worn-shoe love—has stabilized my life.

It's the best treatment I know of for ADD. And for most everything else.

■ ■ ■

Q: Can an ADD spouse make a good coach?

A: For those readers unfamiliar with the term, a coach is someone who meets with the person with ADD three or four times a week for ten or fifteen minutes to go over obligations and plans. The coach offers encouragement as well as practical assistance—prodding and reminders.

It is very difficult, but not impossible, for a spouse to fill this role. A spouse is usually too busy being a spouse to take on the additional role of coach. (For the same reasons, it is difficult for a parent to be a coach.) Sometimes, however, the spouse is the only person available to fill the role. In these instances it should be made very clear from the outset what the deal is. The ADD person is asking the spouse for help. Only in response to this request for help is the non-ADD spouse offering his or her coaching. Therefore, the coaching cannot be mistaken for nagging, *since the ADD person has requested it.* Only if this request is clear and unambiguous does the spouse stand a chance of succeeding as a coach.

■ ■ ■

Q: What one single technique works the best in helping ADD couples get along?

A: Humor. It is also the second-best and the third-best technique. Humor makes lemonade out of lemons and sweet marriages out of bad dreams.

For more advice see appendix III at the back of this book, which contains twenty-five tips on the management of ADD in couples.

■ ■ ■

Q: My husband has ADD. He is a really creative man—works in advertising, financially successful, great dad, always into some new project at home and at work. My problem is that although he is good to me and pays attention to me in most ways, sexually he pays no attention at all! We don't have sex more than twice a year! Is this normal?

A: Whether we call it normal or not, it is obviously a concern for you. And I would imagine it is a concern for your husband.

I don't know enough about the two of you to say in your case whether or not this problem is attributable to ADD. But I can certainly say that it might be.

What we sometimes see in both men and women with ADD, particularly highly energetic, creative people, is that they get so absorbed in everything else that they all but forget about sex. By the time they get ready to go to bed, all they want to do is go to sleep. They put all their energy into other projects. Some people speculate that creative energy drains off the supply of sexual energy. Since we have no way of measuring either of these qualities, it must remain speculation; however, more than a few creative people, alive, vibrant people whom one would expect to be, if anything, overly interested in sexual activity, report that in fact their frequency of lovemaking is low. When they do make love, they do so without problems and they enjoy it; it is just that they do it rarely. So it is with some men and women who have ADD. They are too involved in everything else to "remember" to have sex.

What is to be done in these situations? First of all, you want to make sure of the diagnosis. There are many other causes of reduced frequency of lovemaking in a relationship, such as depression, substance abuse, or insecurity. Indeed, ADD would rank low on the list of likely causes.

However, if the diagnosis of ADD is correct, then treating the ADD may improve the problem. It won't cure it, but it can help a great deal. Treatment must include more than just medication. It begins with insight and education. The individual needs to understand first of all that there is a problem. People, particularly men, surround sexuality with much pride and embarrassment. To talk openly of problems in one's sex life can be very threatening. The subject has to be taken up delicately, with great tact. It is important that the individual not feel blamed or attacked. Humor can help, as long as it steers clear of ridicule. A dialogue might go something like this:

WIFE: Honey, have you noticed how we don't make love much anymore?

HUSBAND: Not now, honey. Let me finish this first.

W: No, I don't mean I want to *do* it right *now*, I just mean we don't do it much period, you know what I mean?

H: This is what happens after two kids and ten years together.

W: Really? It has to be this way?

H: Honey, I'm wrapped up in this.

W: Well, unwrap yourself, big boy. I want to talk about sex.

H: Big boy? Where'd you get that?

W: Just trying to get your attention. Did it work?

H: Momentarily, at least. I don't know, honey, I guess I let you down on the sex score, don't I? I don't know what it is.

W: Do you find me attractive?

H: You know I do. I think you're the sexiest girl I know. It's my problem. I'm just not into it the way I used to be.

W: You know, sweetheart, you were never *that* into it. I mean I think you are an incredible hunk, but jumping my bones was never at the top of your list.

H: Really? Even when we were dating?

W: Yup. I had to convince myself that you were attracted to me. You didn't look at me the way guys do, you didn't put moves on me—I even wondered if you were gay and didn't know it.

H: Really?

W: It's the truth. I found out differently, of course. When you want to be, you're very turned on. It just doesn't happen that much.

H: Then why did you stay with me? I mean there were lots of other men, as I recall, who were plenty interested in you.

w: What a male question! "Well, if you couldn't get enough off of me, why didn't you look somewhere else?" Because it was *you* I wanted, stupid. It was *you* I was interested in. It was *you* I was falling in love with, Alex. The fact there wasn't that much sex was just one factor I had to live with. Only problem is, I still do. And I didn't know how much it would bother me.

Now let's assume that Alex has ADD. And let's assume that this is why he has always been so engaged in other projects. Now that Nancy has skillfully presented the problem and let it be talked about in such a way that the two of them did not get into a fight, a path has been cleared to pursue a diagnosis. They could see a couples therapist, who hopefully would recognize the ADD.

After that, treatment could begin. Structure alone might do the trick, without even using medication at all. Building on the insight that it was ADD—not some hidden psychological problem—that was causing Alex's lack of interest, structuring time for lovemaking during the day—or in the morning or in the evening—might activate a degree of interest in Alex he didn't know he had.

If that did not work, medication might be tried because sometimes it is a lack of focus that leads the individual not to be interested in sex.

All this is said with full acknowledgement and awareness that in most cases like the one described it is *not* ADD that is the cause. However, when it is, it is good to know about because it is so treatable.

■ ■ ■

Q: How does a non-ADD spouse help an ADD spouse without bugging him or acting as if it's a parent-child relationship? Examples: I'm always saying "Don't forget to . . . ," or "Did you remember to . . . ?" just as I say to my kids. My husband resents this, and I don't like doing it, but on the other hand, if I don't, nothing gets done.

A: The key here is for your husband to ask for the reminders in advance. If they are not asked for, then they become annoying, like a mother fussing over her grown-up child. If, however, the couple agrees that life will go more smoothly if the non-ADD member can remind the ADD member of his or her plans and obligations, then the reminders are just that—asked-for, helpful reminders, not nagging by-products of a parent-child relationship grown up.

■ ■ ■

Q: I have ADD and I'm forty-six years old. My husband of twenty-two years doesn't want to hear about it at all. What can I do to gain understanding from him? He doesn't agree with medication or anything. I feel so alone in my effort.

A: It is not uncommon for one member of a couple to have trouble understanding the meaning of ADD in his or her spouse. What you need to do—which can be very difficult—is find out *why* the spouse is having such trouble understanding.

Often the dialogue goes something like this:

RHONA (wife): Honey, I want to talk to you about my attention deficit disorder. Remember, I told you I've been diagnosed with ADD?

DON (husband): Yes, I remember, and I think it is bogus.

RHONA: I don't see how you can say that.

DON: Because I think it's your excuse for not caring enough to get things done, if you want to know the truth. You accomplish a lot when you want to.

RHONA: That's not fair.

DON: I know, and I'm a mean, unfeeling man, just like all other men, unable to get in touch with their wives' feelings. But Rhona honey, what do you think the IRS would say if I said, "Oops, sorry, I haven't paid taxes in ten years because I forgot, but don't hold it against me, I have ADD." Do you think that would fly?

RHONA: Of course not. You really are not going to even try
to understand, are you?

DON: If that means "Am I going to cave in and agree with
you?" then the answer is no, I am not.

Let's stop the dialogue at this point. Rhona is not getting anywhere with Don because she hasn't addressed the underlying cause
of Don's skepticism, which is, believe it or not, envy. He thinks
ADD is too good to be true. He'll be darned if he'll let Rhona have
such a neat excuse.

Rhona needs to show Don she does not intend to use ADD as an
excuse. Rather, it is a rational explanation for why so many things
have been difficult for Rhona, and in turn for Don. By stating she
has ADD she is not trying to get out of doing work—or out of paying taxes. She is simply explaining why certain matters have been so
difficult. If Rhona can put Don's mind to rest on this point, so that
he will not feel as if he is being left out of a good deal, he might be
better able to offer some understanding.

■　■　■

Q: I have ADD and I can't have an orgasm. Is there a relationship between the two?

A: There may be. Some women with ADD are anorgasmic. They
sometimes incorrectly believe this is due to an emotional conflict
they have about sex. However, it is often not due to some emotional problem but due to the ADD itself. In order to have an orgasm, one needs to be able to pay attention, to focus on the
lovemaking and the fantasies that go with it. If, instead, one's mind
is on tomorrow's shopping list or what you're going to tell your
employees about next month's sales meeting, then it is difficult to
reach the sexual heights. Treatment for ADD may cure this problem
by restoring your ability to focus on the present moment.

■　■　■

Q: How can I persuade my husband to get help? I am *sure* he has ADD, but he refuses to go for any sort of evaluation. He says I am just caught up in the latest fad, that he always got good grades in school, that he pays attention just fine most of the time. Well, I love him dearly, but he is dead wrong on this. Yet he won't budge. Any ideas?

A: This is a common problem. I have three main solutions. Persist, persist, and persist. If he has a male friend you can convince of the validity of your point of view, that male friend may be able to talk to your husband, who may feel less threatened by the friend. Or a book may succeed in getting through to your husband where your words have failed. Or your family doctor might get through. Or your child. Or your child's schoolteacher. Whatever you do, don't give up. Persist. Don't waste your energy and get into a struggle. Just keep backing up, regrouping, getting more support, and coming at the issue from different angles.

■ ■ ■

Q: The following letter came from a woman desperate for help with her marriage:

Dear Dr. Hallowell,
My husband and I have been married for twelve years. Four years ago our son was diagnosed with ADD and at that time my husband was diagnosed as well.
He has done OK with treatment, but his ADD is not cured. Worse than that, though, is my reaction to it. I just can't stand it! I am so fed up with his endlessly forgetting things, not picking things up, interrupting, talking about himself, not being there in conversations, only remembering what concerns him, never what concerns me, that I could *kill* him! Don't worry, I won't. This is not the letter of a crazy person. But some days I think it might be.
He has really driven me to the end of my rope. I cannot believe that ADD could make a person so selfish, and yet

our doctor says that is what is going on. If that is the case, then something has to be done.

For example, the other day I came home from work—we both work—and the kitchen was a complete mess because he had got home first and made himself a snack. Do you think he might have cleaned up? No way. It wasn't just the mess that bothered me. It was that he basically ignored me when I asked him to clean up. Said he was into some project and he'd do it later. Well, I couldn't feel right until it was cleaned up, so I cleaned it up. But that really made me mad. He apologized and said he would have got around to it and that he was sorry he aggravated me so much and that he would try to do better. *But I have heard all that before!*

It wouldn't matter if this happened once or twice. But this is a way of life for us. This may sound petty to you. I hope not. It's just that it happens so often! I can't rely on him for anything. He is lost in his own world so much of the time, and he forgets things or just doesn't do things so often that I'm starting to hate him! This upsets me because I really do love him, if you can believe that.

Maybe he's just a jerk, or maybe I'm a jerk, or maybe we're both jerks. What can you tell me that might help?!

A: I don't think the answer is that either of you is a jerk, and I do believe you love him. Why else would you take the time to try to get help?

Sometimes the treatment for ADD offers only marginal gains. Sometimes it doesn't work at all. This is quite rare, as there usually is some progress, either from medication, or insight, or structure, and you say in your letter there was some progress, just not nearly enough.

I wish I had a magic cure for you, but I don't. There are some cases where ADD persists as a really bad problem, despite all efforts to treat it. Some men and some women just never get over their forgetfulness and distractibility, and they have these symptoms to an extreme. At their worst, these people seem selfish and uncaring, interested only in what comes close to them in the present moment. They lack all sense of consideration and anticipation of others' needs, and they offer no help without being prodded or repeatedly asked.

This sounds as if I am describing a jerk. But what separates this person from jerkhood is remorse. Does he feel badly about the way he is? Does he want to reform? In your husband's case you said, yes, but you were fed up with resolutions that didn't produce results.

This is tough. If nothing else, you need some empathy. As one of my old and best teachers taught me, "Never worry alone." One of the best ways to "treat" an unsolvable worry is to share it with someone. If you sit and brood over it, it will eat a hole in your liver—or some other important bodily part—and you will get furious not only at the problem but at your inability to solve it. Who knows, you may have written me that letter in such a mood.

At these moments it is best to do what perhaps you did. Share the worry with someone else. The someone else will not be any better at solving the problem than you, but you'll be surprised at how much better two heads are than one. Even if a solution is not forthcoming, just the act of communicating your worry and having it understood by a sympathetic outsider can relieve most of the pain. It can put the problem back into perspective. And sometimes the outsider does indeed come up with an answer you haven't thought of before.

So join a support group, talk to a friend, speak more to your husband's doctor, call a sibling, talk to someone whom you trust. Above all, never worry alone.

■ ■ ■

Q: Sometimes I feel as if my wife, who has ADD, is speaking a different language than I am. Is there a special ADD dialect? My question is only half in jest.

A: Your question brings to mind a scene from James Thurber. In "A Ride with Olympy," the American narrator, who speaks little

French, is trying to explain to a White Russian handyman, who speaks mainly French, how to drive his car:

> He put his foot on the clutch, tentatively, and said "Embrayage?" He had me there. My knowledge of French automotive terms is inadequate and volatile. I was forced to say I didn't know. I couldn't remember the word for clutch in any of the three languages, French, Italian, and German, in which it was given in my "Motorist's Guide" (which was back at the villa). Somehow *embrayage* didn't sound right for clutch (it is, though). I knew it wouldn't do any good for an American writer to explain in French to a Russian boat specialist the purpose that particular pedal served; furthermore, I didn't really know. I compromised by putting my left foot on the brake. "Frein," I said. "Ah," said Olympy, unhappily. This method of indicating what something might be by demonstrating what it wasn't had a disturbing effect. I shifted my foot to the accelerator—or rather pointed my toe at it—and suddenly the word for that, even the French for gasoline, left me. I was growing a little nervous myself. "Benzina," I said, in Italian finally. "Ah?" said Olympy. Whereas we had been one remove from reality to begin with, we were now two, or perhaps three removes.

How many conversations in the world of ADD sound like that! It is not a special language of its own, but it is a special way of getting lost, of starting only one remove from reality and ending up several more removes away.

■ ■ ■

Q: Recently, my boyfriend was diagnosed with ADD. He is so forgetful that he sometimes forgets what we're talking about *while* we're talking about it. Sound familiar?

A: This can be very annoying. Consider a conversation like the following one, during which Bob forgets why he is calling Judy:

Hi, Judy, this is Bob calling. I'm fine, how about you. No, I didn't see it but maybe I will tonight because I have the night off. That's why I'm calling. I was wondering if you had Mary's phone number. No, I wasn't the one who recommended you, but I sure am glad you got the job. You're going to love working over there. The new plant manager will really give you all the freedom you need to put in some of your ideas. And I know how much freedom means to you. Boy, what a jerk that guy was at Billings and Stern. You know, I think you'd have a legitimate lawsuit against him. Seriously, he had no right to let you go like that just because you disagreed with him a few times. What a jerk. But you'll be better off at Hennesey anyway. Anyway, I hate to cut things off, but I'm late and I've got to run. Nice talking to you. Hope to see you soon. Bye.

Bob hangs up without getting Mary's phone number. Even after he hangs up, he still doesn't remember that he forgot to get her number. He is so caught up in his ideas about Judy's new job and his aggravation at her losing her old job and his warm feelings in talking with her that he completely forgets he wanted to get Mary's phone number from her so he could ask Mary to go to the movies. In fact, he completely forgets he wants to go to the movies. After he hangs up, he knows he is in a hurry, because he has just told Judy he is in a hurry, so he starts hurrying around his apartment, picking up his car keys, turning off the lights, locking the front door. Only after he is in his car with the engine running does he realize he doesn't know where he is going. He goes blank for a minute, trying to reconstruct the immediate past events that might explain to him why he is sitting in his car, engine running, with the feeling that he is in a hurry to get somewhere.

This is confusion, so common in ADD. Cousin to creativity, confusion fills the interstices of the ADD life. Transitions, moments of decision, turning points—these are all marked by confusion. As the mind embraces a new concept and begins to perceive its many intricacies, the underpinnings of reality begin to come unhinged. As the

ADD mind takes in a new concept, it often hyperfocuses on the new concept and leaves the rest of reality behind.

■ ■ ■

Q: My husband has ADD. What is the best way to handle his sudden bursts of anger or bouts of sadness? I try to analyze what is going on, and even when I'm right on the mark, it doesn't help.

A: Analysis and insight at these moments is actually counterproductive. It tends to drive the bad mood deeper. Even if it is accurate, as you say, it rarely helps. The best time for insight with someone who has ADD is during periods of calm, of emotional neutrality.

In the heat of emotion what helps most is reassurance. One of the big problems people with ADD have is that they can lose perspective so suddenly. Something that is in the background of their life can suddenly project itself front and center so that it is impossible to ignore. Listen to this example:

> Anna and John are having a quiet afternoon together. They are sitting on their porch sipping iced tea. John has his feet up on the railing and Anna has hers tucked underneath her. They are talking about the weekend they just spent with friends in Vermont.
>
> "Wasn't Debbie adorable?" Anna asks.
>
> "Yes," John says.
>
> "Should we invite them down here before the summer is over?"
>
> "I don't think we need to. Unless you want to."
>
> "It might be nice," Anna says.
>
> Abruptly, John swings his feet off the railing. "Well, if you feel that way, why don't you just get on the phone right now? Invite them for the rest of the summer. Tell them they can just move in. It doesn't matter that I have work to do. What do you care about that? All that matters is that we observe the social propriety of returning their in-

vitation. Have to keep up appearances, don't we? By all means, call them right up, bring them on down. Why don't I just move out to a hotel? I'm sure you wouldn't miss me as long as you have Debbie and Harold to keep you company."

"John, honey, please—"

"Oh, I know, I'm being irrational and difficult. Blame it all on me. But I do have a point, you know. Why do we always have to reciprocate immediately?"

"We don't," Anna protests.

"Then why did you just ask me if I minded if you invited them down here?"

Here Anna has a decision to make. She can follow one of several options. She might tell John he is being a jerk and go back into the house until he calms down. That might make the most sense. Or she might analyze why he is suddenly so threatened by the thought of Debbie and Harold coming to visit. Perhaps he needs some private time with his wife after spending a weekend with other people. However, it will probably not help for Anna to offer insight at this point. If she has the patience, she might offer John reassurance. She might tell him something simple like "Honey, don't worry, we do not have to have any guests, I promise," or "It's OK, I understand," (even if she doesn't), or "I know how hard it can be to have them to come visit when you are trying to get work done."

These reassuring responses can be difficult to offer when someone is being as impossible as John. Getting away from him may be best.

But in general, reassurance is what the ADD person needs at these moments of irrational anger, sadness, or fear. The moments can come out of nowhere. They are usually accompanied by an abrupt loss of perspective, and they catch the partner unaware, quietly sipping her iced tea.

My best advice to the partner is, if at all possible, don't explode. You are perfectly justified if you do; these moments are not fair. But if you can bite your tongue and see it as a problem of your mate's without making it a problem of yours, then the moment will pass sooner.

■ ■ ■

Q: Is there an innate tendency in ADD to be drawn to complexity?

A: The ADD brain thrives on complexity. It eats up complexity the way a horse eats up oats. This love of complexity can be exasperating for a spouse.

I have listened to many couples in couples therapy where the ADD member analyzes a situation in the most incredibly complex fashion imaginable. While the analysis is often brilliant, it is also usually stupefyingly dense, almost impossible for any but the most ardent student of human affairs to listen to, certainly too much for a somewhat disgruntled spouse (or a weary psychiatrist).

Listen to such a couple: "What Louise is really saying," the ADD spouse says to his wife, "is that my tendency to forget when I said I'd be coming home is annoying to her, that is, it is annoying to her on her terms according to the value scheme set up by her family, a family that really valued promptness and took being on time as proof of devotion to each other, and lateness as proof of the opposite, while my family, on the other hand, was in love with chaos, or if not in love with it at least unable to escape it, so that the idea that any event might start on time was so far from the realm of the possible that it would be ludicrous to entertain the idea, much less hold anybody to it. So what Louise sees as an annoying habit, if not a downright infuriating habit [at this point Louise is vigorously nodding her head yes] is no more than my habituated response to what I used to know as a child growing up. Furthermore, it would not bother me if she were late. [Now Louise is vigorously shaking her head no.] It would not bother me in the slightest. However, I have observed over time that what does annoy me is her projecting onto me, her applying to me her sets of values and traditions as if I were supposed to buy into them, one, two, three. Is that fair? No, of course it is not fair. [At this point Louise is beginning to feel lost, and she doesn't know which way to shake her head.] But it is not the fairness or the unfairness of the situation that bothers me. It is that I have to spend my time worrying about it when I know that in fact neither of us really wants to spend our time in this way, whether we are on time or late. Do you see my point?"

Louise opens her mouth, but nothing comes out. She is stuck. I intervene and say: "I can't agree that I do see your point, Jerome. Perhaps it would be more clear if you tried to put it into one sentence, one simple sentence."

"But I can't do that," Jerome protests. "My point is more complicated than that. I can't possibly put it into just one sentence."

"May I try?" I humbly ask.

"Be my guest," Jerome replies, sitting back in his chair, a little out of breath.

"Well," I say, "Louise is angry with you because you are never on time, and you are angry at Louise because you were brought up not to care about such things and you don't want to start now. Is that a fair summary?"

Jerome pauses, looks at me as if I had just told him the cosmos is not infinite after all, and says, "Well, what you said sort of sums up what I said, but it misses something essential."

"And can you tell me what that is?" Louise interrupts. "As far as I can see, Dr. Hallowell just miraculously translated your gobbledygook into plain English. The only thing essential he left out is all the nonsense you put in."

"May I suggest," I intervene, "that you both are right? Jerome, it is very difficult for Louise or anyone to listen to you at times because your thoughts are always branching and vectoring. And Louise, it is almost painful for Jerome to hear his thoughts reduced to their bare essentials because what is essential to him is never bare. It is always complex."

And that is how life so often is in the ADD brain. Complex. We turn a triangle into an octagon. We see hidden shapes within simple forms and hidden messages within plain statements.

Why this attraction to complexity? We love branching here and darting off there, like a never-ending Scrabble game, always a new word, a new space, a new combination, and there are always new letters to be taken from the bin. It happens spontaneously. It is not done to infuriate our spouses, although it may seem that way.

But we also like to keep it simple. We can become enraged when someone has trouble getting to the point—unless it is we ourselves who are having trouble getting to the point. This is not selfishness; it is due to the way we process information. We can only take in so much at a time. So if someone else has trouble getting to the point, we know we are on the brink of stimulus overload and shutdown, so we get aggravated, wanting to get to the point before shutdown occurs.

On the other hand, if we are making a point, we may not get to it right away because so many stimulating side issues divert us along the way. And we are not able to shut them out. So we follow them. We are charmed from one diversion to the next. And what was the original point? Often we do not know.

.9.

Taming the Big Struggle

ADD AND THE FAMILY

■ ■ ■

Q: What should we watch out for in the siblings of a child with ADD?

A: First of all, make sure they do not have ADD themselves. Since there is a heavy genetic component in ADD, it is worthwhile to check out the whole family. I have treated a few families in which *all* immediate members had ADD, plus numerous extended members.

Second, if one child is being treated for ADD, make sure the non-ADD siblings do not feel left out. What often happens is that parents get so preoccupied with the problems of the ADD child that the other children take a backseat. The whole family comes to center on Johnny's problems, and pretty soon everyone resents Johnny—Mom, Dad, brother, and sister alike.

If the diagnosis never gets made, this unfortunate situation can go on for years, until the child leaves home and in subtle ways even after that.

If the diagnosis is made, however, the family gets the chance to reorganize. It is important that all the children be a part of this reorganization, not just the child with ADD.

A short course of family therapy can help. Give the siblings a chance to speak their feelings, how fed up they are with all the attention Johnny gets, or how fed up they are with all the disturbances Johnny causes, or how worried they feel for Johnny. Siblings

167

typically have these feelings, and more. They need education along with the rest of the family, and they need time for venting emotion and for proposing solutions. All this can happen most productively with a referee present, as in family therapy.

It is a mistake to address only the identified patient, the child with ADD. ADD is always a family affair. The whole family must be taken into account when treatment begins.

■ ■ ■

Q: Do most families get into struggles around ADD, or just mine? I know you'll say most families do, but I need to hear it.

A: Most families get into struggles, period. When you have a group of people living together for a long time, struggles are inevitable. This is normal. You should not feel your family is "dysfunctional" (or some other buzzword) if you get into arguments from time to time. Families necessarily struggle. I remember a cartoon that showed an enormous assembly hall with a giant banner over the podium that read CONVENTION FOR NONDYSFUNCTIONAL FAMILIES. The audience consisted of one man, sitting by himself in the huge hall.

If all families struggle, is there anything special about the struggles in families where one or more member has ADD? I think there is. I think the struggles are more intense and more frequent. They can be so frequent as to feel continuous and uninterrupted. This is what I call the Big Struggle. It is what families with ADD need to work to avoid.

Why do ADD families struggle? I think the reason is in the nature of ADD. The symptoms of ADD can be so annoying to others and seem so volitional that it is almost impossible not to get into arguments.

Take a family and set it in motion as follows:

> Peter, who has ADD, comes home from school with his
> tennis racquet in hand and a smile on his face. He walks in
> the back door and the screen slams shut behind him.

"Peter?" his mom calls from upstairs. "Did you bring home Mr. Thomas's comments?

"Oh, no," Peter mutters under his breath. "Yeah, Mom, they're in my bookbag." Later at dinner Peter's mom asks him for the comments. "Later, Mom," Peter says, eating.

"Do you have them?" his father asks.

Peter puts his fork down and pounds his fist on the table which makes his younger brother and sister giggle. "Why don't you guys just get off my back? I can't even have dinner in my own home without being bitched at by one of you."

"I beg your pardon, young man, but that language is unacceptable."

"Yeah, Dad, well you're unacceptable, if you want to know what I think. When was the last time you helped me out with anything?"

"Are we going to hear more excuses, son? Do you have the comments or not? You know, in just one more year you'll be applying to college and colleges aren't going to give a damn about your excuses."

"Is that all that matters to you, Dad? Whether I get into the right college, and we all know which one that is? What if I don't get in? What will you do then? Have three martinis instead of two when you get home?"

"Son, why don't you leave the table until you can calm down."

"Dad, why don't you fuck yourself until you can get a life?"

Peter's father reaches over and grabs his son by the scruff of neck and begins to drag him out of his chair. Peter comes up quickly, and shoots a right jab into his father's face, breaking his glasses in two and opening a cut across his nose. The two younger kids watch wide-eyed, no longer giggling. Peter's mother shrieks, "Harry, you're bleeding." Peter picks the pieces of his father's glasses up off the floor. "I didn't mean to hit you," he says, putting the glasses on the dining-room table.

"I don't care," his father barks. "Hit me again, if it will help you. You're so screwed up. You're ruining your life. And all you can do is try and beat up your father."

"Dad," Peter says, "be glad I don't try," and he storms out of the house.

This is the Big Struggle writ large. Strong language, violent behavior—it can sound like the description of an R-rated movie. It is not uncommon.

In the scene above, the problem was that both the parents thought Peter was behaving irresponsibly and Peter felt his parents were simply making demands on him without understanding what he was going through. This is typical in the life of most adolescents, but ADD only accentuates it.

When an adolescent has ADD, the normal power struggles tend to intensify. Voices raise. Tempers flare. No transaction is simple. Every sentence becomes loaded with emotional baggage. Every word carries an inner meaning. Each glance is taken as a reproach. Everyone is tense, on edge, wondering who is going to explode first.

And explode someone will. Usually over something trivial, as in the example above. Whatever Mr. Thomas's comments were that Peter was supposed to have brought home and apparently forgot, it is doubtful they were worth coming to blows over. It is doubtful that Peter or either of his parents would have said, "Yes, let's have a fist fight at dinner over Mr. Thomas's comments." Yet that is exactly what happened. It might have been Mr. Thomas's comments or a request from Peter to use the car or a teasing remark from one of the younger children or a simple sigh. When a family is waging the Big Struggle, anything can set off an explosion.

So the answer to your question is yes, yes, a thousand times yes. Families in which there is ADD do struggle, and they struggle intensely.

■ ■ ■

Q: I've heard you talk about the Big Struggle in families. How do we stay out of it?

A: It is impossible to stay out of it altogether, but there are some steps you can take to reduce the fire.

First of all, recognize what is happening. Use insight. If the struggle occurs over and over again and solves nothing, you might try to abstain from the struggle. Don't rise to the bait. What you must realize is that unwittingly many kids with ADD are drawn to the struggle. It is stimulating. It is exciting. At some level, painful as it may be, it is fun. It is therefore up to the adult not to rise to the bait, not to vent the rage and passion that he might feel. Instead, step back. Say to yourself, "This is the Big Struggle. It is useless. All that happens is that people get hurt. I will not join it." That is the constructive use of insight. With practice, you can get good at it.

Use humor and perspective. Remember that you were young once. Remember that it is hard to be told what to do. Remember that you actually like your child's spunk and iconoclasm, except when it's fired at you. Back off. Tell a joke. Don't engage at that blood-blind level that causes you to treat your child as if he or she were an enemy, encountered on the street.

In downtimes, when the family is at peace, work on negotiating plans for the future and rules of behavior. An excellent book about negotiating is *Getting to Yes* by Roger Fisher and William Ury.

In appendix II of this book there are twenty-five tips on managing ADD in the family; many have to do with ways of staying out of the Big Struggle.

■ ■ ■

Q: Sometimes I worry for my family's safety. My son can get so out of control that I'm concerned he may really hurt one of the other children or me. What should I do?

A: You cannot let this situation continue as it is. You cannot be a parent and feel in danger from your own child. He needs more intensive treatment than he is getting. You must present your case to your pediatrician or family doctor in as urgent terms as you possibly can. Family violence can be avoided, but you must speak up and others must respond. If all else fails, speak to a lawyer, speak to the police, speak to a judge. Trust your instincts as a mother. It will be

as tragic for your son as it will be for the rest of the family if someone gets hurt. If he is out of control, he *wants* to be brought under
control. The most loving step you can take is seeing to it that he
finds that control before he does damage.

■ ■ ■

Q: The younger kids tease my daughter, Maria, about taking
medication for her ADD. They call it her "stupid pill." She
wants to keep it secret from them and pretend she's not taking
it anymore. What do you think?

A: I think it is unwise to keep it secret. All that does is perpetuate
a feeling in Maria that the medication is shameful, something to
hide. Instead, I would work with the other kids and Maria together
to help them understand what the medication really is, and what
ADD really is. If they are calling it her "stupid pill," that means they
don't understand.

■ ■ ■

Q: This is more a comment than a question. I would like every
mom and dad out there to know that there is hope. We were a
family on the brink of breaking apart when my middle son was
diagnosed with ADD. At first, nothing changed. The medication did not work. He's one of the kids no medication works
for. But we got into family therapy. That, plus a structured approach to Timmy's ADD, has brought us back together. Without knowing about ADD, I never would have understood
Timmy, and without understanding Timmy, I never would have
been able to deal with him or explain him to his father, who
had totally given up. Now he and Timmy are best pals. That's
probably the best part of all. I just wanted you to know so you
could tell others.

A: I reprint this letter—and I could have reprinted many like it—
so that others may know. I'm also aware that diagnosing ADD is

not the answer to all life's problems, and I know that it is not always easy to treat once diagnosed. But at the same time, I agree with the letter writer when she says, "I would like every mom and dad out there to know that there is hope." If this diagnosis applies to someone in your family, no matter how dire your situation may be, there is hope.

■ ■ ■

Q: We are looking for a family therapist. How much should we assume the therapist knows about ADD, and how much does it matter?

A: Assume the therapist knows nothing. You need not find a family therapist who is expert in ADD. The most important thing is that you find a therapist your family feels good about, a therapist who is qualified in general, who can laugh, and who is smart. You can explain what ADD is to your therapist. In fact, the process of explaining it, during a family therapy session, can be quite therapeutic. The same principle applies to individual therapists, too, I believe. What's important is the quality of the therapist. He or she can learn about ADD. To make an analogy from the world of professional football, it is like drafting the best athlete available, instead of drafting for a particular position.

■ ■ ■

Q: I'm marooned in a family full of people who have ADD. My husband has it. My two children have it. My father-in-law has it. Should I just give up now?

A: It is hard, no doubt about that. You have to watch for the following traps the "non-ADD savior" can fall into:

1. Don't take on the job of doing everything for everybody else. Just because you *can* do it doesn't mean you should. In fact, you shouldn't. You need to work with the others to help them learn how to do for themselves.

2. Don't go it alone. You need a family consultant or therapist, at least until life gets stabilized and a routine develops. Then put your consultant on hold until things destabilize again, as they inevitably will.

3. Don't become humorless. If you lose your sense of humor, meltdown will ensue.

4. Don't lose a sense of what is possible. Given your family, it is probably not *possible* for certain expectations to be met. Better to change your expectations than to grind your teeth down to your gums trying to make things happen that won't.

■ ■ ■

Q: Is there any way to use the family to enhance my son's self-esteem instead of tearing it apart as it does now?

A: Your question makes a good point. The family can be as powerful in a negative direction as it can be in a positive one. To turn the family around can be like reversing the direction of the *Queen Mary*. But it can be done. Call everybody's attention to what is happening. Have a few family conferences. Plant ideas strategically in various members' minds. Use extended family to help out. If you can produce a positive bath of family feeling for the ADD child, that is one of the best treatments I know of, if not the best.

■ ■ ■

Q: We can't find anyone to be an ADD coach outside the immediate family. Is it OK for my husband or me to take that job?

A: You do already. As a parent, you already are a kind of coach. That is why I think it is important for someone other than a parent to be the coach. A parent should not be his or her own child's coach for the same reasons a doctor should not be his or her own child's physician. It is not impossible, but it is far from ideal.

Try instead someone in the extended family. Or make a swap with a parent of another child who has ADD; you each coach the other's child. Or see if a teacher or secretary or other ancillary personnel at school might be available. Usually, if you think creatively, you can find someone other than yourself.

.10.

The Unfinished Symphony

ADD AND CREATIVITY

■ ■ ■

Q: If there is a relationship between mental illness and creativity, where does ADD fit into that equation?

A: There is a relationship of some sort between mental illness and art. It is a commonplace observation that an inordinate number of creative people have been emotionally disturbed, if not crazy. We are left to speculate on what this relationship might be.

In his review of a recent biography of F. Scott Fitzgerald, John Updike closed with the following extraordinary sentence: "The early death of a writer, besides shortening by a few unwritten volumes the shelves of books that weigh on our consciences, confirms our instinct that art, especially the literary art, should be sublimely difficult—a current from beyond that burns out the wire."

I can't think of a better description of madness than "a current from beyond that burns out the wire." It brings to mind the formulation Elvin Semrad had of psychosis: "the mind's last defense against unbearable affect." Semrad, one of the great American teachers of psychiatry in this century, understood mental illness in the same terms Updike understands art. The mind, in the case of both the madman and the artist, is trying to bear the unbearable, carry something too heavy for these mortal coils, comprehend something too vast to be taken in.

As the mind comes close to that which is commensurate with its capacity for wonder, it either recoils or it heats up, as if approaching the sun. As the mind heats up, as feelings intensify, as experience sharpens, the mind needs a way of bleeding off its excess energy. It needs a cooling system or a switching station, some kind of altered circuitry to help carry the added voltage it is now asking itself to carry.

For some, the cooling system is madness. In Semrad's formulation, as the mind buckles under emotion it cannot bear, it creates psychosis to take on the added burden, twisting reality into a shape the mind can accommodate. For others the coolant is some kind of substance such as alcohol, as it was for Fitzgerald.

But others find a better avenue. They channel their intense experience, their added voltage, into a creative act. While this current from beyond may ultimately burn out their wire, in the meantime it burns through the tough membrane of the banal and into the land of art. Whether it be poetry or prose, painting or sculpture, music or ballet, whether it be the artistry of a great short-order cook at work at his grill or the artistry of a juggler doing his act, all art draws upon this "current from beyond" to carry it to the level beyond ordinary experience.

If the creative process is a high-voltage act, then ADD may be the perfect high-voltage modulator. Some of the disadvantages ADD imposes in everyday life may actually become advantages in the creative process. The switching from idea to idea, so annoying in everyday existence, may act as a kind of internal circuit breaker for the artist, letting the mind heat up without burning out in any one sitting. The ability to hyperfocus, so common in ADD, may assist in the creative process at those moments when an extra jolt is needed. The capacity to live in uncertainty and ambiguity, so common in ADD, is annoying when one is stopped at an intersection wondering which way to turn, but may assist the artist in his effort to see a scene in a new way. The disorganization that bothers so many adults with ADD may assist the artist in shifting perspective, the disorganized state being a necessary prelude to a new focused field of vision.

■ ■ ■

Q: What do you mean when you refer to "creative ADD" as a subtype of ADD in general?

A: This is the syndrome of a highly creative, highly distractible individual who is stuck, unable to make the most of his or her talent. Most people with ADD are quite creative, but these people, the ones I refer to as having "creative ADD," are gifted. Typically, he or she—and it seems to be evenly divided between both sexes—comes to see me because underachievement has become a big problem. The talent is there, and there in spades, but for one reason or another the results are not.

Listen to Lisa, whose story is representative. "I know there are so many pictures I want to paint and stories I want to tell. I go to sleep at night and wake up in the morning thinking of children's books. I have story line after story line. And I have the illustrations to go with them. Sometimes the story comes first, sometimes an image will suggest a story, sometimes they pop into my head at the same time. I don't know. It must be the same for songwriters who compose their own music and lyrics. One day you're humming a tune, the next day the words hit you first. So I'll get an idea and I'll go to my desk and try to make a sketch or write a paragraph. But then, that's when the pretzels start to break. That's my phrase for what happens to my mind. You know how when you have a box of pretzels and you get down to the bottom of the box, all you've got is this half-inch of fragments of pretzels and lots of pretzel dust. That's what happens in my head when I sit down. All my formed pretzels start to fragment and the next thing you know all I've got is dust.

"I'll want to reach in for a fully formed pretzel, thinking there's one in there, thinking there's an image waiting for me to sketch or a paragraph waiting for me to write, but all I'll come out with are these little bits of pretzels. It's pathetic. I get really angry. That doesn't help either. You'd think I'd have given up by now. But there's no quit in me. Lord knows why."

Lisa's tenacious effort, and her frustration, are typical of ADD in creative people. They have the vision and the inspiration—qualities that make them artists in the first place. And they have the elusive third ingredient that usually separates the successful from the unsuccessful in the arts—perspiration. They are willing to work hard. They do not give up. But why, with all three in place—vision, inspiration, and perspiration—do they fall short of their goals so often?

It is because their focus fails them at the crucial moment. Their pretzels, to use Lisa's image, crumble.

The diagnosis and treatment of ADD in these people can help reassemble the crumbled pretzel so it can be brought out of the box and into the light of the world.

■ ■ ■

Q: What is the biological basis of creativity?

A: In order to write this chapter I had a conversation with one of the best neurobiologists I know, Dr. Jeff Sutton, who is both a psychiatrist on the Harvard faculty and a physicist on the M.I.T. faculty. He is smart. He is also honest.

I asked him what the latest thinking was about the biological basis of creativity. He responded, "We really don't know. Neurobiologists usually don't use the term 'creativity' because it sounds too psychological, and they take pains to separate themselves from the psychologists. Turf and prestige, you know. Instead, they talk about 'unsupervised learning' when they mean creativity. That's OK because terms like 'learning' and 'attention' have some biological underpinnings. 'Unsupervised learning' means there is learning going on in the brain that has not been planned, that is not being 'supervised,' so to speak. Some part of the brain is simply generating new material. This is what we mere mortals would call creative thinking. But there must also be consciousness at work—some selection process—for it to be called creativity instead of garbage that simply disappears. This is what is so intriguing to me, the combination of unplanned activity with reflective consciousness. These are two quite different neural networks being activated simultaneously. It is sort of like getting lost and reading the directions at the same time.

"But we haven't really pinned much down scientifically," he went on. "You know it's funny—there was a huge amount of research done on creativity a few years ago, peaking around 1988. And if you look at the history of brain research, there is a peak in the number of papers published on creativity about every fifteen years. In other words, there is a repetitive cycle, peaking every fifteen years, in creativity research. If you think about it, that corresponds approximately to one peak for every new generation of researchers. I think what happens is that when the senior researchers have done all their studies that made them famous and they've got comfortable and are sitting around in administrative positions wondering why they aren't as creative as they used to be, they get their grad students to start doing research into creativity. What they are really studying is themselves, trying to figure out what has gone flat in their brains, where their creativity has gone to and how to get it back. It's sort of like the scientists' equivalent of looking for the fountain of youth, this search for the roots of creativity. Anyway, the last peak of papers didn't give us the answer. Ask me again in about ten years when there's a new cycle and maybe I'll have a better response."

That is typically honest of Jeff. So if we don't yet have the biological explanation, we're left with psychological—and biological—speculation.

■ ■ ■

Q: How might we speculate on the relationship between ADD and creativity?

A: I think there are several connections between ADD and creativity. First of all, there is the empirical observation that enhanced creativity is part of ADD. No matter how annoying ADD behavior might become, almost invariably the parent, teacher, or spouse of the person with ADD will add, "But I have to admit that Albert is one of the most creative people I've ever met." So we start with this bit of data: ADD and creativity go hand in hand.

But why? To start with, consider one of the core symptoms of ADD, impulsivity. What is creativity but impulsivity gone right? If an impulse leads one to do something annoying, then we call it impulsive or obnoxious. But what if the impulse leads one to find a new solution? What if an impulsive remark, perhaps intended as a joke, leads the business meeting to the discovery of a new marketing strategy? What if a petri dish left unattended overnight leads to the discovery of a new antibiotic?

We do not plan to have a creative thought; it happens on its own. It happens impulsively. It happens, as my friend Jeff said, by spontaneous electrical activity in the brain accompanied by some degree of selection and self-consciousness. There must be enough self-consciousness to pick up the creative thought as it swims by, like a fish underwater, but not so much self-consciousness that the fish fears to swim by at all. The conditions that enhance or facilitate creativity are similar to those that allow for play; play and creativity have much in common. It is no coincidence that people with ADD are also often described as playful, too playful at times perhaps, but certainly playful. Impulsive, creative, playful—this is ADD.

If creativity is impulsivity gone right, creativity may emerge from a state of confusion in an impulsive act or thought. Haven't we all had the experience, at one time or another, of being lost, driving in our cars, feeling horribly confused, even panicked, with no idea where we are or how to get straightened out, only on an impulse to make a sudden right turn and find ourselves precisely where we wanted to be, then arrive bragging that we had discovered a wonderful shortcut to our destination?

I think that metaphor serves as a good model for the creative process itself. We embark on a project for which there is no road map. We are going to concoct a new spaghetti—or should I say pasta—sauce, or we are going to write a poem, or we are going to try to rig up a special lighting fixture next to our bed, or we are going to wing it for a while on the new computer rather than read the directions. Whatever the new project is, we let go of the traditional way of doing it, we throw away the cookbook and the road map, and go at it. We get there first. We cannot be guided because no one has done it before. As the critic William Hazlitt said, "He who imitates the divine *Iliad* does not imitate Homer." That is because Homer had no model. His was the first epic poem. No one had been there before. Whether yours is the first epic or the first spaghetti à la you, when you set out on your own, you are like the man driving who gets lost.

You usually go through a period of confusion, even panic, as you realize what you have got yourself into. Let's listen to the inner thoughts of our spaghetti-sauce maker for a moment as he stands in his kitchen concocting his new brew:

> OK, now stay calm. But what is this going to taste like? Spaghetti sauce without tomatoes, without anything red at all? They're going to laugh at this. The kids are going to hold their noses and say, "Grrr-osss." Helen is going to say, "Richard, the next time you want to get creative, keep it in the bedroom, OK? At least there you don't endanger the children's health." No, she wouldn't say something that catty. No? No.*What* did you just add? You put cauliflower florets in the olive oil? Do you remember what the kids said the last time cauliflower came near their mouths? But it will taste different in this sauce. A little garlic, no a *lot* of garlic. Oh, my god, this is a disaster, it looks like cadaver parts swimming in formaldehyde and it smells like it, too. Some black olives, now that's a good idea. Some chopped parsley, that's good. And some grated cheese. . . . I think this might work after all. Will they name it after me? I wonder if there's a book in this. Richard's cookbook.

And so spaghetti à la Richard is born. But not without some pretty scary moments.

We have to get lost in the woods in order to find a new way out. We have to give up on the old ways in order to try a new way. The advantage people with ADD have is that they cannot help but get lost from time to time, so they are forced to use their wits to try to come up with a new way, a new solution, a new spaghetti sauce.

■ ■ ■

Q: I have found that I get my best work done in those unpredictable moments of hyperfocus you have written about. Is this common in ADD?

A: Yes, it is. Who of us hasn't become so engrossed in a task that we forget what time it is, what day it is, where we are, or even who we are? Who of us hasn't had moments, even minutes or hours, of such intense focus that we leave the world altogether and merge with the project? A psychologist from Chicago whose name I can't pronounce (Mihaly Csikszentmihalyi) wrote a brilliant book about this moment, and he called it *Flow,* both the book and the moment, the time when we are so involved in what we are doing that we forget our worries, our concerns, our bills, our cavities, our enemies, our cravings, and we join our project so completely that we become it for a time.

At these moments we forget self. We transcend the bounds of time and place and become our task. I don't know that there are any happier moments in one's life. It is ironic, if not paradoxical, that in these happiest of moments we are unable to be aware that we are happy. Were we aware, we wouldn't be happy; we would be aware instead. We wouldn't be in flow; instead we would be in a state of self-conscious awareness.

In the state of flow, or hyperfocus, that we with ADD know so well, we are not aware of anything except the thing we are doing— the painting we are painting, the pie we are baking, the garden we are raking, the baseball we are pitching, the person we are stroking, the slope we are skiing, the instrument we are playing. Since we are aware of nothing else, we are not explicitly aware that we are happy. The moment we apprehend that we are happy, we are, by definition, aware of something else, namely ourselves, our self-conscious selves, and the spell is broken. But we can remember how happy we were during it, just moments ago, or even years. Isn't it strange that we can remember the happiness, but not actually be aware of that happiness as it is happening?

However, when it does happen, as you leave reality behind, you also must deal with confusion. Confusion on the way out and confusion on the way back. Haven't we all had those embarrassing moments of being "found out" as we drifted off into a reverie, forgetting the people we're with or even the conversation we supposedly are in?

Confusion might be thought of as the waste product of hyperfocus. The hyperfocused state, we might speculate, requires so much mental energy, draws so heavily on the brain's turbochargers that a residue of waste develops around it. This waste creates confusion, or the forgetfulness and distractibility all who have ADD know so well.

Richard focused on the spaghetti sauce so closely, albeit briefly, that he forgot where he was and what he was doing. All he could be guided by was his mental momentum. It carries some people into new careers, into new countries, into new situations altogether. Many people with ADD swim through their days guided much of the time only by mental momentum. They are moving from one state of focus to the next, negotiating the many states of confusion in between only by the momentum of their prior mental movements.

It is a strange way to live, but it can be productive, if it is channeled properly, or it can be very, very frustrating.

■　■　■

Q: The way you talk about structure allowing creativity makes great sense to me. I've always resisted structure, though, thinking of it as stifling. I'm still wary of it, but I'd like to hear more about creating my own structure while maintaining my autonomy.

A: Many creative people understandably fear imposing restrictions on their creativity. However, the right kind of structure will enhance creativity, not limit it, and will promote autonomy, not inhibit it.

Too often we associate structure with stultifying bureaucratic procedure. However, it does not have to be this way. Structure can be the creative person's best friend. A bit of structure as simple as a daily schedule can make the difference between being productive and frittering your time away. Lists, reminders, clocks that are on time, a computer you can use—these all can make the creative life more creative.

What you have to remember is that you are in charge of the structure, not vice versa. That is the big difference between a system you set up and a bureaucracy. While the bureaucracy may seem to run you, you run your own system.

.11.

Fact or Fad?

THE DIAGNOSIS OF ADD

■ ■ ■

Q: How do you respond to people who say ADD is a fad, the disease of the nineties?

A: What I would really like to do with those people is invite them to sit next to me in my office for one day. Join me when I arrive at 7:30 A.M. and say good night to me when I leave at 8 P.M. and talk to all the people I talk to in between. Spend one full day sitting next to me listening to the stories I hear. That is where the refutation of the notion that ADD is just a fad truly resides. In the stories of the people who have ADD. In their faces, in their tears. In their gutsy tales of getting up for work knowing they're going to falter during the day, or heading off to school knowing they're going to be called down in their first class.

I listen to these stories all day—from parents, from children, from spouses, from friends. I presented many of them in *Driven to Distraction,* and I wish I could present all the rest here.

Think about it. Imagine having a condition that makes it hard for you to focus your attention or stay on track so that you spend your whole school and work life underachieving, knowing you could do better, but having to say "I don't know" all the thousands of times you are asked why you aren't doing better. Imagine toughing it out, not giving up, even when you'd all but lost hope, just because you didn't believe in giving up, or just because a part of you said, "No,

damn it, I refuse to give in. The world will have to shoot me first."
Imagine spending most of your life struggling but not even knowing you were struggling, thinking instead that that was just life, as if
wearing leg irons was just life.

Then imagine someone came along and cut off those irons.
Someone came along and said, "Look here. You'll be better off
without these things. Why don't we just cut them off of you?" And
they were cut off. You'd feel pretty good. You'd want to run around
and use your newfound talents.

But then imagine how you would feel if somebody else came
along and said, "Hold on, now. If you were born with leg irons,
there was a reason for that. Leg irons are good for you. Don't tam-
per with nature. All these people taking off their leg irons are just
part of a passing fad. Pretty soon they'll all discover how much better off they were in shackles. Leg irons will come back as soon as
people come to their senses. Some people are simply meant to be
slow, that's all. It's best to learn to accept one's lot in life."

ADD is no fad. It is a medical diagnosis. Undiagnosed, ADD can
cripple an individual.

■ ■ ■

Q: Are there places where ADD is overdiagnosed?

A: I'm not sure I can name specific places, but it is true that in
some places the diagnosis of ADD captures the local imagination.
As crucial as it is not to miss the diagnosis, it is also dangerous to
overdo the diagnosis. I once saw a woman who had been told she
had ADD when what she really had was a tumor in her adrenal
gland, called a pheochromocytoma, which caused symptoms similar
to ADD. That incorrect diagnosis nearly killed her.

Remember, only about 5 percent of the population has ADD.
That means that 95 percent do not. If in one class at your school or
in one work site in your town half the children or adults are diagnosed with ADD, you might want to question some of those diagnoses. It is possible, of course, for 50 percent of a large, unrelated
group of people to have ADD, but it is *highly* unlikely.

The great damage that is done when ADD is overdiagnosed is

that the diagnosis itself is called into question. It becomes trivialized. This can only hurt people with true ADD.

It is for this reason that we are radical about maintaining a moderate position concerning diagnosis. We feel strongly that one should not become an ADD enthusiast, seeing ADD behind every lapse in attention, nor should one become an anti-ADD zealot, denouncing the diagnosis as a sham. ADD is not an article of faith, nor is it a political diagnosis. It is a scientific one. It must be made on the basis of science, of objective evidence. As long as we keep to that, we will be fine.

■ ■ ■

Q: What is the best test to diagnose ADD?

A: The best test for ADD is the oldest test in the history of medicine: the patient's own story. More reliable than any paper-and-pencil test or psychological test, more reliable than any technical diagnostic procedure, the patient's history contains the diagnosis of ADD. If possible, the history should always be taken from at least two people—the identified patient plus a parent or spouse or friend.

In the case of children, teacher reports should always be reviewed. Grades are largely irrelevant, as one may get excellent grades or poor grades or, more often, a combination of both in ADD. But what the teacher has to say about how the student learns is invaluable. Is distractibility an issue in the classroom? Impulsivity? Inconsistency? *Apparent* lack of effort? Restless or impatient behavior? These are among the telltale signs in teacher reports.

In the case of an adult, a spouse or close friend can give reliable information where the patient may forget, overlook, or simply not recognize important information about himself. Those of us with ADD are not good self-observers. We may think, for example, that we are usually on time, or that organization is no problem for us, or that we pay attention perfectly well; our wives may have a slightly different, more accurate version of how we actually are.

Once your doctor obtains your history—from you and from someone else—then he is in a good position to make a diagnosis.

Sometimes, but not often, additional tests are needed. Sometimes a blood test is needed to investigate some potential medical problem. Sometimes an EEG is needed to look into the possibility of a seizure disorder. Sometimes psychological testing may be ordered, particularly if there is a question of an associated learning disability. But most of the time the diagnosis of ADD can be made in the doctor's office via the history.

The history is such a powerful and reliable tool that it should always take precedence over any other test. For example, often a teacher will report all the standard symptoms of ADD in a child in her classroom, only to be contradicted by the psychological testing report. What usually happens then should actually *never* happen: parents believe the testing report over the teacher's report. The teacher's report is based upon weeks and months of close observation in many settings. The testing report is based upon a few hours of observation in a highly structured setting where the child is motivated to pay attention and "do well." It is the teacher's report that is the more reliable. The teacher's observations deserve greater credence than any testing report.

The same is true for adults, although the mistake is made less frequently. For some reason we tend to trust our observations of adults better than of children, and so we are less frequently misled by psychological testing or other test data.

All these various tests have great value as long as they are used properly. Psychological testing is extremely useful in diagnosing a host of mental problems. ADD, however, is not one of them. The history is the best diagnostic test for ADD.

■ ■ ■

Q: Recently, I had an MRI to diagnose a knee injury. I was amazed at how fine the detail is. Since my son has ADD, I was wondering if they've done any studies of the brain using MRIs in kids with ADD.

A: Yes, they have. The MRI, or magnetic resonance imaging, technique has given us a closer look at the anatomy of many medical problems, from those in the knee to those in the brain. A number of studies have been done using the MRI in attention deficit disorder, notably by George Hynd, by Jay Giedd, and by Margaret Semrud-Clikeman. These studies have revealed various morphological differences—or differences in shape—in certain parts of the brain in subjects with ADD as compared to normal controls. The differences are very small, but the small differences are significant. They are mainly in the part of the brain responsible for communication between the brain's two hemispheres called the corpus callosum, which may help to explain why we see slowed responses at times in individuals with ADD. The studies all found that the corpus callosum was smaller in certain areas in individuals with ADD.

So far, unlike the orthopedists who used the MRI to diagnose your knee injury, the psychiatrists and neurologists do not use the MRI to diagnose ADD. It is mainly a research tool, and a very exciting one at that.

■ ■ ■

Q: I have heard of a study that showed a change in brain metabolism in ADD. Is this a diagnostic test now?

A: No. The study you are referring to is a landmark study in the history of ADD done by Alan Zametkin at the National Institutes of Mental Health in 1990. Zametkin showed there was reduced glucose uptake in the brains of adult subjects with ADD as compared to normal controls. This was one of the most important studies in establishing a biological basis for ADD, a measurable, real difference between the non-ADD brain and the ADD brain. Of course, that there is a difference does not tell us where that difference comes from or what it means.

Interestingly enough, when Zametkin extended this study to adolescents, he did not find the same global differences, but he did find there was reduced glucose uptake in his female subjects compared to controls. That finding points up the need for intensified research into females with ADD. There is a lot of catching up to do in this regard. Since research began in this field in the 1930s, almost all of it has focused on males, long thought to be the only ones to have ADD. We now know this is altogether false.

Also of interest is that the glucose-uptake study was repeated on and off medication. Although the patients in the study who took stimulant medication for ADD noted improvement of their symptoms after taking medication, there was no difference found in the glucose uptake before and after medication. This suggests that whatever the medication is doing, and we know from the fact that the patients improved that it is doing *something,* it is not at the level of cellular energy consumption.

Like the MRI, the glucose-uptake technique is a research tool, far too elaborate and invasive—and unnecessary—to be used diagnostically.

■ ■ ■

Q: What are the chances of finding a "litmus test" diagnostic procedure for ADD? I know that there isn't one now, but I would feel a lot better about getting diagnosed if they had a surefire test.

A: The chances are good. As mentioned in the first two questions above, there are a number of potential biological procedures or markers that might develop into diagnostic tests someday. These include studies of cerebral blood flow, studies of eye-movement patterns in ADD, and refinement of tests of attention. As of now, however, none of these is precise enough to be a diagnostic "litmus test."

■ ■ ■

Q: In an adult, does the acquisition of an ADD diagnosis even matter, provided one's balance and compensatory skills are sufficient enough to generate a productive, fulfilled life?

A: If it's not broken, don't fix it. Certainly, if one is productive and fulfilled, diagnosis and treatment would seem superfluous.

Sometimes people are interested to learn they have ADD even though their symptoms are causing them no problem. It is of intellectual interest. I would say you are always better off knowing your brain as well as possible.

■ ■ ■

Q: What about concomitant physical illness?

A: There are a number of physical conditions *associated* with ADD in children and adults, such as being male, being left-handed or ambidextrous (medically termed mixed dominant), having asthma, having thyroid abnormalities, having sleep disturbances, having dyslexia, or having a history of early ear infections. None of these is of diagnostic value, however.

Sometimes a physical illness can look like ADD and so confuse the diagnosis—or the diagnostician! For example, hyperthyroidism, a not uncommon condition, or the manifestations of pheochromocytoma, an uncommon, potentially lethal condition affecting the adrenal gland, can produce symptoms similar to ADD. This is why a medical evaluation is an essential part of the diagnostic workup.

■ ■ ■

Q: In cases of equivocal diagnosis, is a trial on medication appropriate, and, if effective, can anything diagnostically be concluded?

A: The answer to this question requires a simple risk-benefit analysis. Is the risk of a trial on medication justified by the potential benefit? If the medication is Ritalin, and it makes sense that it should be, since Ritalin is the drug of choice for most people in treating ADD, then the answer is yes. The risks involved in a trial of Ritalin are very small; any side effect that might occur is reversible by stopping the medication. And the potential gain is high, because when Ritalin works, it is very helpful indeed. The only true way to know if it will work is to try it; there is no sure way of predicting its effectiveness in advance.

The diagnosis, however, cannot be based on a medication trial. If the Ritalin works, all you can say for sure is that the Ritalin works. The diagnosis has to be based upon the individual's history. The diagnostic criteria for ADD do not include a response to any particular medication. However, most authorities would agree that a favorable response to Ritalin contributes evidence for a diagnosis of ADD.

■ ■ ■

Q: How can one differentiate between a state of mind that is due to depression and one that results from ADD?

A: This can be a difficult distinction to make. Often depression and ADD occur together. Sometimes they both need to be treated pharmacologically; the combination of a stimulant medication such as Ritalin for the ADD plus an antidepressant such as Prozac for the depression can be quite effective. At other times the treatment for ADD will also take care of the depression. And sometimes no medication is needed; psychotherapy and structure suffice.

In order to distinguish depression from ADD, you must carefully review the history. The pattern of ADD symptoms will go back to childhood, whereas depression usually will not. The ADD symptoms of distractibility, impulsivity, and restlessness may appear in depression, but in depression the chief complaint will be of sadness, hopelessness, and gloom rather than of loss of focus. It is a difference in emphasis.

If you are depressed, and you can find no evidence of ADD in your history, particularly your childhood history, then it is likely your depression is just that—depression. But if you have a history of ADD or ADD-like symptoms, then ADD may be the underlying cause of your depression.

Above all you should rely on your doctor, not yourself, to make these determinations.

■ ■ ■

Q: I was diagnosed with ADD a year ago at age thirty-nine. Treatment has helped me a lot, but I still need the medication. My family doctor says he doesn't want to keep prescribing the Ritalin unless I go back to see the specialist who first diagnosed me to make sure I still have ADD. Does this make sense?

A: Yes and no.

Yes, it makes sense to have a yearly review by a specialist to assess how you are doing. Your medication requirements may change over the course of a year. Your target symptoms may change. You may be improving more than you think you are. Since your family doctor is not an ADD specialist, he wants someone who knows what questions to ask and what answers to look for to have a look at you. I think that makes good sense.

However, your ADD is not going to go away. You are not going back to the specialist to see if you still have it, because you will always have it. ADD in adults does not go away. But it may get much better. With treatment—and remember, treatment includes more than just medication; it also includes education, structure, insight, coaching, and the various tips outlined elsewhere in this book— with treatment, symptoms may improve to the point that you don't even need the medication anymore. Or you need less medication. Or, sometimes, you need more medication. Or a different medication. In any case, your ADD may change, but it will not disappear.

■ ■ ■

Q: You stress the importance of the history in making the diagnosis. But in my daughter's case it wasn't at all clear from her history what was going on. She had done great in school until the tenth grade, when she began to tail off, both academically and emotionally. She was just not a happy kid anymore. But these changes were concurrent with her feeling angry with us about setting too many restrictions and with her having many expanding interests—boys, music, and shopping being the main ones. We went through two years of intense struggle. We chalked all this up to adolescence, until my daughter's twelfth-grade English teacher suggested an evaluation for ADD. Bingo! It was the missing link. We got treatment for her, and all our lives changed for the better.

She still has all her many "interests," we still struggle (with about three megatons less intensity), but she is back on track, near the top of her class academically, and, most important, happy again.

But my question is this: since her symptoms of ADD were not apparent in her history, is there any way we might have made the diagnosis sooner?

A: Yours is a very good question. While I do stress the importance of the history in making the diagnosis—and the history does remain the best "test" we have for ADD—history alone sometimes is not enough.

With some children the onset of the problems caused by ADD is slow and insidious. While their ADD has been present since birth, these children have been able to cope with it so successfully that there has been no problem. At some point along the way, however, they begin to encounter problems, as all children do. When there have been no prior warning signs of ADD, it is almost impossible for the diagnosis to be made by history alone.

Your daughter's scenario is a common one, especially among bright or gifted children. The problems caused by ADD intertwine imperceptibly with the problems caused by normal development. Hence one ascribes all the problems to everyday life, like ascribing the peeling of paint on your house to the salt in the air, without knowing there may be a problem in the paint itself. You set about solving the problems in everyday ways, repainting with the same paint. With adolescents this usually means what you did—struggle and try to set limits.

The insidious onset of ADD can deceive even the most experienced doctor or other practitioner in the field. When we watch a play, we usually get right into the characters and the plot, without stopping to think about the lighting. And yet the lighting profoundly influences how we see the play. ADD is to life events what lighting is to a play. It precedes the action, and its influence is seen everywhere. Yet it may never consciously be noticed.

In a case such as your daughter's, the diagnostician must use more tests than just the history. This is where neuropsychological testing becomes invaluable. There are a variety of tests of distractibility and impulsivity that a neuropsychologist uses. Some are basic, like the Wechsler intelligence test. Typically, in ADD there is a greater than ten-point split between the scores of two halves of this intelligence test, the performance half and the verbal half. Also certain subscores typically are lower in ADD. These are the subscores for coding, arithmetic, and digit span.

Then there are other tests that try to assess more specifically the symptoms of ADD. These tests have various names with initials, like the TOVA or the CPT. It would be too cumbersome to describe them all in detail here, but basically each assesses attention and distractibility in a different way. Some use puzzles. Others involve solving problems. In some, the subject watches series of flashing lights and tries to click a switch when, and only when, a certain pattern flashes. In others the subject tries to pick out letters in a camouflage, rather like looking for Waldo. None of these tests alone is definitive. However, when used in combination as a battery of tests, they can uncover hidden evidence of ADD and help clarify the diagnosis where history alone was insufficient.

As to your making the diagnosis sooner, perhaps you might have. But it would have been difficult. I think you—and the English teacher—did well to pick it up at all. Most individuals like your daughter *never* get diagnosed.

■ ■ ■

Q: Can ADD and manic-depressive illness [bipolar disorder] exist in the same person?

A: Yes, indeed. There are estimates that as many as 10 percent of individuals with manic-depressive, or bipolar, disorder also have ADD.

■ ■ ■

Q: Can you have a conduct disorder in a child who also has ADD?

A: Yes. Both oppositional defiant disorder and conduct disorder can exist with ADD in children.

■ ■ ■

Q: Can children who have fetal alcohol syndrome look as if they have ADD?

A: Yes. Some babies who are born to mothers who drank too much alcohol during pregnancy develop a condition referred to as fetal alcohol syndrome, resulting from the toxic effects of alcohol upon the fetus while still *in utero*. It is characterized by certain phys- ical abnormalities as well as neurological symptoms that resemble attention deficit disorder. Medication can help, but in general ADD secondary to fetal alcohol syndrome doesn't respond as well to treatment as genetically transmitted ADD.

■ ■ ■

Q: Our school psychologist referred to something called "cen- tral auditory processing disorder," and said our son may have that instead of ADD. What is it, and how does it relate to ADD?

A: Central auditory processing disorder, or CAPD, refers to hav- ing problems with deciding how to use what you hear. CAPD does not include individuals who have hearing impairment or who are in- tellectually slow. The problem in CAPD is not that you can't hear or that you aren't smart enough to know what to do with what you do hear, but that you have a problem in processing what you hear.

Let me digress here on a matter of vocabulary that is central in the world of learning problems. I want to discuss the word "process" and its contemporary derivatives.

In decades gone by, "process" was a noun. It referred to a set of steps that were customarily followed to reach some goal, as in "the learning process" or "the legal process." The use of "process" as a verb was restricted to only the most dreary bureaucratic centers, as in "Passport Processing Center" or "Draft Cards Processed Here."

Then process got processed (about the same time, by the way, that impact got impacted and became a verb in vogue). The word "processing" arrived in common usage with the Cuisinart, I think. It originally had to do with grinding up food quickly and into varying consistencies and shapes. Soon after the food people conscripted what used to be a noun and turned it into a verb, as in "to process" potatoes, it was then returned to the land of nouns, but now in a verb form, as in "food processor," where the noun "food," is used as an adjective to modify the noun "processor," which is itself a processed verb.

Then the information and computer people stole "process" and its derivatives from the food people. This was a sad day in the history of clear speech and writing. Now, instead of trying to describe as precisely as possible what happens to a bit of information as it enters a machine or a brain, it became acceptable to say it gets "processed." What does that mean? That the bit of information undergoes some process? Well, yes, probably, but what kind of process? Is there any specificity to the word? No. That's the great beauty of it. It can be used anywhere. It is even vaguer than "nice" or "incredible" or "big." What does it mean? No one really knows. The human brain might be described as an information processor. What does that mean, that the brain takes in information, transforms it in some way, then stores it or uses it? Why not say that, if that is what is meant? Is processing the same as thinking? Is it the same as seeing? Can you "process" if you can't read? Can you "process" in your sleep?

So from food processors we went to word processors; then the psychologists gave us the idea of information processors and the inevitable "disorders" of information processing trotted by. We now use that slippery word "processing" blithely, as if we knew what we meant by it; it is good to stop and reflect that we don't. Or at least to confess that information processing means nothing more exact than food processing. You put the information in the processor—the brain—and then you wait as the information gets ground up. The brain has different blades and can perform various functions, but exactly what is going on as it "processes"—that we don't know.

If you feel confused by the term "central auditory processing disorder" you have every right to be. It is a fancy term. What it means is anybody's guess. It was defined in 1992 by the American Speech-Language-Hearing Association as "limitation in the ongoing transmission, analysis, organization, transformation, elaboration, storage, retrieval, and use of information contained in audible signals." People with CAPD hear, but they have problems with storing and responding properly. This syndrome can look a great deal like ADD; in fact, some people argue that CAPD and ADD are slightly different expressions of the same disorder. Studies have estimated that as high as 50 percent of children with CAPD also have ADD. So not all children with CAPD have ADD. They need proper diagnosis and treatment rather than being lumped together with the ADD population.

CAPD is a real disorder. Like ADD it is hard to define precisely. However, there are people who cannot use what they hear effectively, and their difficulty does not result from being cognitively impaired or hard of hearing. Some of them also have ADD. A big problem is that different medical disciplines diagnose and treat ADD and CAPD. CAPD is diagnosed mainly by audiologists or speech and language specialists, while ADD is diagnosed by psychologists and psychiatrists. This means that many of the professionals who know enough to diagnose CAPD do not know enough to diagnose ADD, and many of the people who know enough to diagnose ADD do not know enough to diagnose CAPD.

We can only diagnose what we know about. Knowledge is growing so fast that not only do you need a specialist to treat a certain disorder, but you need a specialist to have even heard of it. The reason people with ADD have had such a difficult time getting the right diagnosis is that, until recently, most doctors had never heard of ADD. Even specialists. I completed my residency in psychiatry without ever hearing of ADD. Not until I began subspecialty training in child psychiatry did I encounter ADD.

This is not the fault of doctors. They work as hard as any profession to keep up with their field. However, it is impossible for one doctor to know everything. It is even impossible for one doctor to know enough about everything to know when he should make a referral. Particularly in the field of learning disabilities, where very little is covered in the traditional medical curriculum, you cannot expect your doctor to know all the latest developments.

Without getting into a long, technical discussion, the best advice for you is to enquire of your evaluator if he or she is aware of CAPD, and if not, whom you should consult. Psychologists, especially those with expertise in educational testing, should know when to make a referral to an audiologist to diagnose suspected CAPD.

■ ■ ■

Q: My child was given a battery of educational tests (IQ, etc.) before we knew she had ADD. If these tests are given to an uncooperative child who isn't taking the proper medication, how valid are the scores?

A: They may be way off. One of the problems with testing is that factors like motivation, mood, and the degree of structure and novelty in the testing situation can all influence scores. Also it is widely accepted that children can score quite differently on and off the right medication. Testing is useful, but we must always read the results knowing how variable they may be.

■ ■ ■

Q: Is there a correlation between ADD and learning disabilities? My daughter (sixteen years old) was diagnosed last year with ADD but no testing was done for LD.

A: There is a greater-than-average chance that if your daughter has ADD she also has some learning disability (LD), such as dyslexia or a math disability. It is also true that if a person has some LD there is a greater-than-average chance that person also has ADD. However, ADD and LD are not synonymous. They may coexist in the same individual or they may occur separately.

Usually, when testing is done for ADD the examiner also looks for LD. However, this is not always the case. If you have reason to believe your daughter may have LD, by all means take her back for more testing. While the history is the best way to diagnose ADD, testing is the best tool to diagnose LD.

■ ■ ■

Q: Is a problem learning foreign languages part of the diagnosis of ADD?

A: No, not strictly speaking. Problems learning foreign languages are not part of the diagnostic criteria for ADD.

However, many children and adults who have ADD also have great difficulty acquiring foreign languages. Try as they might, they stumble at every attempt to learn any language but their native one. This is a common, but not invariable, associated finding. Some people with ADD are language geniuses. Their rapid-fire switching ability lets them hop from tongue to tongue!

■ ■ ■

Q: Who can best determine the diagnosis of ADD—pediatrician, psychologist, neurologist, or psychiatrist?

A: All can, as long as they know what ADD is and what it isn't.

The best diagnostician of ADD is a professional who has a great deal of experience with ADD, but who also is enough of a generalist not to mistake some other condition for ADD and not to overdiagnose ADD. To a person who has a hammer, everything can start to look like a nail. Make sure the professional you see has more than just a hammer in his toolbox.

As to which discipline the professional should come from, that does not really matter. An M.D. should definitely be involved in the process at some point to evaluate medical factors, but an M.D. need not be the main evaluator; psychologists are well-trained to diagnose ADD, as are some social workers, occupational therapists, and nurses.

However, be careful. As ADD grows in the public's awareness, more and more people represent themselves as experts in ADD. As one of my patients said to me, "ADD has become a growth industry." Not every self-proclaimed expert knows ADD from ABC. Be particularly wary of people who charge large fees and require fancy tests to make the diagnosis.

The best way to find the right clinician is through your family doctor or a friend who has already seen the doctor and can vouch for him or her. Another reliable source for a referral is a medical school. All states have medical schools, and many have several. You can call the department of psychiatry or pediatrics as a starting point. Most medical schools have clinics on site that deal with ADD. If not, they can suggest where you might go.

■ ■ ■

Q: What physical tests should be done to make a diagnosis of ADD (e.g., physical exam, blood tests, X-rays, scans, etc.)?

A: Most authorities would agree that no tests beyond a physical exam and standard blood tests (including thyroid function tests) should be routine. Some authorities would contend that even these tests need not be routine. The automatic ordering of more expensive, advanced tests is unnecessary.

Other tests should only be done when the history or physical exam indicates they are needed or if they are needed before treatment can begin. For example, if your doctor suspects a seizure disorder on the basis of your history, he may order an EEG. Or if on your physical exam your doctor detects a neurological abnormality, he may order a scan of some sort. If your mental-status exam suggests memory problems, additional blood tests may be indicated or a skull X-ray. Or if your doctor decides treatment with tricyclic antidepressants is in order, an EKG must be performed first.

■ ■ ■

Q: Can you suggest an appropriate evaluation setting for an elementary-school student with ADD?

A: Three settings come immediately to mind: the classroom, the dining-room table, and the bedroom. (One of the worst places is the doctor's office. Kids aren't themselves in doctors' offices.) The classroom is probably the best place of all. If your evaluator cannot come to the classroom or have dinner with you and your family or watch your child as he or she gets dressed and ready for school in the morning, as most cannot, then the next-best thing is for the evaluator to be given detailed accounts of what happens in these settings. Teacher reports are particularly valuable. I think teacher reports are the single most valuable piece of diagnostic data I can receive.

■ ■ ■

Q: No offense intended, but how do I know you know all you need to know to make the correct diagnosis?

A: No offense taken; you ask an excellent question. The fact is, I don't know enough. I don't know that anyone does. Many people know a great deal more than I do, but I don't think anybody knows everything in this field.

The problem is that "this field" is in fact many fields. The diagnosis and treatment of learning and attentional problems draw upon the latest information from many disciplines. To name a few, all of which publish their own specialty journals and convene their own conferences, there are the disciplines of neurology, pediatric neurology, neuroscience, neurochemistry, pharmacology, psychopharmacology, biochemistry, neuroimaging, neuroradiology, psychiatry, child psychiatry, psychology, child psychology, cognitive psychology, learning theory, experimental psychology, audiology, speech and language pathology, behavioral therapy, school counseling, pediatrics, developmental pediatrics, family medicine, internal medicine, ophthalmology, pediatric ophthalmology, ophthalmologic neurology, occupational therapy, recreational, dance, and other movement therapies, social work, educational psychology, educational theory, reading theory, phonetics, not to mention the questions treatment always raises in philosophy, ethics, and epistemology.

All those disciplines contribute to "the field" of learning and attentional problems. No one is expert in all those disciplines. Few people are even conversant in most. What we have is a situation that is increasingly common in today's world of knowledge boom. Not only does no one know all, no one can even know how much he or she doesn't know. We have legs in diverging rowboats all the time. The best one can do is to be in touch with specialists in disparate fields, skim a wide variety of journals, have easy access to computer networks and the "information super-highway," and above all, be humble.

■ ■ ■

Q: Can you look at an EEG signal and identify a person with ADD?

A: No. There is no EEG (electroencephalogram, or brain-wave test) pattern characteristic of ADD.

■ ■ ■

Q: Our psychologist ruled out ADD because no hyperactivity was present. Is that correct? Does a person have to be hyperactive?

A: No. You may have ADD *without* hyperactivity. These people are very daydreamy, even serene.

■ ■ ■

Q: What is meant by comorbidity in relation to ADD?

A: "Comorbid" is an adjective from the medical lexicon. If you are not familiar with medical jargon, "comorbid" might sound like something to do with death, maybe a variant on codependent.

All it really refers to is a coexisting pathological condition. "Co-" means more than one; "morbid" means sickness. When you hear people talk about the "comorbidity" associated with ADD, they are referring to the fact that other problems often accompany ADD. One may have ADD plus substance abuse, or ADD plus depression, or ADD plus anxiety disorders, or ADD plus panic attacks, or ADD plus psychosis, or ADD plus learning disabilities, to name a few.

It is imperative that the person evaluating you look for comorbid conditions, as they are often present.

.12.

The Brain's Behind It

THE BIOLOGY OF ADD

■ ■ ■

Q: Doesn't everyone have symptoms of ADD?

A: Many people recognize their own behavior and feelings in the ADD syndrome. But to receive the diagnosis, an individual must have a large cluster of symptoms that have been present since childhood, and that seriously affect their ability to function in school, at work, and in social relationships. Feeling disorganized, being prone to procrastination, and having trouble with intimate relationships is not enough to receive the diagnosis.

In our experience, people who seek help for what they suspect is ADD *do* have symptoms that are severe enough to significantly impair one of the major spheres (job, personal relationships, pleasure, self-esteem). The United States is certainly a country demanding that we all live ADD lives. But not everyone has it. "ADD symptoms" have a real impact only on the lives of those who have the inner biological machinery producing many, if not all, of the symptoms in a consistent and debilitating manner.

■ ■ ■

Q: Is ADD a biochemical problem?

A: Yes and no. Most experts believe that disorders like ADD stem from biochemical malfunctions. Those with ADD, they believe, don't have the right amount of neurotransmitters in the gap (the synapse) between nerves in the brain. However, such explanations lead to the false hope that all science has to do is determine the right cocktail mixture, and then correctly package it and deliver it, in order to fix the problem. The widespread celebration of Prozac as a "transforming" medication has led people to believe what is still just wishful thinking: that all one has to do is correct a neurochemical imbalance and the demons will be gone.

Unfortunately, it's not so simple. PET, SPECT, and EEG studies show that in ADD brains there are not only biochemical anomalies but also geographical, or structural, differences.

■ ■ ■

Q: What symptoms of ADD can structural brain differences explain?

A: There are neurobiological differences in ADD that researchers believe do contribute to the symptoms of impulsivity, hyperactivity, distractibility, and perhaps even risk-taking behavior. These differences exist on three different levels of brain operation: the macro level, or differences that affect the overall functioning of brain processes; the regional level, or differences that are apparent in particular structures and interfere with the way parts of the brain communicate with one another; and the molecular level, or differences that have been found in the genes of those with ADD and which influence cell function.

1. *The macro level:* In some ADD-ers there is diminished blood flow to the frontal cortex, which means that there is diminished activity and less glucose utilization (glucose is fuel for brain cells and its use indicates that the cells are active). This has led some to see the ADD brain as being sleepy or in need of arousal in order to operate efficiently. This is significant, because the main job of the frontal cortex is to inhibit, or to slow down, those messages coming from other parts of the brain, and to sculpt the final product that

comes into consciousness. Thus we see disturbances in the area of the brain that is crucial to maintain arousal and attention. The frontal areas of the brain also help modulate emotional responses originating in the lower parts of the brain, and perform executive tasks like planning, following through, and anticipating consequences. Obviously, a sleepy frontal cortex limits one's ability to keep emotions in check and to set and achieve goals.

Those with this type of ADD could be described as chronically underaroused. They may consistently seek high stimulus experience in order to increase the level of frontal brain activity. The intensity of the high stimulus event awakens the sleepy cortex and allows it to function normally. So despite the risk that, say, sky diving, vertical skiing, or gambling entails, those with this type of ADD don't feel anxious or diseased while engaged in such activity, as their brain systems are actually experiencing a kind of stabilization.

There is another type of decreased functioning, whose physiological basis has been observed by Dr. Daniel Amen and colleagues using the SPECT scan. In this case, the ADD-er has a normal blood flow through the frontal cortex *until* he needs to pay attention. Only then does the blood flow diminish. Of course, this is the opposite of what one would expect in the normal brain or, for that matter, in the brains of those with ADD, since usually whenever there is an increase in stimulus, there is a corresponding increase in brain activity and thus in blood flow. In other words, just when this type of ADD brain is supposed to respond, it goes dead, as if it has hit a "disconnect." This certainly mirrors the reports of those ADD-ers who feel focused until they are supposed to read or sit through a lecture. Then their brain turns to cotton wool. Amen has shown that this cruel joke of nature is measurable.

2. *The regional level:* Different groups of investigators have found there are two brain structures that are abnormal in ADD. These are the caudate nucleus and the corpus callosum. The caudate nucleus, which is deep in the middle of the brain, has been shown in three studies to be significantly different in a group of ADD children as compared to normal children. The caudate is responsible for initiating, inhibiting, and sculpting our movements and our attention. The caudate is one of the structures that deteriorates in

Parkinson's disease, the disorder made famous by Oliver Sacks in *Awakenings*. Here the patients had a difficult time starting to move, stopping their movements, and refining them to fit the pattern that they are consciously attempting to produce. The medication used to treat Parkinson's is L-Dopa, a dopamine replacement. The normal caudate is rich in dopamine and is definitely deficient in Parkinson's disease.

The caudate, with its rich connections to the frontal cortex, may also play a role in guiding attention. In ADD, the left side of the caudate appears to be smaller, and the blood flow through it is diminished. A study by Dr. H.C. Lou and colleagues found that the blood flow through the caudate became normal when Ritalin was given. What is striking is the similarity between an underfunctioning caudate, which contributes to the cognitive symptoms of ADD, problems with initiating, stopping, moving and sculpting our attention, and the physical symptoms of Parkinson's. It's worth noting that we use dopamine enhancers to treat the ADD symptoms of inattention.

The corpus callosum is the structure in the brain that allows the left and right hemispheres to communicate. Its function has been linked to the amount of arousal and attention that each hemisphere has at any one time. Two research groups have shown that the volume of the corpus callosum is lower in ADD children than in normal children. This could imply that the two hemispheres cannot communicate efficiently, which would lead to some of the symptoms or complaints we hear from ADD-ers.

For example, many ADD-ers complain that they cannot articulate the insights or ideas that come to them. They seem trapped in their right hemisphere and can't get their beautiful, holistic notions over to their left side to detail them, describe them, and logically convey the facts. Thus they often can't share with the world, their employers, their mentors, or their teachers the amazing discoveries they've happened upon. Often ADD adults say that if they could only convey their wisdom, they could make the world better. But they are blocked, and they and those around them suffer.

3. *The molecular, or genetic, level:* Another line of research indicating that biological differences are at work in ADD brains is more

biochemical than anatomical. The gene that codes for a specific type of dopamine receptor has been found to be abnormal 60 percent of the time in ADD patients. It is a defect on one of the versions of the D2 receptor gene, and is also found to be abnormal about 60 percent of the time in alcoholics, cocaine addicts, those with posttraumatic stress disorder, and patients with Tourette's disorders. This particular abnormality only appears in about 6 percent of the population overall.

The genetic mistake in question could lead to the production of ADD symptoms. Dopamine is an important neurotransmitter throughout the brain but especially prominent in the "attentional neural network," interconnected nerve cells that run throughout structures in the brain and involve arousal, motivation, and attention.

Because many areas of the brain contribute to fixing and sustaining attention, it is not necessarily one abnormality that is the cause of everyone's ADD. In the next decade we will undoubtedly use new technologies and techniques to further refine biological subtypes of ADD, meaning that we might be able to determine which structures or systems are malfunctioning in which individuals. We may find that some of the abnormalities, or various combinations of them, are causal links to deficits in brain function and subsequently to symptoms. This would be a guide to effectively tailor treatment strategies.

■ ■ ■

Q: You've referred many times to a relationship between ADD and intuition. What is this link?

A: Families, friends, and especially teachers frequently comment that ADD-ers live by their intuition. I agree. In fact, I like to think that having ADD means having a hypertrophic intuition muscle in the brain, which the ADD-er has been exercising since birth. For an ADD-er it isn't a matter of *choosing* to get better at intuition, it's a matter of *needing* to get better at it in order to get by. Due to such ADD symptoms as distractability, inattention to details, and the compulsion to move onward, ADD-ers must depend on intuition to fill in the blanks in their observations. They more or less guess their way through life.

Using intuition means constructing perceptions, or reaching conclusions or decisions, without relying solely upon objective information or rationality. It can involve disregarding available information, ignoring external stimuli, or processing it much more rapidly than is normal. Usually we perceive, solve problems, or anticipate consequences by integrating past experiences with present ones. We make moment-to-moment predictions based upon old memories and confirm or adjust those predictions by using relevant sensory information—the seeing, hearing, smelling, and feeling data of the present moment. Most of the time our behaviors are guided by this process.

The typical ADD-er perceives only a small percentage of relevant sensory information. The rapid-transit ADD brain puts the ADD person three steps ahead of the moment and prevents the accurate perception of information. Because the ADD-er is rapidly traveling past pertinent information, the usual information-processing procedure is skewed in the direction of prediction. That is, ADD-ers are prone to invent information in order to fill in those gaps created when they have not paused long enough to apprehend the event. Thus they encounter reality through a rapid reconstruction process. This process is necessary because they are never really in the moment—they are always channel-surfing their way to the next stimulus or reality frame. Since ADD-ers do this constantly they become well practiced and quite good at taking small bits of information and instantly developing a perception or a problem-solving strategy.

When they engage in these rapid reconstructions they are called intuitive. Often ADD-ers' intuition is sound. But sometimes they can be dead wrong. Yet the ADD-er cannot take the time to critically evaluate his conclusion. He cannot stop, observe, and use conflicting evidence to self-correct. So there are times when the ADD-er makes the grossest mistakes, and yet believes and insists that he is absolutely right.

Lastly, many ADD-ers are more right brain than left and have a distaste for logic and linear reasoning. They recognize patterns quickly.

They get the whole picture from a little information. Some find it difficult to translate the whole picture into details, which they find frustrating and time consuming. They do not want to spend time thinking in sequences, using words, or making judgments. Right-brain people, whether or not they have ADD, use the visual and the emotional to construct their ideas. They think in images and rhythms rather than in words. They depend on pattern recognition and pattern completion rather than incremental steps to reach an understanding. It could be said that they tend to leap to the whole and ignore many of the parts. When they pull it off, we call them artists, creators, pioneers, and leaders. We find many of them in the ADD population.

■ ■ ■

Q: I've heard a lot of mixed reviews about using biofeedback to treat ADD. Does it work?

A: Biofeedback seems to help some people with their ADD symptoms, but others have been disappointed when treatment did not produce any long-term benefits.

Biofeedback obtains data from your body and brain by monitoring physiologic measures like electrical brain activity. The patient observes the changes in the data and is taught to remain in the "alpha state," the brain state that is indicative of being optimally attentive. This reduces overall bodily stress and helps maintain a steadily focused brain. The aim is to raise and stabilize the brain's arousal state while lowering the arousal of the body. Biofeedback offers the possibility of control and regularity without medication.

The debate over biofeedback concerns whether or not the treatment leads to a generalized change in attention span when the patient is not being monitored by the machine. Some people feel that its effect is only temporary. The zealousness of proponents is matched only by the vehemence of their detractors, so more studies need to be done. And although the cost of the treatment remains an issue, this will change as home machines become available and affordable.

■ ■ ■

Q: Are ADD and LD the same thing? Is there a biological link?

A: Learning disabilities can exist without ADD. And ADD can exist without LD.

But 30 percent of LD kids will have ADD and 30 percent of ADD kids will have a learning disability. Is there a biological link? One recent study showed that of all the possibilities as to why ADD and LD frequently are found together, the statistically strongest reason was nonrandom mating—that is, people with ADD tend to marry people with LD more than would be predicted by chance alone. Some people claim this is not surprising since ADD-ers and LD-ers recognize kindred spirits and delight in each other's nonlinear encompassing of life's richness.

■ ■ ■

Q: Is there any evidence of environmental factors causing or affecting ADD?

A: The brain's ability to attend and focus is a final common pathway involving the interaction of many regions of the brain. Environmental factors that disturb normal brain activity can affect the attentional network and look like classic ADD. Some 90 to 95 percent of people diagnosed with ADD have inherited it—that is, their ADD is genetically based—while the other 5 to 10 percent develop it as a result of external factors.

The rapidly developing and very plastic brain in utero and in the young baby is particularly sensitive to injury, trauma, or toxins, and thus taxing events during this time, such as prematurity, difficult labor and delivery, and early head trauma, can all lead to an ADD-like picture. Throughout life toxic chemicals, radiation, trauma to the brain, seizures, tumors, and strokes can all produce or worsen ADD. In addition, temporary changes caused by infections, drugs, allergic states, hormonal abnormalities, and acute psychiatric disorders like anxiety, depression, mania, OCD (obsessive-compulsive disorder), and psychological trauma will all create an ADD-like state or make resident ADD worse. The knowledge that these influences from the environment can create ADD-like symptoms underscores the need to obtain a proper medical diagnosis that would rule out these other causes and establish the legitimate condition before treatment is begun.

■ ■ ■

Q: What about asthma and ADD?

A: There is a higher incidence of asthma in people with ADD. This is important to recognize because we know that theophylline, and other drugs used to treat asthma, can impair the attention of kids and adults, thus complicating our attempts at treatment of the ADD. When possible, alternate treatment strategies for asthma should be explored.

■ ■ ■

Q: Is there an association between ADHD and thyroid disorder?

A: The thyroid and ADD are natural companions, as the psychiatric symptoms of hyperthyroidism, or too much thyroid, match those of ADD. In fact, any child or adult who has a sudden onset of ADD without any history of it in the past should be checked for thyroid abnormalities.

Recently Peter Hauser, Alan Zametkin, and their group at the National Institutes of Mental Health found an association between another thyroid disorder and ADHD. Generalized resistance to thyroid hormone (GRTH) also creates symptoms matching ADHD. This disorder is autosomal dominant in its transmission, which means that the only way to get it is to inherit it—and many offspring will.

The study found that 50 percent of the adults in the sample who had GRTH also had ADHD, and 70 percent of the children with GRTH had ADHD. This finding is exciting as it could possibly lead to some helpful gene studies that could contribute toward our understanding of ADHD.

GRTH is a relatively rare disorder, found in only fifty families in the United States, and should not lead to rampant thyroid testing of all ADD children. Though some authorities recommend that all ADD children be screened for thyroid dysfunction, the authors and others do not recommend widespread screening unless there are suggestive symptoms or family history.

■ ■ ■

Q: If ADD isn't diagnosed until adulthood, is it harder to treat?

A: Biologically speaking, no. Medications can work just as successfully for adults as they do for children.

On other levels, the ADD adult brings special strengths and vulnerabilities to the treatment situation. Treatment is often forced upon children, which leads to mixed results. The adult, on the other hand, is more likely to collaborate with the clinician. Due to their increased awareness of their problems, and their troubled past, adults are more likely to take the disorder and its treatment very seriously.

Most adults with ADD have been searching their whole lives, knowing something was wrong, but being unable to identify the cause of their distress. However, this very issue is what can make treatment a bit more difficult. The adult's history of failure, confusion, and unhappiness usually results in deep-rooted pain and low self-esteem. Coexisting anxiety or depressive disorders are common, as is substance abuse. Treatment becomes as much about rebuilding an entire sense of self as about medication and behavioral management.

■ ■ ■

Q: Can those who seemed to be "cured" of ADD after passing through puberty regress in later life?

A: Adolescence can resolve many of the symptoms of ADD. As the brain develops, some of the weakness of the attentional network can, on a biological level, be adequately compensated for or fixed directly. The brain continues to develop throughout life and the frontal cortex, an important part of the attentional neural net, finishes much of its growth during adolescence. The myth that as the brain matures, so does the person, is true for some.

Symptoms could reappear later, due to stress, life changes, or further brain changes. For instance, one of my patients, Mary, had stopped taking Ritalin at the age of sixteen. She was doing well in school and socially and continued to thrive after stopping medication. She was the captain of her soccer and basketball teams and even ran the Boston Marathon in her senior year in high school. But at college she fell apart. She did not make the varsity sports teams, and her poor school performance had her on probation.

What happened? She had hit the unstructured college life, lost her vigorous exercise schedule, and had too much time on her hands. The busy, crammed time of high school had provided the external structure that her brain needed, and her strenuous exercise had helped control her distractibility and kept her emotionally stable. Without these aids, and with the increased demands of college work, her ADD resurfaced. She needed to start supportive therapy and medication once again to help get back on track.

■ ■ ■

Q: My ADD seems to affect everything, even my level of consciousness. At times I am almost unconscious and unaware of what is going on around me. Is there a biologic explanation?

A: Perhaps. Some interesting new work by Francis Crick and Cristof Koch on the neurology of consciousness might contain some clues about this phenomenon. They speculate that human consciousness can be reduced to attention and short-term memory.

Disturbances in these two brain operations, which together comprise the general concept of awareness, can lead to an altered state of consciousness. As we are painfully aware, ADD is defined by disturbances in attention and short-term memory, making it likely that the conscious state of the ADD-er will be different than normal.

Some patients with ADD will complain of frequently being out of it, unaware of what they just did or what was going on about them. We have called these ADD-ers "ahistorical selves"—they have a shifting sense of who and what they are and do not seem to have a sense of their formative past. This may be due to an "ADD state of consciousness," which distorts their sense of time and place.

■ ■ ■

Q: I have a hard time making decisions. I'm always able to see everyone else's point of view, but I have no real views or preferences of my own. My first therapist told me that I had a defect in my inner self. I now have been diagnosed with ADD and I wonder if there is a connection between it and my indecisiveness?

A: Many people with ADD have trouble making up their minds. They are the proverbial "fence sitters." In fact they seem to have no enduring set of values or ideas of their own, but rather embrace those of whatever group or individual they are currently engaged by. And when there is more than one set of views vying for their attention, they find themselves agreeing with one side and then with the other side. In fact many politicians have ADD-like qualities and their ability to "shape shift" allows them to appeal to many groups with diverse views.

Is this due to early childhood problems in parenting or due to the workings of the brain? A Freudian account would say that early trauma had overwhelmed the developing ego, leaving the individual unable to repress competing impulses or interests. Such an individual would be bound by every stimulus that might come into his awareness. Object relations theorists would characterize an individual with these traits as lacking a cohesive sense of self due to a childhood absence of supportive, consistent mothering. Similarly, the self-psychology school would find the person defective in the formation of his "true self" due to a deficient "holding environment." However, I would describe the problem this way: such an individual, like many ADD-ers, has an historical self. These ADD-ers often forget the choices they've made in the past and/or why they made them. Their outlook can easily be reshaped by any force or person in their current environment who is sufficiently compelling. This is not to say that these ADD-ers are weak-willed. Rather they seem to be suffering from "environmental dependency syndrome." This recently defined syndrome results from damage to the lower regions of the brain's frontal lobes. Patients with this affliction imitate the behavior of those around them.

A similar disturbance in the frontal lobes may have some of the same effects on the behavior of many with ADD. These ADD-ers do not look inward or to the past to determine what they should do, but rather are guided by the values and goals of whatever group or institution they are part of at the moment. Since they rarely stop to consider their own goals, their behavior is almost never shaped by their individual aims. In fact, they avoid grappling with important personal decisions at just about any point in their lives, e.g., they frequently end up in a profession suggested by someone whose reasons sounded good at the time.

However, ADD-ers who are "environmentally dependent" have one decided advantage: they are great in a crisis. Since they are not preoccupied by their own goals, they react quickly, and often creatively, to the demands of the moment.

■ ■ ■

Q: Is there any treatment to help me be less influenced by my surroundings? I avidly pursue any challenge that's presented to me, while neglecting other tasks and pursuits that are of greater importance.

A: Treatment begins with recognizing your environmental dependence. You need to be your own "environmental engineer" and create the environment that will inevitably drive you. Here are three major elements to consider in constructing the right personal environment.

Structure. First, you need to structure your physical space so that it works for you rather than against you. If, like most ADD-ers, you are easily thrown off course by physical distractions, try such strategies as making your office soundproof, facing a wall (not a window or door) while you work, and throwing out the television. Next, devise the most helpful psychological space. Decide whether you work best solo or as a team member. Many ADD-ers find they need to work closely with other people who stimulate them, modulate their sometimes excessive enthusiasm, and help them hone their ideas. If you find the presence of others more of an undermining distraction than an enabling support, you will still find it beneficial to have a coach to check in with regularly to reinforce your commitment to your short- and long-term goals.

Obligations. ADD-ers function best by putting themselves under obligation. Choosing the right set of goals and then making them obligations is crucial. An obligation can mobilize "good guilt" that will help you meet the goal you set with your coach or team. This "good guilt" focuses you, and because it functions as a demand for action, it lets you escape from the trap of procrastination.

Missions. Another method is to make goals into missions, and then break them down into large and small ones. Changing the nature of each duty by making it more interesting, more competitive, allows the ADD-er to remain excited and attuned to the task at hand. Dr. Thomas Gaultieri describes this as a process of "limbic tagging," a way to increase the brain's focus and attentiveness to the otherwise unremarkable task. What actually occurs is that the part of the brain that controls emotions, the limbic system, becomes stimulated, and in turn activates the frontal cortex, thereby increasing attentiveness to the material at hand. By breaking down each goal into large and small challenges, and instilling energy into each activity, the ADD-er can more often meet goals that had originally seemed overwhelming. Not only are deadlines easier to stick to, but also feelings of genuine satisfaction accompany and reward the task well done. Without these methods, the ADD-er's search for a meaningful goal becomes the mission—the focus—when the focus should be on actively pursuing the chosen goal itself.

■ ■ ■

Q: I never get to tend to my own life! Most of my female friends have successfully shifted their roles. They have become more independent and can set and achieve self-fulfilling goals. In contrast, I continue to use all of my energy accommodating others and managing everyone else's life. I know many women still have this problem, but does my ADD play a part in keeping me so firmly fixed in my role?

A: Yes, your ADD can definitely add to your tendency to easily adopt available roles and make it harder for you to emerge from them. Many ADD-ers are completely driven by cues from their environment. Women ADD-ers find it especially difficult to free themselves from their assigned role, having become addicted to its safe harbor. The rigid social expectations embodied in the role of the caretaking, sacrificing female actually have helped many women contain their ADD symptoms for years. Pouring energy into handling the daily demands and emergencies of one's family can become a welcome structure, a mission that is hard to challenge.

The ADD-er must become her own environmental engineer, deciding for herself what role to pursue. She needs to be aware that her resistance to others' demands is compromised from the statrt, and that she is prone to being trapped in a role without noticing, while losing sight of her own hopes and dreams.

■ ■ ■

Q: My daughter has a horrible time making and keeping friends. She wants them desperately but can't do it. Are there always problems in social relations with ADD? Are there biologic roots to this problem?

A: Unfortunately, many ADD-ers seem to have attributes that get in the way of forming successful friendships. Some ADD-ers may recognize the conventional form of social communications but can't shape their own verbal and physical responses to others accordingly. They end up alienating those with whom they'd like to be friends. These ADD-ers don't pay attention to the cues and nuances of social interaction necessary to sustain a discourse. Often they "seize the floor" and then tell what should be a funny story, and yet fail to communicate the punch line. Sometimes they space out, leaving their friends and acquaintances feeling confused. Often their frustration at not being able to sense the rhythms that shape a group's interactions manifests itself in angry outbursts, rudeness in speech and action, and restlessness: traits that do not add to their desirability as playmates or long-term friends. The defenses ADD-ers build up to protect themselves from further rejection only make matters worse. They may attempt to control people and the environment around them through bullying or demanding behavior. They can seem narcissistic or arrogant. And their poor self-image may cause them to denigrate others in order to bolster their own diminished sense of worth.

Most of these unwinning characteristics stem from neurobiological differences found in ADD. Poor information-processing and lack of ability to brake inappropriate impulses contribute to the social awkwardness, restlessness, and communication difficulties that many with ADD regularly experience.

Just as there is a definite subset of ADD people who are interpersonally dense, unable to form or sustain friendships, there is also a subset of ADD-ers who are charismatic and interpersonally intuitive. Both subsets are driven more or less by differences in their brains' operating system. In any case, I would predict that one of the growth industries in psychological services is going to be social skills training, not only in ADD children—where the greatest impact will be made—but for ADD adults. Many of our adult ADD patients desire help with their interaction and would welcome close coaching and group work.

■ ■ ■

Q: I have few friends because I drive them crazy with my chatter. They say I glue on to them and won't stop talking. I end up making no sense and no friends. Is this related to my ADD?

A: One of the distinct subtypes of ADD is characterized by overly sustained focus on one person or topic. ADD-ers of this type get hooked on a subject or just talking in general and can't stop themselves from going on and on. At the same time, they seem oblivious to the listener's response (which often is frustration or just plain boredom).

Their behavior is driven by the biology of ADD. The underfunctioning of the frontal lobes makes these ADD-ers prone to particular problems in sustaining attention, and while they seem to be obsessively attentive to one topic or audience, it's precisely because they can't focus long enough to assess whether their point has been made that they keep nattering on about the same subject.

Recognizing that these ADD-ers' behavior is the result of a particularly lazy frontal lobe can reduce its annoyance factor, and having their problems pointed out by professionals or others who know about their ADD can help them to monitor their behavior more closely. Finally, medication with stimulants can dramatically ameliorate the problems.

■ ■ ■

Q: I have a hard time developing emotional closeness with my mate. I can't seem to listen closely and respond to her. I worry that I am incapable of loving. What role does my ADD play in my dilemma?

A: Of course, the expression of ADD in an individual is as unique as his or her fingerprint. The form ADD takes is dependent upon a complex interplay of biological and environmental forces. What is remarkable is that despite the many faces of ADD, the problems that ADD people have in their relationships seem astonishingly similar. This suggests that there is a "biology of intimacy."

If the story for those with ADD has the same ending each time, either the starting materials or the developmental process must be influencing the plot in a predictable manner. The diversity of social, political, and economic backgrounds within the ADD population rules out developmental processes as the sole cause of their problems with intimacy. We are left to consider the starting materials, the biological tendencies present at birth.

Particularly evident in adults with ADD is a consistent overreaction to emotional triggers. For instance, when contradicted by a loved one, the ADD-er may see it as a supreme rejection and lash out, dumfounding their mate. While this overreaction may appear immature or in other words as a problem in psychological development, it is caused by a deficiency in the natural inhibitory control of the brain. The lack of "cortical control" in ADD may interfere with an individual's efforts to establish and maintain healthy relationships in a number of ways:

Physiological barriers. There is a physiological restlessness that stems from the inability of the frontal cortex of those with ADD to inhibit motor output, which creates the dis-ease, the pressured uneasiness characteristic of the ADD syndrome. The restlessness can dramatically interfere with the quality of the individual's intimate relationships. We have some clients who cannot be physically close to another individual for an extended time without feeling trapped. Some are supersensitive to touch. Others feel an urgency to move or to act, which manifests itself in pacing, wandering off, or fleeing. One of our clients once sadly commented, "How can I be heart to heart when I can't even be eye to eye?"

Cognitive barriers. The restlessness of the ADD syndrome includes not just physiological urgency but also a cognitive discomfort with sameness. Like ADD children who crave—and perform best with—new and varied stimuli, adults with ADD generally report an overwhelming desire to move on to the next cognitive frame, the next new thing, the next idea or thought.

The tendency to move ever faster makes it almost impossible to register the other's thoughts or feelings, let alone reflect on them. It's as if people with ADD cannot "study" the other person or the situation any better than they can study their textbooks while in school. Since ADD-ers frequently carefully consider the messages they receive from others or the cues apparent in their environment, they are prone to developing false perceptions about people, characterizations that owe more to the ADD-er's inventive imagination than to reality. Sometimes ADD-ers, in their compulsive hurriedness, simply assign an unfair label to another person. The inaccurate label takes on a life of its own, becoming a generalized script that guides the ADD-er's reactions, so that the boring interpersonal exchange becomes generalized as a boring partner, or the painful event becomes the painful relationship.

Emotional barriers. Just as there is the need to move forward to the next cognitive frame, so there is the need to extinguish an existing emotional state and move on to the next. This creates intimate relationships that can be alternately intense and demanding, and distanced and cool. Interpersonal situations become events, where affects must be discharged all at once, to "get it over with." The phenomenon seems related to two factors, the first, already mentioned, being the need to move onward from current stimuli and states to new stimuli and states. The second factor is the seeming inability or unwillingness on the part of the ADD adult to postpone a reaction until after the "internal processing" warranted by the situation has taken place. Perhaps this is because ADD adults do not consider a particular emotional state or situation dynamic to be accessible at a later time. Thus the tool which many of us find essential to shaping our inner lives—namely, time—is unavailable.

The major work and reward of intimacy is in creating and having a mutually protected holding environment where one feels attended to, listened to, and comforted when necessary. When someone with ADD attempts to create this holding environment with the other person, the distractions, the "what's next," the movement, the wanting to get to the bottom line—the hurriedness of it all—clouds acceptance and love, and makes the other feel devalued, uncared for, and unlistened to. Since the ADD-er tends to experience intimate relationships as a series of events, these relationships take on a "chunky" nature: they are segmented or broken down into discrete, nettled encounters instead of existing as a continuum over time. The quiet times of an intimate relationship, the harbors, do not develop. Thus there is no continuous sense of emotional security for either partner.

■ ■ ■

Q: If problems with intimacy have a biological basis for people like me who have ADD, what can I do about them?

A: First of all, identifying and recognizing relationship problems as due to the ADD, rather than to interpersonal incompetency or "selfishness," goes a long way toward helping both participants in the relationship. It allows them to develop techniques that can help them get through the times that before were unmanageable. The strategies that work best for a couple or family might be suggested by therapists or a support group. However, the biology of ADD can defeat even the most motivated ADD-er's valiant attempt at change. In that event, medication can be helpful.

Here is an example of one ADD-er who found medication helped save her marriage. When Jane started medication, her marriage was near the end point. Her inability to listen to her husband, her tantrums, and her lack of organization that had always caused problems in the marriage had now become intolerable. Her interactions with her husband had become a series of small crises, with each interaction seeming to provoke her into a testy, nasty, doubting attitude. She described herself as "a porcupine ready to shoot her quills." Whatever current real-life problems might have exacerbated Jane's ADD then, there was no possibility that she and her husband could solve them together until her ADD symptoms were modified.

After a month on the medication, Jane reported the following: a cessation of paniclike responses, crises, and outbursts in her marriage and a diminishment of the "peaks and valleys" in her emotions. There was an increased relaxation, playfulness, and enjoyment within her marriage. She felt that she was more flexible and had more time to reflect both on what was said by her husband and what she herself felt. She stopped making snap decisions about what he was feeling, which promoted an ambiance of openness and mutuality. Her husband felt that she was more available, more responsive to his needs, and better able to listen to his troubles. This new emotional stability enabled Jane and her husband to structure a newly strong and nourishing marriage.

■ ■ ■

Q: How can an ADD adult pursue happiness? It seems that so much is stacked against us.

A: Long ago William James observed that happiness was proportional to success over pretensions. He claimed that if we increased our success or decreased our pretensions we would be happier. Knowing about your biologically driven limitations can lower your pretensions and give you the freedom to accentuate your strengths while dealing concretely with your weaknesses. This is the path to more success. With a reduction in overblown expectations and an increase in successes, we have an increase in happiness.

.13.

Whence It Came

THE GENETIC BASIS OF ADD

■ ■ ■

Q: Why are adoptees more prone to ADD?

A: An adopted child has an over 30-percent chance of having ADD. This is staggering and there are many speculations as to why this may be. The high percentage fits in well with psychodynamic theories that saw the disruption from the biologic mother and father as being causative in creating ADD in a child. That is to say that earlier theories assumed that the trauma of such an early and crucial separation created hyperactivity and behavioral problems.

Of course, we now see ADD much more clearly linked to the biology of the brain than to the psychology of the mind. We also know that ADD is a genetic disorder that is often inherited. Thus the best explanation for the high rate of ADD adoptees might be found in the genes of the biologic parents of the adopted children. One assumes that most pregnancies that produce children given up for adoption are the result of impulsive action. Thus it seems reasonable to think that the parents of these children may well have ADD, which the children then inherit.

We also know that children sometimes are put up for adoption when their lives, and the lives of one or both parents, are particularly tenuous or unhealthy. Circumstances might include substance abuse, violence, or extreme poverty. In these cases, the chaotic circumstances of the environment might have an effect on the development of the brain, both in utero (during pregnancy) and during the early life of the neonate. The plasticity of the brain is such that it is especially vulnerable to outside influences during its early development, and untoward circumstances could potentially alter development sufficiently enough to contribute toward ADD.

■ ■ ■

Q: What are the chances of ADD parents passing the ADD on to their children? What if both parents have ADD?

A: After conducting a number of studies, Dr. Joseph Biederman, and colleagues at the Massachusetts General Hospital estimate that there is a 30- to 80-percent chance that the children of an ADD parent will have ADD. One would expect this percentage to climb if both parents have the disorder, but to date there are no studies that confirm this.

■ ■ ■

Q: Has anyone identified a gene responsible for ADD?

A: A number of investigators are approaching the problem from several angles. David Comings, along with a number of other gene hunters, is looking at the genes that direct the development of the dopamine receptors in the brain. David and his wife, Brenda, headed a nationwide team of investigators who identified an uncommon gene that is found in 10 percent of the normal population but occurs in 55 to 65 percent of the ADD population. This is big news, as the dopamine receptor is the major one targeted by the stimulants used to treat ADD. It seems as though our treatments may be trying to correct a genetic variant that is instrumental in causing the symptoms of ADD.

A group led by Peter Hauser at the National Institutes of Mental Health has reported a compelling association of ADD and a rare genetic disorder of the thyroid. The disorder, generalized resistance to thyroid hormone (GRTH) is rare in both its occurrence (1 in 100,000) and in the fact that the name describes the problem—that is, the body is resistant to the action of thyroid hormone. It is confined to approximately fifty families in the United States, and those that have the disorder have a 50- to 70-percent chance of having ADD. The ADD may be caused by the thyroid problem in that it doesn't allow the brain to develop normally. Or it may be due to another gene defect that goes along with this gene problem. In any case, these studies are continuing to strengthen our perceptions that ADD is a brain problem and not due to TV, bad parents, or poor socioeconomic circumstances.

■ ■ ■

Q: If one child has ADD, and one parent does, would that mean there is a greater chance that the next child would have ADD?

A: No. Each child in the family has the same chance of having ADD as any other child in the family. Each chance is a new roll of the dice and the same odds always apply in each case. Some studies have indicated that there is a 35 percent chance of the next sibling having ADD if the first has it. These studies look at the phenomenon from a different perspective than the studies that have examined the probability of an ADD parent having an ADD child. But the incidence rate of 35 percent still falls within the 30- to 80-percent inheritance rate mentioned earlier in this section.

■ ■ ■

Q: Why are so many Americans diagnosed as having ADD? The incidence is far smaller in the rest of the world.

A: It is likely that we in America have a greater concentration of ADD genes in our collective gene pool. Dr. Frank Farley, past president of the American Psychological Association, has a hypothesis regarding the "T type personality." These people are constantly searching for big thrills or the next big adventure. They are risk takers, relentless in their pursuit of the next high-stimulus activity. Farley argues reasonably well that the United States is genetically loaded with this personality type.

There is a lot of overlap between the "T type personality" and the person with ADD. Like Farley, we similarly could argue that the United States has an especially high concentration of ADD genes. This is genetic drift—when the separation of groups within a species due to circumstances leads to slightly different genetic characteristics—and it is seen throughout history, across many species.

So why might the United States be loaded with ADD? Since our gene pools are made up of immigrant genes, that must mean our forebears had to leave their homeland, looking for adventure and a new world. They were restless movers and shakers and probably could not stand being fenced in by either the lack of opportunity or threats to their freedom. This probably selected a gene pool of people who are chronically curious and willing to risk traveling down new pathways of exploration. Sounds like ADD to me.

The Europeans, especially the British, are not very excited about ADD and see it as a curious American phenomenon. I'm fond of responding that ADD people couldn't stand the repressive bureaucratic structures of the developed countries and left to settle the wide open spaces. For instance, the pursuit of big sky and the attitude of "Don't fence me in" may be one of the reasons that Idaho leads the nation in per capita prescriptions of Ritalin for school-age children.

.14.

What's in a Pill?

TREATING ADD WITH MEDICATION

■ ■ ■

Q: What behaviors or brain functions can medication help?

A: The stimulants such as Ritalin, Dexedrine, and Cylert allow ADD-ers to inhibit their behaviors, allow them to put on the brakes, to slow down, to pay attention, and to increase focus. The stimulants accomplish this by "waking up" the frontal lobes of the brain. Research now indicates that the frontal lobes of those with ADD do not work as efficiently as they should. This is probably a critical factor in the ADD syndrome because the frontal lobes are normally responsible for regulating behavior by acting as the gate-keeper for the rest of the brain—they let the right information in, and usually only let appropriate information from other parts of the brain out. The frontal lobes also serve as the master planning station, integrating information from the outside world and from other parts of the brain in such a way that situations can be accurately assessed and goals or appropriate courses of action can be reasonably determined.

Needless to say, the improved functioning of the frontal lobes that the stimulants afford alleviates many ADD symptoms. Impulsivity, distractibility, and hyperactivity are diminished as the frontal lobes more adequately prevent the lower brain's impulses from running amok. Overreactions and tantrums decrease as the frontal lobes put a halt to the primitive instincts of the emotional center of the brain. And although the stimulants work directly on lower brain structures as well, the improved functioning of the frontal lobes increases the overall capacity of the brain to receive information, integrate it, store it, and retrieve it, thereby decreasing some memory problems and increasing the ability to learn from one's past behaviors.

It is important to note that medication alleviates many important ADD symptoms in some people but not in others. Below are three common symptom clusters that are often positively affected by medication.

Mental clarity. This item is crucial and can have two different components. The first is the background of fog, or as one patient aptly put it, "my smog of the brain." In this funk it is hard to function and people feel as though all their thoughts and actions come out of a cloud. The other common characteristic of consciousness that can be affected by medicine is that of noise. The noise may be similar to what is called tinnitus (a humming or whistling), but more often it is the clash of too many thoughts all at once. The normal state of consciousness of some ADD people is the crackle of a rushing brain in a hurry to get nowhere. The noise can be so loud that some ADD-ers think they are hearing voices and must be crazy. This is the only inner state that they have ever known. Medicine can be an immediate and lasting relief. The clouds can disappear and the discordant music is silenced. With some patients, the quiet that results is the most cherished effect of the medicine.

The ability to come and go. The ADD brain involves the frontal lobes not acting as they should. One of the major functions of this area is to help us engage and disengage our attention when we should. The ADD person can't stop one activity to get into something else. They know how painful it is to start and know from experience that if they stop a task, they will never return to it. I had a patient, a professor, who really suffered from this disability. He would not take phone calls, would not stop his typing for lunch, and could not stop and talk to his wife when she returned home. He was driven by the panicky feeling that he couldn't stop to do something else or else he would never re-engage. He fiercely protected his train of thought and would yell and carry on to keep intruders out. On medication he became much better. He made time for lunch with friends, he could stop and chat with his wife, and he knew he could go back to his work at a later date.

The minipanics. ADD people are at the extremes of the startle response. The startle response is a natural prepanic response that is with us at birth. When we are startled by loud noises, quick movements, or any surprise or sudden change in the environment, our brain is thrown into a hypervigilant state with a rush of anxiety. Any change or transition can lead to a disruption of an ADD-er's flow of consciousness, and this can cause an extreme overreaction with a heightened state of arousal bordering on panic. This causes distress and adds to the difficulty of staying on task and living normally. Many with ADD continue to overrespond to every new stimulus. Medicine can lessen these responses and even eliminate them.

■ ■ ■

Q: My daughter gets irritable and has tantrums in the evening after her Ritalin wears off. Any tips on how to manage these periods?

A: There are a number of options to consider. First, you can have her do scheduled periods of cardiovascular exercise every evening to help with the off periods. A good burst of exercise helps maintain concentration, plus it reduces anxiety, stabilizes the mood, and increases the ability to stand frustration. If this is impossible or fails to help, then you should try a dose of Ritalin later in the day to help her manage the evenings better. A crucial issue is arriving at the right dose and regimen for Ritalin, and trial and error is the only way to establish the best way to use your daughter's medicine. If the added dose interferes with sleep onset, then you have to use less in the evening, or give it a bit earlier. The next option is to switch to other medicines that act right up until bedtime. You can have your doctor try Cylert, long-acting Dexedrine (which lasts from six to eight hours), Tofranil, Wellbutrin, or long-acting Ritalin as an afternoon dose.

■ ■ ■

Q: I have a severe anxiety disorder along with my ADD. In my case, Ritalin worsens the anxiety while increasing my attention. The rise in anxiety tends to cancel out the benefits of an increased focus. I have tried Inderal but this tends to dampen my cognitive functioning, even though it short-circuits the anxiety. Help!

A: "Comorbid" is a lousy term but conveys the impression that another problem like anxiety makes the ADD worse. The treatment of comorbid disorders is often critical in obtaining optimum treatment of ADD. Anxiety and panic disorders are often associated with ADD (30 percent of ADD patients will qualify for an anxiety diagnosis). The primary goal in using medicine to treat ADD is to improve attention and other cognitive functions like short-term memory and mental clarity. Using these targets as a guide helps to select the right medicines. The traditional drugs used to alleviate anxiety have been the benzodiazepines like Valium, Ativan, and Xanax. They work well for anxiety but always slow cognition, make memory worse, and can cloud the conscious state. If possible, one should avoid using these drugs.

The trial of Inderal is a good idea, but its central effects on the brain can slow the brain down. Our first choice is to use Corgard (10–80 mg/day) or Tenormin (25–100 mg/day) as an additional medicine for anxiety and irritability. These are beta-blockers that stay mainly in the body and out of the brain. They act by lowering bodily anxiety and tension, often without dampening any brain function. Our next choice is the use of Buspar (20–60 mg/day in divided doses), a nonbenzodiazepine antianxiety drug that doesn't have depressant effects on the brain. The benzodiazepines are good drugs, but most psychiatrists are prescribing them less often as more alternatives with fewer side effects become available. Our next choice is to use the SSRIs (selective serotonin reuptake inhibitors)— that is, the notorious Prozac and her sisters Paxil and Zoloft. These are especially useful in treating panic disorder but may greatly help generalized anxiety as well.

■ ■ ■

Q: When should I as a parent resort to medication for my child? Are there guidelines for when "discussion," "negotiation," and "compromise" don't do it?

A: There are no definite answers except for you to trust your overall assessment of when enough is enough. When you've tried structure, check-in sessions, and education—and still find that your child's life is derailed by her lack of focus—then medication should be started. A trial of medication is an attempt to make things better for your child and not a life sentence. The medication trial should be evaluated on a cost-benefit basis. Are the side effects too great? Does the procedure for taking the medicines cause too much shame? Is taking medicine a mark of weakness in your or your child's mind, offsetting the benefits gained by their use?

Most people would not hesitate to use eyeglasses to treat nearsightedness. Similarly, parents don't balk at using medicine for allergies, asthma, seizures, or diabetes. Yet they have problems in using medicine that affects the brain and behavior of their child, especially since ADD is a hidden disability. We cannot see it. It doesn't come in dramatic, discrete packages, and often the child appears to be in little acute distress. Therefore, its treatment seems less pressing. But there are times when the use of medication to treat ADD is essential to the child's well-being.

■ ■ ■

Q: I've tried both Ritalin and Dexedrine and their effectiveness seems to decrease over time. Can people become resistant to ADD medications, and if so, is there a solution to this? Would combining medications help?

A: First, most people do not find that these medications become less effective over time. Rather, they use a smaller dose than they were originally prescribed as they get better at determining when they need their medication.

However, some people do experience a declining therapeutic effect with these medications. I have found that alternating Ritalin and Dexedrine can work: once one stimulant's effect wears off, the other one is used. For example, I have had two patients who quickly accommodated to both Ritalin and Dexedrine—and we had to switch medicines every two weeks. We tried adding other drugs like Norpramin, Wellbutrin, and Prozac, but these didn't prevent the erosion of the stimulant's effect.

Switching from the stimulants to high doses of Norpramin (150–300 mg/day), Wellbutrin (400–450 mg/day), or standard doses of Parnate (10–40 mg/day) are other options. Using more than one stimulant (Ritalin, Dexedrine, Cylert) at a time can be attempted but only under close supervision of your psychiatrist. Not every psychiatrist would feel comfortable doing this.

■ ■ ■

Q: When I exercise in the morning, I can actually read better for a couple of hours. Why does exercise seem to help my ADD?

A: This is a common experience and accounts for why we include exercise as a key element in our treatment program. Many of our patients report that they do their best thinking during or soon after their daily exercise. Some who have a difficult time reading can only read while they are on their stationary bike, StairMaster, or treadmill. Others see an improvement in symptoms that can last four hours or more following their exercise period.

Exercise research is just coming into its own, so "scientifically correct" data regarding this issue are spotty but compelling. What we do know experimentally is that people who exercise regularly show a decrease in depression scores, a reduction in anxiety, and an improvement in their ability to handle stress. Also there is a small improvement in some measures of learning and memory with a regular exercise program. Many of these effects were thought to result from the "runners' high" or endorphin rush that prolonged exercise can produce. However, recent studies indicate that these mood, anxiety, and cognitive changes are probably due to changes in the production of dopamine, norepinephrine, and serotonin and are not related to whether or not the endorphin high was obtained.

The stimulants we use to treat ADD act by increasing dopamine and norepinephrine. Thus exercise could be a natural means to correct deficits. Further, one investigator found a specific area of the brain, the caudate nucleus, where the enzymes necessary to produce dopamine were significantly elevated with chronic exercise. It is this area that is involved in adjusting and controlling our attention, and it is found to be significantly different in people with ADD.

ADD often has components of anxiety and depression that complicate attempts to stay focused, so a regular exercise program makes the ADD-er more fit to deal with the world. A good workout makes the person less anxious, reduces panic and anger, improves the mood, and chases the gloom. With this new balance and flexibility, the exercised person can better stand the frustration of sustaining attention. Additionally, exercise improves both short- and long-term memory and shortens response time to new material.

The effect of exercise is so powerful for ADD that I often wonder whether some patients would need medicine if they could exercise three or four times a day. Students and employees alike often say that if they could just move about, their performance would be better. As Thom Hartmann has suggested in *Attention Deficit Disorder: A Different Perception,* people with ADD are hunters in a farmer's world. Rather than roaming and moving constantly as our ancient relatives had to do, we are asked to sit quietly in front of our computer screens, at our desks in school or at work, and read and write to function and succeed. Frequent and regular exercise may be the correct answer for ADD-ers living in a quiet world.

■ ■ ■

Q: I started off on Ritalin and got a great response. Then, after about a year, the medication didn't help anymore. I tried other medicines, but none worked. What can I do?

A: Your story demonstrates one of the reasons we stress the non-medication treatment of ADD. When the medication works, it's great. But it does not work for everyone, and it does not work continuously for those people it helps. Therefore, the best approach to treatment is to combine medication with serious attention to the nonmedication approaches to treatment.

It is entirely possible that you will be able to do well with the nonmedication approaches alone. Try them. There is a natural tendency to despair if the medicine stops working. However, the medication may still be working; it is just not as dramatic because you have grown accustomed to it. Or it may not be working as well. But if you master the nonmedication methods of treatment, you should do fine.

■ ■ ■

Q: How do I know if my dosage of stimulant medication is too high?

A: "Too high" is defined by the presence of side effects that are intolerable. Mild appetite suppression, for example, is tolerable as long as you maintain your caloric intake and do not lose weight. An occasional mild headache may also be tolerable.

Examples of intolerable side effects that would warrant lowering the dosage or discontinuing the medication altogether if lowering the dose does not make side effects go away include: severe headaches, nausea, sleeplessness, irritability, weight loss, tremors or tics, severe agitation, mania, elevated blood pressure, palpitations, elevated heart rate, or altered blood chemistries.

The possibility of these side effects is one reason it is important that a physician monitor you while you are taking stimulant medication (or any medication prescribed for ADD).

■ ■ ■

Q: What is your opinion about food playing a role in ADD— such as described by Dr. Benjamin Feingold in *Why Your Child Is Hyperactive* and Dr. Doris Rapp in *Allergies and the Hyperactive Child*?

A: The fact that certain foods or diets have a negative or positive effect on ADD is not proven. We all know that eating a balanced diet makes sense and that a concentration on one food group or another can have an effect on mood and energy. At this point, however, studies do not show that changing the diet can reduce the symptoms of ADD. There is no question that some individuals have what we call an idiosyncratic reaction, where changing the food or timing of meals has a pronounced effect on all aspects of the person's functioning and experience. This effect is statistically "washed out" in large samples of children, though, and thus one cannot generalize. However, we heartily recommend a balanced diet with regular meals and urge an avoidance of sugars and fats.

■ ■ ■

Q: How do you know if you are getting a positive response to medication?

A: For children there are scales like the Conners' Parent and Teacher Rating Scales that help determine whether the medication is working. In our experience, subjective reports from parents, teachers, and occasionally the child, are the best guide to evaluating effectiveness.

Often my adult patients have a difficult time defining the exact effect the medication has on them. To help in this evaluation many patients use a journal, a part of a page of their organizer, or develop their own symptom checklist and rate the medication's effect. We have developed the following scale to serve as a reminder to patients to evaluate their medication. We offer this scale to those who may want it, but we also rely on the overall subjective impression from the patient and those close to him. Each week is rated on a scale of 0 to 2, with 0 being no change, 1 being a small change, 2 representing a large change. All changes are from the baseline nonmedicated state.

MEDICATION RESPONSE SCALE

Rate each category on a scale from 0 to 2 (0 = no change, 1 = small improvement, 2 = large improvement) from your baseline nonmedicated state.

	Week 1	Week 2	Week 3	Week 4	Week 5	Week 6
Memory						
Attention						
Mood						
Impulsivity						
Restlessness						
Productivity						
Victories—give examples						
Side Effects—give examples						

■ ■ ■

Q: If an adult responds well to Ritalin, does that confirm the diagnosis? I happen to know that depression can also respond to Ritalin. I think I'd rather be diagnosed with depression.

A: Response to medicine does not confirm the diagnosis, but it is obviously suggestive. Some depressions do respond to stimulants, but one must look at the total symptom picture before and after treatment.

There seems to be a bias against making the diagnosis of ADD. No one wants to have a brain that is different and unchangeable.

Our hubris, our pride, our belief that we should all be on a level playing field is drilled into us culturally and socially. But brains and people are different, and accepting that fact leads to the ability to use the gifts one has as well as deal with differences or deficits. If you have problems organizing, concentrating, and attending, and were impulsive and hyperactive as a kid, and respond to Ritalin, it is likely you have ADD. This does not have to be a life sentence of misery. Many people find ways to manage their ADD and go on to have happy, successful lives.

■ ■ ■

Q: If Ritalin did not work for me, does that mean Dexedrine won't?

A: No. If one stimulant does not work, another might. We do not know why this is so, but it is. This phenomenon is true in all fields of medicine, by the way. If one antiallergy medication fails, another may work, for example, or if one anti-high-blood-pressure medication fails, another may work. The important message for you and your doctor is, Keep trying.

■ ■ ■

Q: Are any new medications being developed?

A: All the time. New medications are coming out and old medications are being used in new ways. The whole field of psychopharmacology is new and exciting.

■ ■ ■

Q: If Ritalin is not harmful in regular doses, why is it a controlled substance? I've heard that prior to 1970 it was not controlled tightly.

A: You're right. I've talked to some older doctors who told me that when they were starting out Ritalin was handed out freely. It was probably handed out too freely and for the wrong reasons, which led to its being made a controlled substance.

Being a controlled substance does not mean that a drug is harmful at regular doses. Other controlled substances, the painkillers and the sedatives, for example, are not harmful when given properly. They are controlled because it is believed there is the *potential* for abuse or harm if the substances are not carefully regulated.

■ ■ ■

Q: Can medicines be combined? If one helps my mood and another my distractibility, can I safely take a combination of both?

A: Only under careful medical supervision. But under supervision, yes, a combination of medications sometimes works well. In general, we like to prescribe as few medications as possible. But in the situation you describe, where there is both a mood problem as well as a problem with distractibility, the combination of an antidepressant, such as Prozac, and a stimulant, such as Ritalin, can work well. Other common combinations include a stimulant plus a beta-blocker, when aggressive impulses heighten the distractibility, or a stimulant plus an antianxiety agent when extreme anxiety joins ADD.

■ ■ ■

Q: Is it true that brand-name Ritalin works better than generic methylphenidate?

A: It shouldn't be true, but it seems to be true for most people that brand-name Ritalin works better. Try the experiment for yourself under your doctor's supervision and see which works better for you. The advantage to generic methylphenidate is that it is less expensive than Ritalin, but obviously this is an advantage only if the medication works as well as Ritalin.

■ ■ ■

Q: Should I discontinue drinking coffee while on Ritalin?

A: Ritalin, and all the stimulants, tend to work better if you do not drink caffeine simultaneously. This means you should discontinue coffee, cola, and any other beverage or food containing caffeine. Be careful, though. Do not discontinue caffeine abruptly or you will get a horrible headache. Taper off it over a couple of weeks.

■ ■ ■

Q: Is there any problem with my taking my son's Ritalin to see how it will work on me? I know you'll probably give me a "proper" medical answer, but is there any *real* reason not to?

A: The real reason is the proper reason, and the proper reason is the real reason. I understand the impatience with proper procedure inherent in your question, and I often feel the way you do.

However, when it comes to taking prescription medications, I'm afraid I'm an advocate of doing it by the book. Proper procedure is, in this instance, your best guide. Sure, you might get away with it without a disaster, but you'd lose a great deal. There are too many factors involved that you have no awareness of for you to make an informed medical decision without a doctor's consultation. And by shortcutting the correct way of getting diagnosed and then treated, you shortchange yourself. You miss your chance to be seen by an expert who can tell you if some other condition you don't even know about may be affecting you. You miss out on the chance to get some information and education, to hear the latest thinking. You miss out on the chance to get some counseling or psychotherapy. Even if you don't think there's any way you'd want *that,* you miss out on the chance to decline in person. And finally, you expose

yourself to the significant medical risk of taking a controlled substance without a proper diagnosis or any medical supervision.

All that risk and missed opportunity just to take a shortcut? It is
foolish. It isn't worth the time you save.

■ ■ ■

Q: Is Cylert as good as Ritalin? What are the differences?

A: The biggest difference is that Cylert works for six to seven
hours for children and all day for adults, whereas Ritalin typically
works for two to four hours. Cylert efficacy studies were done
twenty-five years ago and the majority showed no statistical difference between Cylert and Ritalin in terms of usefulness in treating
symptoms of ADD. Cylert has never caught on, however, because
there was a mild overall difference in favor of Ritalin in the efficacy
studies; and, over time, most clinicians obtained a more reliable response from Ritalin. Also, Cylert causes an elevation of liver enzymes in some patients so that the *Physicians' Desk Reference* (the
famed PDR) suggests monitoring liver functions during ongoing
treatment. Added to this concern were a number of rare reports of
hepatitis and a few reports of liver failure (resulting in death in a few
cases). However, Ritalin also carries with it a monitoring suggestion
in the PDR, since Ritalin can lead to red-blood-cell problems. Clinical experience suggests that this is an incidental finding with rare
clinical consequences. In our experience, Cylert and Ritalin have
similar side effects, including hyperactivity or hyperarousal, sleeplessness, and headaches.

My own preference is to do a trial of Cylert before trying Ritalin
in adults, as they find the once-a-day dosing a true blessing. Many
people have to be switched to Ritalin, however, since the percentage
of adult ADD-ers that respond to Cylert is less than 50 percent, versus the 75 to 90 percent of patients who get a good response from
Ritalin.

■ ■ ■

Q: Have you ever encountered ADD-type symptoms that are due to allergies?

A: Definitely. Some children and adults can have ADD-type symptoms due to allergies. Allergies can have a cloudy, dreary effect on our conscious state and all of our perceptions. An allergic state can be like having a thorn in your foot. This can make us more distractible and restless, lower our frustration tolerance, and drive us to act impulsively. Thus, allergies can create ADD-like symptoms or worsen the underlying condition.

But there is good news. Some diets and allergen elimination programs are very successful in eliminating the distorted perceptions and the general blahs that allergies induce. Most often, treating the allergies leads to a clearer head, which makes it easier to think and read. Since ADD and allergies are often found together, however, correcting one problem still leaves the other problem present.

■ ■ ■

Q: My pharmacist is always running out of Ritalin and I often can't get my prescription filled. Why do they always have such a short supply of Ritalin on hand?

A: The stimulants, as potential drugs of abuse, are controlled substances. Their production is limited by yearly and monthly quotas intended to keep the supply under control. The limited supply keeps each local pharmacy on the brink of being out of stock much of the time. This sometimes has led to problems. For example, in November and December of 1993, there was a national shortage of Ritalin as the quota had been exhausted. Patients were panicking, and were switched to other stimulants. Some patients deteriorated and protests were raised. This spurred the FDA to allow the drug companies to make more Ritalin available.

Some patients have abandoned trusting the regulators and are hoarding a store of Ritalin to guard against anticipated shortages. It is worth mentioning that because more children and adults are being diagnosed with ADD, a shortage could happen again unless FDA quotas are altered.

■ ■ ■

Q: Whenever I go to get my prescription of Ritalin refilled, I get a lecture from the pharmacist about how I shouldn't be taking Ritalin as an adult. I have to show my ID and give my Social Security number every time I get a refill. I am made to feel like a criminal. Is there anything I can do to avoid this experience?

A: This was a frequent complaint from our patients when we first started prescribing the stimulants for adults. They were made to feel suspect by pharmacists who lacked information and familiarity with the disorder in adults.

Things have changed recently, to the point where some pharmacists give how-to pamphlets to my adult patients. In many parts of the country this education process is just starting. To speed it along you can bring literature about adults with ADD to the pharmacist. You need to understand that the public, many clinicians, Rush Limbaugh, and many pharmacists need to be educated about the disorder and its persistence into adulthood.

■ ■ ■

Q: In *Driven to Distraction* you recommend a one-week medication holiday every 4 to 6 months. How does the child and family cope for that week when after only one day (or six hours) it is clear that medicine is needed?

A: If the situation becomes intolerable for your child and family when medicine is not used, then it shouldn't be stopped. In most cases, however, dire consequences do not result and many clinicians recommend an annual reevaluation of the need for medicine. Enough structure and behavioral changes may have been incorporated into the lives of the patient and his family to make medication unnecessary or, upon retrying, another dosage level may be more satisfactory. Frequent retrials also remind everyone involved that ADD is a serious issue and one that needs attention. This is useful, because one of the frequent contributors to poor long-term outcomes is forgetting that the person has ADD. That is to say, once things are going well, the patient and significant others can become complacent and retreat to bad habits. The holiday experience may lead to a redoubling of efforts by everyone to work with ADD-related problems.

Q: Will I need more and more Ritalin as time goes on?

A: Not likely. After a set regimen and dosage schedule is established, we almost never see the requirements for successful treatment go up. Instead, we find that people actually use their short-acting stimulants less frequently. They target their use of the medication to when they need it.

Many clinicians fear that their adult patients will need an escalating number of pills and prescriptions, and they are troubled by the fear of addicting their patients. These worried clinicians underprescribe and increase the dose very sparingly. In reality, most people need less medicine as time goes on.

Q: I've been on Ritalin for years now with a good response. Is there any reason to try another drug?

A: A better effect might be obtained with another drug or another combination even if one has attained a good, comfortable dose and regimen. Of course, it is entirely up to the patient and his or her psychiatrist to try and maximize the effect of medications. For instance, it may be that the longer-acting strategy provides a more even state of attention and may be more desirable. The longer-acting strategy means using drugs that work all day long like Cylert, Norpramin, Tofranil, Pamelor, Parnate, or Wellbutrin.

The major reason for switching is persistent side effects. Ritalin can have a troubling side effect of feeling "wired," and this may necessitate a change. Also, if there are associated symptoms such as temper tantrums, depression, anxiety, panic, or obsessive-compulsive behavior, a better treatment strategy might include treating the ADD and the comorbid condition with one drug.

A patient of mine could serve as an example. Mark has been on 10 mg of Ritalin three times a day for two years. He was more organized at work, and his wife was very pleased with his being more "there" at home. However, he came in complaining that he still had temper tantrums on a regular basis at home. As a child, he was called "Attila" by his parents, and though the years mellowed him considerably, he still could get so mad that he became afraid of what he might do. I explained that we could add Corgard (my favorite medication for anger) or a serotonin-acting drug like BuSpar or Prozac to the Ritalin in order to help him with the tantrums. Or we could switch him from Ritalin to Norpramin or Parnate, which may treat the ADD and his tantrum potential. He chose Norpramin and had a very good response at 200 mg per day. He retained the positive effects on his concentration and lost the short fuse that had plagued him. Such tailoring of the drug regimen to each individual patient often has positive effects.

■ ■ ■

Q: I take only half of a 5-mg Ritalin in the morning and I am fine for the rest of the day. If I take more, I feel too wired and can't get to sleep that night. What gives?

A: I have seen fifteen to twenty patients who have what we call "sensitive brain syndrome." These people cannot take medicine in normal doses, as even a tiny amount is far too much for them. They do not use coffee and avoid anything with caffeine. An aspirin can give them a high and antihistamines put them to sleep for an entire day. They do not typically use alcohol, for a sip can make them tipsy. They present knowing that they have this condition and usually already have pill guillotines to carefully cut their pills into the smallest doses possible.

These people would be called "crocks," "help-rejecting complainers," or people who have a "negative therapeutic reaction" in other eras. Their families, friends, and professionals doubt their wish to use medicines and even doubt that they have a disorder to treat. In truth, they do have a disorder and they can respond to treatment. This is where creative and careful management is needed, since it is clear that these people want to get better but have a history of being thwarted by their own physiology.

Diane, a forty-one-year-old education specialist, had been engaged in psychotherapy for fifteen years to try and get her life on track. She had the advantages of the best prep schools and an Ivy League college but couldn't settle on a career or a life for herself. She was at various times depressed, anxious, and very unhappy. She had all the symptoms of ADD and had a severe math learning disability that kept her from attempting the graduate degree she desired. She was referred to me by her psychiatrist with the caveat that she had tried many medicines but couldn't tolerate any of them.

She had never tried Ritalin and did so now with much trepidation. She said that she knew herself well enough to guess that she should take half of a 5-mg tablet. It turned out that this was too much for her, as it made her feel speedy. She adjusted the dose downward and took one-fourth of a tablet in the morning. She eventually took three of these doses a day, and now occasionally tries to increase her "chip" to a full half of a pill. She has had many successes over the past nine years and remains content taking less than a full tablet a day.

■ ■ ■

Q: Occasionally, I find that my ADD medicine doesn't seem to work for a day. I am reminded of how foggy and cluttered my experience used to be. The next day the medicine regains its magic. What is happening?

A: Many patients report a similar experience. One patient named these occasions "bad brain days." When they occur, people try doubling their doses of medicine, skipping medicine altogether, exercising, meditating, prayer, and doing their most tedious tasks (a strategy that sometimes works to improve focusing for the short term), all to little avail. We would recommend a prolonged and more vigorous exercise session followed by a short nap—although we know this is difficult in the ADD person's hectic world.

■ ■ ■

Q: With children, you give 0.3 to 0.7 mg per kg per day of Ritalin. What is the formula for adults? My husband gets a little help from 10 mg three times a day but he and I feel he could use more.

A: The only study that has been done regarding this issue is by Joseph Biederman and colleagues at Massachusetts General Hospital. They found that the formula was 1 mg of Ritalin per kilogram per day. So an adult who weighs 154 pounds would need 70 mg per day and one weighing 200 pounds would need 90 mg per day.

This is much higher than the dosage range we use. We find that most adults respond to 10 to 15 mg three or four times a day. However, some adults do seem to need more. The issue of dosage seems to become one of common sense. One usually tries raising the dosage until the desired effect is obtained or side effects occur. The major dosage-limiting side effect is feeling too "wired" after the dose is taken. It is an inner feeling of restlessness and may actually be increased muscle tension, similar to having too much caffeine. The mistake that many clinicians make is underdosing for fear of getting the patient addicted or encouraging the patient to abuse the drug. This attitude results in some patients complaining that the medicine doesn't work.

The problem of underprescribing is based on a number of different assumptions that just do not hold—e.g., adults have a milder case of ADD than children and thus need less; adults actually don't have ADD and it's better to use just a little to placate them; the more stimulant they use the more likely they are to abuse the medication or become addicted. As experience and information grow, the remaining myths surrounding ADD will be exposed, and eventually the facts might deter the problem of underprescribing.

■ ■ ■

Q: How long can a child or adult take Ritalin?

A: In most cases the desired effect of the stimulant and/or the antidepressant does not wear off. Thirty-some years' experience in using these medicines suggests that there are no long-term side effects, thus making continuation of the medication a question of need rather than fear of doing harm to the body.

■ ■ ■

Q: Should I take my Dexedrine before exercising?

A: Most people take their medicine after exercising. They find it a waste of the medication's effect to take it while engaged in repetitive physical activity. These drugs do improve performance in certain sports, and sometimes patients will take them to improve concentration as well as improve physical dexterity. But there is controversy over whether children should take their medication for after-school activities. Most of the time, the medication is prescribed to cover regular school hours only. This leaves the late-afternoon and evening hours unaccounted for, and many children need the stimulant to study as well as to engage successfully in sports. Each case is different and the medication plan should be worked out with your doctor to get the best results.

■ ■ ■

Q: How can I convince my psychiatrist to let me monitor my own medicine? He got angry with me for increasing my dose of Ritalin to 20 mg in the morning while skipping the afternoon dose. Should I fight my psychiatrist on this, or just switch to someone else?

A: Educate, educate, educate. There is ample literature suggesting that there is no one dosage range for any one patient. Everyone is different, with different drug-absorption patterns, drug-metabolism characteristics, and perhaps even different needs at the active sites in the brain.

All clinicians have menus of particular drugs we try in given situations along with the approximate dosage range within which we expect the medication to work best. These are "best guesses" and one needs an active experimental partner in the patient to get to the best regimen for them. Rather than leaving or fuming, I would suggest you inform your psychiatrist about the latest information. The information may conflict with their clinical experience, and you may never get them to change their views, but you shouldn't leave without trying.

■ ■ ■

Q: I have had a paradoxical response to all medicines that I've tried. For example, I became more hyperactive and less focused on Ritalin and Dexedrine. What can I do next?

A: First, I would recheck your diagnosis. This is always a good idea and in your case it would be imperative. The next step is to try smaller doses of medicine, as you may have an oversensitive brain. If this is not successful, then a trial of one of the antidepressants like Norpramin, Pamelor, Wellbutrin, Effexor, or Parnate may be in order.

■ ■ ■

Q: My psychiatrist has me on Prozac and Ritalin. Is this dangerous? What is the maximum dose of Prozac I can take?

A: There are a number of reports in the medical literature stating that the combination of these two drugs may be beneficial. Not only is there no danger found in the combination, but the two drugs may act synergistically with one another. Prozac acts on the serotonin system while Ritalin and the other stimulants act on the dopamine and norepinephrine system. There is little overlap. In some cases, having the action on both systems is highly effective, especially when treating an ADD person with persistent depression or troubling obsessive-compulsive thinking or behavior. Prozac alone can have a beneficial effect on many associated ADD symptoms like the minipanics, the mood swings, the overresponsivity, and the anxiety. Ameliorating these associated symptoms leaves the person more cognitively able and has little direct effect on concentration.

■ ■ ■

Q: I have found that my individual psychotherapy has gone much better since I've been on medication for my ADD. Do others find it helpful?

A: Yes, most definitely! Many of my patients have been in ongoing psychotherapy when the diagnosis was made and medicine was tried. The therapy usually improves significantly. The patient is better able to sustain their attention on memories and feeling states. They are more comfortable exploring the nuances and less likely to quickly close off discussion of painful items. In general being less distracted allows for a more thorough and deeper exploration of the material. Also, there is an improvement in the relationship between therapist and patient. There is more eye contact; the patient is less frustrated and better able to accept interpretations. Patients also report that they are better able to listen and remember contributions from the therapist. The diagnosing and the treatment of ADD often serve to renew the vigor in the therapeutic relationship for both patient and therapist. As the patient is less distracted and more goal oriented the therapist is less bored and both feel a closer mutual commitment to their work.

■ ■ ■

Q: I'll arrive in a room and won't know why I am there. Can you use any medication for absentmindedness?

A: The lack of working memory in ADD can be positively influenced by the stimulants. Most of the time, the Swiss-cheese memory that ADD-ers have is related to the brain whizzing along at breakneck speed. This impairs the brain's ability to perceive information accurately and to store it adequately. Some patients report that the stimulants decrease their absentmindedness and this probably is due to the brain inhibiting better and slowing down enough to focus on present stimuli. The paradox is always that we are using medicines in the treatment of ADD to stimulate an underactive brain that when stimulated can slow the rapid-shifting attention and allow us to put the data into short-term memory.

■ ■ ■

Q: Can I go into withdrawal if I skip a dose of my Ritalin?

A: Since Ritalin has a half-life of three to six hours, you are technically in withdrawal every evening and every morning (before you take the next dose). Indeed, some people experience an acute withdrawal from Ritalin. They feel tired, irritable, and their ADD symptoms are magnified as the drug wears off. This can happen within an hour after taking Ritalin. But it is a rare phenomenon. Most people notice only a gradual ebbing of the positive effects. And most people notice very little difference when they forget a dose, or a day, or even a week. What they typically find is that when they miss their dose they are just back to their familiar ADD.

■ ■ ■

Q: In trying to keep the dosage of Ritalin to a minimum, how much can parents request or require of the child that he exert some degree of self-control? Is this a false hope of parents?

A: To begin with, I would suggest abandoning the myth that it is important to keep the dose as small as possible. There is no minimum or maximum effective dose. Some people need one-fourth of a pill per day while others need 20 pills per day. How much and how often can only be arrived at by trial and error. A conviction that "less is best" defeats the purpose of using medicine in the first place.

But we would add that of course parents need to require self-control from their ADD child. Both you and your child need to agree on guidelines related to conduct and behavior. And remember that there can never be enough encouragement to do better, and there should be quick rewards when self-control is shown. The medication's job is to help the child's brain to slow down. It allows him to stop and think before he acts and thus gives him time to reflect and be considerate. Your child's job is to try out better behaviors and, upon failing, to try again. Your job is to act as coach and cheerleader. With this team effort success can occur.

■ ■ ■

Q: I am on light therapy for SAD and it has been marvelous. The winter seemed to make me even foggier and my ADD worse. Is there an association between SAD and ADD?

A: No one knows for sure, but we can report that an observer at our offices would see sadder, more depressed ADD patients in November through March (the darkest and gloomiest months in New England) than at other times. Seasonal affective disorder, or SAD, is a recent addition to the psychiatric diagnostic world, with about 7 percent of North Americans living on the East Coast reporting symptoms. The cause of SAD is yet unknown, but it has been postulated that it is linked to hormonal shifts caused by the decrease in the amount of light available in the fall and winter months. Similar to the case of ADD and PMS, it may be that the ADD brain is much more susceptible to hormonal influences than the non-ADD brain. Since difficulty in concentrating is a symptom of SAD depression, we know that this would only make the basic ADD problems worse. We have recommended light therapy to many of our patients with very positive results. Light treatment is daily sessions sitting in front of a "light box" designed to give off full-spectrum fluorescent light at a prescribed intensity.

If you regularly feel depressed and get more tired and irritable on cloudy days or in the dark days of fall and winter, then it is wise to consider SAD as an additional problem. Discuss it with your doctor, or for more information you can read Dr. Norman Rosenthal's book, *Seasons of the Mind,* or contact him directly at: National Institutes of Mental Health, 9000 Rockville Pike, Bethesda, MD 20892. He will send you a packet of information on SAD.

■ ■ ■

Q: Dexedrine helps with my ability to focus, but I still have a hard time getting motivated. Ritalin seemed to be better with motivation but not as good with the focusing. Is there any medicine that could do both?

A: Unfortunately, a medication that effectively treats one symptom of ADD will not necessarily treat all. Each drug has a different effect on different neurotransmitter systems, and thus will affect different brain functions and ultimately different aspects of the ADD. For instance, sometimes a stimulant will not only improve concentration in a child, but will help her read and remember things. Other times, with other children, there is only an effect on sustaining attention without any additional benefit. The chance of hitting everything and making it all better with one medication is minimal. Empirical trials to obtain the best combination of effects should be considered, and supplementing drug treatment with other forms of therapy will help to maximize treatment.

■ ■ ■

Q: My doctor has me use Ritalin only when I really have to concentrate and not all the time. Is this OK?

A: This is a perfectly fine strategy. As you grow used to taking the medicine, you will be able to target those periods when you need it the most.

■ ■ ■

Q: How are medications chosen for trial? Why does everyone start with Ritalin? Why not Dexedrine?

A: As with many decisions in medicine, tradition determines the choice of Ritalin as the first medication prescribed by most practitioners to treat ADD. Ritalin has a great track record, significantly helping 70 to 75 percent of those who start on it, and it has been around a long time (since 1957). It is a very safe drug: some patients have been on a steady dose of Ritalin for twenty years or more without any adverse reaction.

Dexedrine has been available and used for ADD symptoms since 1937. It, too, positively affects greater than 75 percent of patients tried, but its past is checkered, in that it became very much associated with experimental drug use and the speed culture of the 1960s. It also was part of the diet-pill craze of the 1970s. This history reverberates in the collective consciousness of the prescribers, and the resulting aversion is reinforced by the problems pharmacists encounter with the Drug Enforcement Agency: if there is an increase in Dexedrine sales in a geographical area, the pharmacists and any doctor who has prescribed an increased amount of Dexedrine may be interrogated by the DEA. This makes everyone feel like a criminal. As a result, pharmacists and doctors would rather avoid this drug.

And yet the more experience clinicians have with all the drugs available, the more attractive Dexedrine becomes as a first choice of treatment. Ritalin is more alerting, more energizing, and can be more motivating than Dexedrine. But Dexedrine is a softer drug. It balances the mood better, it is more of a focuser, and it calms restlessness more than Ritalin. In the end, the clinician needs to rely on the ADD-er's self-report regarding the benefits and side effects of each of the stimulants in order to determine the best treatment strategy.

■ ■ ■

Q: What are the advantages and disadvantages of using long-acting drugs like Ritalin SR, the slow-release preparation?

A: The advantages of using long-acting drugs are significant. Having to take medication only once a day (remembering is not an obvious attribute of most ADD-ers), experiencing an even effect from the medication throughout the day, and not having to carry your supply or go to the nurse to get another dose are blessings. Short-acting medication may have some advantage when it's being used to target certain time periods or when there is the need to adjust the dose frequently. But these are minor advantages compared to the constancy of the long-acting-drug strategy.

However, among the long-acting drugs, Ritalin SR seems the least satisfactory. It comes in a 20 mg slow-release tablet and the claim is that one pill will release 20 mg over a four-to-six hour period. This, however, does not seem to be the experience of any of my patients. If they are used to taking 15 to 20 mg of the quick-release form of Ritalin, they find that the 20-mg slow release doesn't help their focus much. Sometimes doubling the dose improves the effect. Dexedrine, on the other hand, has a long-acting preparation that actually seems to deliver the amount promised and can have an effect lasting up to eight hours. Slow-release Desoxyn seems to be useful, with an effect time of six to eight hours. However, Desoxyn is methamphetamine or "crystal meth" and is a favorite drug of abuse, so most pharmacies don't stock it. Lastly, using Cylert, Norpramin, Tofranil, and Wellbutrin are all options worth considering, as they are once-a-day drugs with a constant, smooth effect.

■ ■ ■

Q: I have a great response to my medication now, but I am very worried about being on medicine forever. Is there any chance of my getting off of medicine in the future and maintaining gains?

A: No one can give you a stock answer except that most ADD symptoms don't spontaneously resolve after you reach adulthood. Remember, medication is not a life sentence. Being on medicine and changing your living patterns to optimize your life with ADD can lead to a situation in which you will be able to get off of the medicine. You certainly can and should learn to use structure, variety, and support to help bolster your attempts at living a full and enriched life. I always advise my patients to wait until they are somewhat settled before they have a trial period off of their medicine. Making the right relationship and career choices can significantly improve chances for not needing medicine. In children any attempt at discontinuing medicine should be in the middle of the school year when routines have been established and a baseline of functioning can be assessed. If you find that your ADD symptoms are still disabling, then you can merely restart the medicine. There is no resistance to medicine that will have developed so as to reduce its effectiveness.

The use of medication to treat your brain is a true partnership with your physician every step of the way. Your reports and wishes are the guides to changes, and stopping the medicine should be a mutual decision, with both patient's and doctor's inputs respected.

.15.

A Wretched Excess

ADD AND ADDICTION

■ ■ ■

Q: Why is there such a strong tendency of ADD people to develop addictions?

A: Some of the key characteristics of ADD match the addictive personality profile. These include impulsivity, hyperactivity, restlessness, hyperemotionality, and a vulnerable temperament. When you combine this with high-stimulus-seeking behavior and a dysregulated neurochemical system, you could get a predisposition for the addictive process. Equally important, the dominant feature of the ADD brain is the inability to inhibit, or to put the brakes on certain thoughts, feelings, behaviors, or cravings. Thus it would seem that ADD-ers are particularly prone to developing an addiction, as the internal alarm system that usually tells you to stop a behavior that is risky or harmful is not working.

Add in the anxiety, depression, and panic that most ADD adults experience, and you have a logical reason for them to seek relief. Many of the addictions may therefore be an attempt at self-medication, an idea advanced by Dr. Edward Khantzian. He proposes that some people use drugs to treat an underlying dysphoric state, or a true state of dis-ease. ADD is often accompanied by a gloomy outlook or an anxious, fretful state, and the use of alcohol or other calming and blurring agents can be seen as medicine that the patient is using to treat his inner state of dis-ease. Many patients, for instance, use alcohol to slow down and relax at the end of the day, and to help them sleep. This can lead to a dependence on alcohol as the quantity necessary grows and the use is generalized to help keep them calmed down throughout the day.

The connection that clinicians see between ADD and addiction to alcohol, marijuana, or cocaine is striking. It would be wise for everyone who suffers from ADD to be aware of their built-in potential to get hooked.

■ ■ ■

Q: What are some common addictions that ADD-ers develop?

A: The lack of rate and prevalence studies makes it difficult to determine how many ADD folks develop addictions, or to determine the nature of the addictions. Yet most clinicians working with the adult ADD populations note higher-than-usual rates of alcohol abuse, marijuana abuse, cocaine abuse, gambling, and overeating.

■ ■ ■

Q: I grew up as the class clown. I never could stay still long enough to get interested in school. I goofed around a lot and was soon using alcohol and marijuana to make things more interesting. I haven't had a driver's license in five years because of all the tickets I accumulated. For a while I was into gambling and skydiving, but now I'm a triathlete in the seniors division. My wife says that my ADD can account for all of these disparate facts. Is she right?

A: Not only is this typical ADD, but it can also be seen as a life dominated by addictions. From being the class clown onward, you have been driven to chase the next high-stimulus situation and you have stopped at a highly adaptive addiction, that of exercise. For ADD people the high of the next thrill or dare is not only intoxicating but also focusing and calming.

Because it feels so good to be focused and calm, the ADD-er risks becoming addicted to the behavior. Drug use, high speed and reckless driving, gambling, and skydiving all share the "thrill that focuses." This leads many high-stimulus-chasing ADD-ers to engage in sports such as vertical skiing, bungee jumping, rock climbing, jet skiing, gambling, and daredevil driving. A subtler form of this is seen in the athlete who just won't quit. This type may still suffer from typical ADD-related motivation problems in other aspects of her life, but the potential thrill propels her to constantly try to go one better or go a little faster and a little longer. Of course, high volumes of exercise are a good treatment for ADD and thus the marathoner or triathlete type uses her addiction to good advantage.

■ ■ ■

Q: Is there a biological link between ADD and addictions?

A: Some of the evidence suggests that there is. Many scientists believe that self-medicating with a substance such as cocaine or alcohol is based on biological processes. That is, the introduced substance interacts with various neurotransmitter systems and consequently reduces symptoms of anxiety, depression, or even distractibility. The brain system then craves the substance to maintain its preferred balance.

In addition, the concept of temperament is now recognized as a biological construct. Individuals seem to be born with a tendency to be shy and withdrawn, or overactive and perhaps aggressive, or somewhere in the middle (that is, with a relatively even temperament). Alcohol researchers have found that individuals who have the overactive temperament, which includes impulsivity, hyperactivity, and some conduct problems, definitely are predisposed to substance abuse. Needless to say, this closely matches the temperaments of many ADD-ers.

Some genetic evidence also seems to suggest a biological link. For example, researchers have discovered a defect on an allele of the D2 receptor gene (an allele is a variation of the dopamine 2 receptor gene, and is involved in the dopamine neurotransmitter system in the brain) that shows up in both alcoholics and ADD-ers. This indicates that the underlying cause for developing ADD and the underlying cause for developing an addiction may be related.

■ ■ ■

Q: I am an adult ADD-er and drink occasionally. Should I worry about becoming an alcoholic?

A: Probably not. Yes, ADD-ers can be prone to substance abuse, but certainly most ADD-ers do not develop an addiction. It's also true that most ADD-ers who develop an addiction started their behaviors early on—mostly during adolescence. If you have made it past your college years without a dependence on a substance or on other addictive behaviors, it is likely that you will not develop an addiction. You might always want to be extravigilant in monitoring your behaviors, though, recognizing that your inability to inhibit could still lead to unhealthy or dangerous habits.

■ ■ ■

Q: I have a friend who grew up in an alcoholic home. She claims she does not have ADD, but she has many of the same symptoms I do—distractibility, lack of focus, restlessness, and impulsiveness. Is she right in assuming she doesn't have ADD?

A: Sometimes people who grew up in chaotic, violent, or otherwise abusive homes develop posttraumatic stress disorder. The symptoms of PTSD can look like those associated with ADD. For example, people with PTSD can suffer from hyperarousal or hypervigilance, the inability to modulate feelings or behaviors, lack of concentration or focus, and memory or information-processing problems. It is no wonder you feel your friend might have ADD.

Although heavy drinking by the mother while pregnant can cause attentional deficiencies in her offspring (the most serious example being fetal alcohol syndrome), we cannot say that there is a causal link between alcoholic or abusive homes and ADD. ADD and

PTSD can exist together, and even when not existing together they result in similar symptoms. But it is likely that those symptoms are due to very different things going on in the brains of people with one or the other disorder.

Because of the similarity of symptoms, it is important that the diagnosis of ADD consist of a thorough psychosocial history. A history of abuse should be ruled out as the primary cause of the attentional and hyperactive problems, and hyperactive behaviors or other cardinal ADD symptoms should be in evidence before the age of seven. Neuropsychological testing that reveals learning disabilities could help confirm a diagnosis of ADD.

■ ■ ■

Q: Are there similarities in the treatment of the addictions and the treatment of ADD?

A: Recently, some ADD adults have taught us that there are parallels between the strategies used to manage substance abuse and the strategies we recommend adults use to manage their ADD. The first and most important step in the twelve-step program of Alcoholics Anonymous consists of admitting that one is powerless over the alcoholism and that life has therefore become unmanageable. AA stipulates that alcoholics always remember that their powerlessness means they must actively monitor their behavior and ask for help when needed. They are encouraged to get sponsors—people with good and lengthy sobriety—to keep them on track. And they are encouraged to use AA slogans to help organize and manage their life. The slogans include sayings like "First things first," "Keep things simple," "One day at a time," and "Don't sit too long on the pity pot."

These slogans help alcoholics organize their time and their priorities. They encourage alcoholics to break things down into smaller pieces so that they don't project into the future and get overwhelmed. And they remind alcoholics to pay attention to their limitations and vulnerabilities so that they can better regulate themselves.

ADD adults manage best when they follow similar principles. Constantly being aware of the role that ADD plays in one's life helps individuals separate out negative ADD symptoms from their sense of self-worth; it allows them to realistically assess personal limits and boundaries, and helps in setting goals; it can also help smooth over interpersonal difficulties; and it prompts those with ADD to seek out those that will help them.

In addition, the sponsors that alcoholics use to bolster their sobriety are just like the coaches that we ADD-ers find helpful. Coaches can really inspire the ADD-er and keep him or her focused. Daily check-in sessions work as a reminder of the key tasks ahead, a chance to receive praise and encouragement, and an obligation that solidifies the external structure so necessary for the ADD-er. The simple but powerful AA slogans could have been written for ADD-ers as much as for alcoholics!

■ ■ ■

Q: I am a recovering alcoholic who does the right things—I go to meetings, take things one day at a time, and work the twelve steps. Yet I still find myself struggling with sobriety. I've only recently been diagnosed with ADD. Will treatment for ADD help me?

A: We see this problem a lot in recovering alcoholics whom we diagnose with ADD. Although they are scrupulously following their program, they continue to have problems with their temper, or with keeping their priorities straight, or with relationships. Sometimes they even have problems sitting through AA meetings!

What's going on here is that ADD symptoms are undermining the person's efforts. Treatment for ADD often proves to be the piece that was missing. Learning about ADD and using organizational strategies helps the person prioritize. Medications can help diminish temper outbursts or excessive moodiness. And recognizing the limitations imposed by ADD can help the person with relationships and other issues related to sobriety. For example, an ADD-er might benefit more from a one-hour AA meeting than from the standard one-and-a-half hour meeting.

■ ■ ■

Q: If ADD-ers are prone to addictions, should we be taking medications that have addictive potential?

A: It is true that the stimulants Ritalin and Dexedrine are addictive. In the laboratory, rats will press the lever to get these drugs rather than the food lever and thus starve to death. In humans we know that Ritalin is a street drug often used to heighten the high sought with other substances such as LSD. However, of the many adolescents and adults with past or current abuse problems whom we have treated for ADD, all treat their medication as medicine and do not show escalating demands as some would fear.

The bond between doctor and patient is particularly important in treating an ADD-er with substance abuse. If a good, trusting relationship exists, the use of all medicines can be honestly and closely appraised. If the individual is newly or not yet sober, the first task is to get the individual hooked up with the appropriate recovery program. Then, after a six-month period of sobriety, we would treat them for their ADD. Most often, however, we see people who have years of sobriety under their belt and now realize that they also have ADD. They may not be afraid of becoming addicted to a stimulant but may want to be closely monitored just the same.

One dramatic example of someone with a history of substance abuse who ultimately benefited from medication for ADD is that of Regina. A twenty-three-year old when I saw her, she had been diagnosed with ADD at the age of nine and during her school years had had long stretches of many drug therapies, including Ritalin and Dexedrine, with little success. She was bright, had an IQ tested at 145, and came from an upper-class home with loving parents. However, she was expelled from five private schools before the age of fifteen and finally ran away from home to New York City.

Because she was intelligent, she was able to hold a variety of jobs, but she lived in the drug culture and eventually ended up living on the streets, addicted to heroin, and supporting her habit as a prostitute. She used any drug she could get, lost touch with her parents, but luckily was rescued by Narcotics Anonymous. She returned to her home, stayed sober for two years, and was trying to "get a life" but kept getting fired from her jobs for insubordination. She finally returned to one of the psychiatrists who saw her in her youth. He would not restart her on Ritalin because of her serious drug history. She was tried on a host of alternatives instead, but without success.

When we met, I agreed to put her on Ritalin. She saw me weekly, began going to NA meetings regularly, and kept a job for a month. Ultimately, Ritalin and Prozac calmed her, allowed her to succeed at work, and allowed her to begin college. The medicine obviously helped treat her ADD symptoms. Perhaps more significantly, it helped decrease the cravings for drugs or alcohol. The determining factor in prescribing a stimulant was her commitment to ongoing therapy.

■ ■ ■

Q: In your experience, what is the most dangerous substance of addiction for the ADD adolescent?

A: Without a doubt, it is marijuana. Rachel Gittleman-Klein, a pioneer in studying ADD's course through the life cycle, warns against an ADD child using marijuana even once. Its effects are so compelling for the ADD brain that it seems to become immediately psychologically addictive. It creates a calmness with a heightened sense of adventure—all within the brain. One of the true delights for ADD people is to play with their thoughts and their ideas and build intense and intricate fantasies. Marijuana accentuates the zaniness and doubles the intensity, all within the backdrop of serenity.

We see so many adults in their late twenties who have been addicted to heavy daily doses of marijuana for years, and have seen their great potential wasted in acrid smoke. The irony is that marijuana makes ADD symptoms worse. It makes you more distractible, worsens your memory, increases the tendency to procrastinate, and decreases motivation. It should be avoided at all costs, for it lurks as a temptation that can destroy a life.

.16.

The Gemlike Flame

AGGRESSION AND ANGER IN ADD

■ ■ ■

Q: What is the connection between aggression and ADD? Are we ADD-ers all aggressive?

A: No, not all people with ADD are aggressive. In fact, there are people with ADD who are remarkably unaggressive. They are the ones who are defined as having attention deficit disorder *without* hyperactivity. Instead of being aggressive and assertive, they are often anxious and depressed. They may be passive, even "mousy," and spend their days dreaming. Nor do many classic ADHD-ers, who are very hyperactive, have trouble with their aggression.

Nevertheless, there *is* a strong connection between ADD and aggression. The reasons for this remain elusive, as we do not have adequate terminology or an adequate lexicon of the brain to guide us to the causal link. Metaphorical explanations seem to be too broadly based, either explaining the link as due to tendencies of the personality, or simply acknowledging that aggression is a part of many ADD syndromes. In any case, there is not the kind of understanding that would offer confirmed guides for treating the problem.

I will attempt to approach an understanding of the relationship between the two by viewing this question from the two vantage points. The first is to begin looking at the association by starting with the attention problem. That is, how can attention problems produce problems with aggression? Then I will look at aggression itself and speculate as to why having ADD may make an individual more aggressive. Simplistic tables will follow to offer a visual sequence for our right-brain readers.

ADD-ers are intense and impulsive and often walk in a cloud of trouble. Impulsiveness is doing what you want to do right now, with no regard for the consequences, no regard for the rules. Intense people feel feelings more intensely, feel impulses more deeply, and are always on the verge of action; they vibrate. When they walk into the room, they explode onto the scene. They certainly attract attention. Their qualities can be seen as charismatic, producing fear and avoidance, or lead them to be scorned. The impulsivity, the fast dance of activity, and the social difficulties create a bundle of nervous confusion that can lead to aggression-proneness.

Impulsivity is a trait seen as coming from the deficit in attention. It involves acting quickly on a wish, a feeling, an urge to get it done before the brain quickly fires to the ever-demanding next impulse. ADD people have a desperate need to *do it now* so that they don't forget the impulse or lose it. This can be accompanied by a lack of judgment, due to sequencing and prioritizing trouble, which again stems from an inability to sustain attention long enough to consider, reflect, and order.

The second major characteristic stemming from attention inconsistency is intensity. Often an ADD person's energy is not adequately distributed over the usual field of cathexis points because he can't keep his focus long enough on anything. Then, when something is found that captures his attention, he can really let loose with all that energy. The intensity factor compels the ADD-er to search for a focus, an often relentless search for targets to capture the attention. So this pent-up energy is both the push to find some point of interest as well as the readiness to fully embody it when it is happened upon.

Intensity leads to aggression for several reasons. First, the relentless, demanding nature of the ADD child's or adult's search for targets of attention draws them to any trouble that is present. Or, at other times, their demandingness creates conflict. And trouble with peers—no confidence, no friends, jealousies—leads to aggression.

Second, ADD-ers tend to take risks. They have trouble sequencing and have no inner sense of order, which interferes with their ability to make adequate evaluations or judgments. They interrupt others without considering that this might make hoped-for friends angry. Third, they challenge authority. Such challenges create instant conflict and feed their insatiable appetite for intensity. Lastly, the relentless pressure for the new can lead ADD-ers into desperate circumstances. Their impatience with needing to know what is up ahead pushes them to completely disregard the boring here-and-now reality. Thus they fail to read the usual social and environmental cues that signal safety or danger. Body language, emotional tones, and facial expressions are a blur rather than a guide to appropriate interaction. ADD-ers often find themselves in situations where they feel they must fight or flee to protect themselves. They are much like Charlie Brown's friend Pigpen, only their cloud is trouble.

Anger is a difficult emotion for everyone. Like most emotions, it is just more of a problem for ADD-ers. The lack of normal inhibition in the brain is the root cause of this frightening characteristic. If we first understand the anatomy of aggression, we may then be able to see how ADD further increases the likelihood of the aggressive response. This may provide a framework to understand why aggression is often more common in ADD people.

The standard situation for anger begins with the hurt and then rapidly proceeds through various information-processing stages. Let me propose a model of aggression, or the anatomy of aggression, to describe these stages. To do a proper job of this anatomical exploration, we must use the freeze-frame approach, slowing down the stages of an aggressive action. When looking at the stages up close, we can see where brain characteristics of ADD amplify the aggressive tendency.

The first stage in processing any event is the *perception*. Enough time has to be allotted for us to accurately perceive various stimuli through our senses. We also automatically limit our perceptual field by predicting what we need to focus on. We do not perceive many stimuli fully, as there are too many sources, so we add a bit of prediction to the perception based on what we expect the data to be. Our reality, or what we finally perceive, is a blend of our expectation and our perception.

The inability to sustain attention long enough to accurately perceive a sufficient segment of reality is a particular characteristic of ADD. From birth those with ADD have been taking in less of the actual data that exists in the world than have non-ADD-ers. ADD-ers soon learn to add proportionally more of their expectations to their perceptions than do those with slower-moving brains (that is, the rest of the world!). However, this rapid process makes for many inaccuracies and leads to well-known ADD problems in reading and mishearing and in getting bored. This is also the basis for intuition, as mentioned in the biology section. That is, ADD people become good at using only small bits of perceived data and adding the "rest of the story" to it. They add value to it. They complete the story quickly, without reflection. Sometimes their version is sufficiently accurate. Sometimes it offers new insight into familiar material. Often, though, the hastily sketched picture bears little resemblance to reality.

The next stage is the *evaluation of the input* and the subsequent labeling of the input. We compare the information we are receiving to our past experiences and categorize it accordingly. The resulting definitions and meanings we ascribe to the current event serve as our guide across the vast terrain of behavior options.

By jumping ahead to complete the story, ADD-ers end up evaluating very poorly at times. They miss additional evidence, like the other's body language or emotional tones. Compounding this problem is the baggage that the ADD-er carries around. If the evaluator has had a history marked by failures, and often has been the object of blame, he will be expecting blame to come at him from the environment. It is likely, then, that the "value-added" part of the perception will be biased toward expecting injury, harm, or insult. The ADD-er will end up seeing trouble where there is none, since a deep well of frustration and past failures provokes him to expect the worst. Consequently, he is always ready to respond to yet another condemnation. Of course, all people, even non-ADD-ers, might be prone to similar problems. It's just that the ADD-er is ten times more likely to make mistakes in prediction and processing, and ten times more likely to act out in frustration.

The next state is the *judgment,* where we use our evaluation to decide the context of the situation. Is it good, bad, or neutral? Do we need to be on guard? In ADD, no time is spent on reflecting and perhaps reshaping the experience. Judgment is passed in a heartbeat as the ever-demanding next frame drives the brain onward. This is significant because our judgment of the situation largely defines the *feeling* that will emerge, and the feeling will determine our *response*. For example, in a situation that potentially holds conflict, our initial feeling may be rage. Our judgment might then inform us that the conflict is not all that threatening. Our response is tempered by this information, and although it may include some anger, it probably would not result in an aggressive action or outburst.

But in ADD the judgment, feeling, and response happen simultaneously. The lack of inhibition, or the lack of brakes, in the ADD brain causes judgments to be mostly black or white. The lack of time to reflect, and the unstoppable inner pressure to label the event as good or bad, leads to many misinterpretations. Without a bridle on their emotional brain, intense feelings are immediately released. No foresight is given to possible consequences. And so, too often, they fly into the anger unchecked.

The last two stages of processing an event or an interpersonal encounter relate to the way we internalize elements of the situation and learn from them. First we must *acknowledge* the reality of the encounter. The usual case is to be aware and stay aware of the anger and the action that resulted. The ADD-ers can often not acknowledge that they were angry. They deny it or they forget it. They are already dealing with the next moment, and they are so driven by the external environment that they can rapidly shift into another mood entirely. Finally, since they are already busy with the next piece of business in their awareness, they can't use this incident to gain any *insight*. They seem unable to reflect on the facts and use the issues to repair the broken relationships. And they can be incapable of self-correction. Thus the situation can't be integrated into the person's experience, and the next time a similar situation arises, the ADD-er's response might well be just as premature and just as aggressive.

■ ■ ■

ANATOMY OF AGGRESSION

NORMAL SEQUENCE OF EVENTS	POSSIBLE INFLUENCES OF ADD
1. The Hurt	Rapid-transit nature of perceiving leads to misperceptions.
2. The Evaluation	Encoding problems: no time to reflect about the perception; facial, body cues not fully comprehended.
3. The Evaluator	Past histories of failure cause slights to be interpreted as major threats.
4. The Judgment	Rush to judgment; black-or-white conclusion.
5. The Feeling	Intensity and depth of feeling state; anger addiction.
6. The Response	Propulsion to act, no consideration of consequences, sequencing problems; "the time to act is now."
7. The Acknowledgment	Denial, forgetting, mood shift, poor self-monitoring.
8. The Insight	Quick movement to the next bit of reality, no time for self-assessment, no growth.

Q: My husband constantly misunderstands what I say to him. This leads to many stupid battles in which he becomes enraged. Is this ADD?

A: ADD people constantly misperceive, mishear, and misunderstand others. The same cognitive problems that interfere with reading or listening in class affect every domain in the brain and influence how well ADD-ers perceive and understand the world.

Chances are that your husband always misunderstands you because his ADD brain can't sit still long enough to get what you are saying. You see, the act of taking in information involves both perception and prediction. Our world is far too full for us to take in everything, so we predict what will need our attention. To predict and perceive accurately we need to spend the necessary time on that particular segment of reality (e.g., words, oncoming cars, people in your path). We then can sense it fully and apprehend it. The rapid-transit ADD brain does not linger long enough to acquire many bits of data accurately. There is no time. Your husband's attention is constantly driven to the "next" focus.

"Always in a hurry to go nowhere" results in insufficient time spent on the act of perception. And when the perception is distorted, the predictions that could be used to make sense of things will be inaccurate, too. In addition, when talking with you or others, your husband may not notice, or may misinterpret, all the facial cues and body language that could help him correct his misperception. If he is predicting that your comment will be hostile, because of past history or his own defensiveness, this adds to the possibility that he may misunderstand what you are saying and react with self-justified anger. Then the fight is on.

Getting him to acknowledge that he has a part to play in this repetitive drama is crucial. Blaming it on the ADD often allows for creative ways of dealing with the problem. Calling "Time out," using a whistle, or jumping up and down have worked for some spouses to stop the anger freight train in its tracks and cut short another battle. These signals have to be prearranged and agreed upon when you are having an open discussion about the problem. The more humor that can be added to this nettlesome problem, the better the solutions.

■ ■ ■

Q: Are there any medications to treat temper tantrums?

A: Yes. Large strides have been made in the treatment of anger. In ADD there is a range of possibilities. The first is to treat the ADD itself with the appropriate stimulant. The stimulant often will help inhibit the anger response. Tempers that have been flaring for years, despite the most intense attempts to master them, sometimes have been stilled completely and forever with ADD treatment.

If the stimulant treatment doesn't decrease the tantrums, additional maneuvers can lead to lessening or complete suppression of temper tantrums or irritability. Catapres (generic name, clonidine) is a drug often used as a primary treatment for Tourette's syndrome and can be very useful when used adjunctively to treat aggression. It is added to the stimulant and helps with aggression and impulsive behaviors. We favor the use of the beta-blockers like Inderal, Corgard, or Tenormin. These can be extremely beneficial and aid the action of the stimulant to treat some of the additional symptoms like bodily tension and anxiety. Both Catapres and the beta-blockers are drugs used to treat hypertension, but they have a dearousing effect on the body and inner cognitive state. The beta-blockers work by blocking the action of adrenaline, the hormone released from our adrenal glands. The beta-blockers have many effects on the brain and the body, but in treating aggression we think that a significant effect occurs by reducing the tension in the large muscles in the body. When the adrenals respond and ready you for a fight-or-flight response, adrenaline acts to tense your muscles in anticipation of action. We call this being hyperaroused, and ADD people often are in this state chronically. We have found that by adding the beta-blockers, tantrums, irritability, the fidgets, rocking behaviors, shouting, and impulsive actions of all sorts diminish. They can raise an individual's tolerance for frustration, thus promoting on-task behavior. In some patients, the beta-blockers add a moment to stop and think before the action is undertaken. Catapres affects solely the brain. It turns down the body's alerting system or the sympathetic nervous system by working directly on the brain center responsible.

If these medications are not successful, then our next option is to use the serotonin-active drugs like BuSpar, Prozac, Zoloft, and Paxil. All these drugs combine well with the stimulants and together they can often keep the tantrums at bay. They act in the brain to influence the serotonin system, which can help delay the hasty brain activity that often leads to reckless responses.

Finally, if there is a history of severe mood swings associated with the ADD, then lithium or the anticonvulsants Tegretol or Depakote may be necessary and very useful. The anticonvulsants also can be effective if there is a history of head injury or EEG abnormality, especially in the temporal lobe. Lithium and the anticonvulsants work by stabilizing the brain, which keeps the moods balanced.

■ ■ ■

Q: I am working hard to treat my ADD. I am much better, but I still blow up at home. I am worried about being a lousy role model for my kids. What can I do?

A: First, explore other therapeutic options, such as behavioral therapy, anger-management training, and medication adjustments. If these do not resolve the outbursts, you should use the variant of "Do as I say and not as I do." As soon as possible, apologize after each event. At some point you need to discuss openly with the entire family your problems in controlling yourself. Acknowledge your efforts to deal with your rages. Tell your children that this is not the way you want to act, that you find it unacceptable in yourself, and that you are taking steps to change. Emphasize your worries that you are hurting them and that they will think that it is OK to lose their temper. Involve them in the solution by asking them to generate possible strategies you could use to control your temper. Even if you can't always use these strategies, they will have come up with healthy coping strategies that they themselves could use.

■ ■ ■

Q: Can Ritalin make you more aggressive? I have heard many people say that it will turn me into a killer.

A: Myths like this one are a blend of a little fact and a lot of fiction. Ritalin can cause people to feel jittery, and this can lead some individuals to act more aggressively than they normally would act. Most of the time, of course, Ritalin helps the brain's self-regulating inhibition system to slow the anger reactions and stop tantrums. Controlled studies by a number of different investigators show that Ritalin decreases anger and retaliatory behavior in boys, and produces improved self-control. Ritalin also can improve social interactions, compliance to authority, and the use of nonviolent coping strategies.

Unfortunately, the media tends to blow out of proportion those rare cases in which a person on Ritalin commits a crime. The lawyers seem to capitalize on misinformation, too. They try the "Ritalin defense," which is similar to the "Prozac defense," which is similar to the "devil made me do it." It is important to realize that many adolescents and adults who take Ritalin have conduct disorder and many have a significant history of breaking the law. The Ritalin, therefore, is not the "cause" of the criminal behavior. It is more likely in these cases that the individual did not take the prescribed medication. Teenagers can be reluctant to take a prescribed medication, especially one that needs to be taken more than once a day.

One last note. I have had at least one patient each on Wellbutrin, Parnate, Ritalin, Dexedrine, and Norpramin (at 10 mg) who experienced a paradoxical response. They became more focused, were generally better, but they had a shorter fuse rather than a longer one. Such decreased frustration tolerance usually happens in the initial phases of treatment. If and when this problem is identified, another medication should be tried.

■ ■ ■

Q: My ADD child is very aggressive. Are there any suggestions as to how to help him stay out of trouble in the future?

A: There is no magic answer, but given what we know about those factors that increase the likelihood he will become antisocial, a rational treatment program could be set up as follows:

1. Reduce the conflict between the parents. An ADD child usually provokes as much conflict among other members of the family as between the child himself and any one sibling or parent. The resulting emotionally chaotic environment exacerbates the ADD child's confusion and the aggression that flows from it. So the first step is to create a more stable emotional environment. At times there may be a need for couples therapy, parent support groups, or individual psychotherapy for the parent as an adjunct.

2. Take a course in parent management training. This will help you develop good, effective ways to help your child deal with his ADD.

3. Make sure that everyone in the house who has ADD is being treated to the fullest capacity.

4. Studies have looked at the wide range of treatment modalities and the only factor that has helped forestall antisocial behavior is the consistent use of medication. Adequate dosing and persistence in monitoring the medication are crucial.

5. Consider social skills training for your son if he shows difficulties in forming and maintaining peer relationships. Special educators and occupational and speech therapists often work with children alone or in groups to help train them to succeed socially. The focus is on training children to better assess the social environment and learn techniques to initially engage in social relations, to develop and carry on a conversation and maintain friendships, and to learn techniques to help resolve conflict and manage their anger.

6. Don't worry alone. Where it is appropriate, inform everyone who may provide help to you about your concerns and fears.

7. Keep the awareness of ADD alive and keep the education process constant.

8. Encourage sports, exercise programs, tai chi, and other martial-arts training that focuses on self-control. Martial-arts skills help them learn that they can control and channel their angry impulses and learn to respect others.

9. Use and encourage humor as a way to deal with conflict.

■ ■ ■

Q: My son Billy lies to us all the time. He lies at times when it doesn't seem necessary. It just seems like he *needs* to tell a lie. Is there a relation between his ADD and what appears to be his compulsive lying?

A: After having worked with many ADD adults and families, I've concluded that a fair number of ADD-ers tend to lie, and that there is a neurobiological explanation for this tendency. Because ADD-ers miss many clues in the environment, they often have to fill in the details for themselves. Sometimes this process leads to the invention of the details they missed, and to shaping scenarios that reflect these invented details but not the reality that other participants remember. The ADD-er's efforts are sincere, but due to the disability the results can seem like outrageous lying. In fact, many ADD-ers *do* know their statements may be inaccurate, but they've learned to lie in order to avoid social embarrassment. For instance, they are constantly telling others that they understand what was said to them when often they don't get the message at all. James, a patient often accused of lying, said that if he were to ask "What did you just say?" or "Could you repeat that, please?" whenever he misses the information, as he does in most conversations, he is sure that no one would be able to stand talking to him.

At other times, the ADD-er simply does not remember what he himself said, what he was supposed to do, or what he promised. So he invents in order to escape humiliation or angry recriminations.

■ ■ ■

Q: To me, lying is immoral regardless of what explanation you give for it. Isn't ADD just another excuse disorder that lets people duck responsibility for their actions?

A: Free will and the individual responsibility that goes along with it are greatly valued by our society. However, society also recognizes the distinction between intent and inadvertence. Thus we should ask: Does the ADD-er know he is lying? Of course, there are many parts to this answer, and we should first examine what underlies the telling of a lie. Sissela Bok says that a lie has to have three separate components. First is a consciousness of the falsity of whatever is said. Second is an intention to lie. Third is the presence of a preconceived goal or purpose in lying.

The consciousness of falsity may not always exist for the ADD-er. As explained in the section on the anatomy of aggression, the ADD brain processes information in such a propulsive and faulty manner that an ADD-er is usually forced to reach a conclusion based on a combination of scattered facts and guesswork. If ADD-ers are challenged to reexamine their conclusions, they have such difficulty recalling the details of how they came to their judgments that they either defensively reassert the judgments or make up the necessary details that would logically support these judgments. Often they believe that they are truly recalling what in reality they are desperately manufacturing.

Because the ADD-er often has little or no consciousness about his lie being false, it would appear that the intention to lie is not there. There is no intention to mislead others. ADD-ers believe or convince themselves that they have made an accurate perception and evaluation of reality when, in fact, they have not. Then they offer their flawed version as truth to others. This tendency can be as detrimental to the ADD-er as it is to the listener. For instance, an ADD-er can look at a question on an essay test and misread it. He then sets about answering this faulty version of the question. If asked after the test what the question stated, he will give you his wrong version, convinced that it is right. This can be seen as evidence of misperception. But if this same ADD-er were to pass on the faulty information to someone who is taking the same test two hours later, he would be accused of lying.

■ ■ ■

Q: Is there anything we can do to help our son stop lying?

A: The first step in any treatment plan for any ADD behavior is education. The child or adult may not be aware of the magnitude of their lying problem. Once it becomes a habit, spurred on by the biology of ADD, they stop noticing when they lie. The effect that lying now has on their life and the potential difficulty it may have for them in the future should be emphasized. A good technique is to acknowledge with the ADD adult or child that their ADD might be contributing to the chronic lying, but then to clearly indicate that it is their responsibility to monitor and correct this conduct. The ADD person with this tendency has to work extra hard to adjust this behavior just as the dyslexic reader must expend extra time, energy, and worry in trying to master their reading disability. Educating the adult or child about the possible biological contributions to their problem helps them feel less embarrassed and guilty. It encourages them to self-correct by taking a bit of the burden of "badness" off them. Next a sincere examination of the level of truthfulness in the home should be assessed. Parents and siblings need to look at whether they lie to each other, break promises, keep secrets, or say one thing and mean another. ADD-ers are extremely sensitive to cues and directions provided by their environment, thus it is crucial to make sure that the home culture is one that displays and expects truthfulness. Next, it may be necessary to alert teachers, coaches, and relatives about this tendency, as they can be enlisted to help set up the expectations that the ADD-er *won't* lie, establish clearly that lying is not acceptable behavior, and that lying will have clear and consistent consequences. Finally, medication can help the ADD-er by reducing information-processing errors and by improving their judgment and self-evaluation. Medication also allows the ADD-er to feel more comfortable and confident in general. The result can be that he has less of a need to be perfectly right all of the time.

■ ■ ■

Q: I have been told that my ADD son will grow up to be either president or a master criminal. What is the likelihood that ADD children will end up in legal trouble?

A: There are conflicting reports as to whether having ADD affects the chances that your son will be a law breaker. Pushing the envelope and being impatient with rules and restrictions typifies ADD life. This, combined with intelligence and exposure to the excitement of problem-solving, can lead one to become a real innovator. The appeal of the dangerous, the thrill of the chase, and the need to control one's own destiny sets a background for the development of the charismatic leader, for good or for ill.

We do know that the crucial element is that the child who ends up in legal trouble must also show conduct problems or oppositional behavior before earning a place in the high-risk category. These additional problems often develop as the child grows. Careful studies have found that ADD children who have hostile aggression toward others, in contrast to provoked tantrums, were much more likely to develop conduct disorder in adolescence. Additional risk factors for conduct problems were severe symptoms of the ADD, family history of antisocial behavior, increased peer rejection, marital discord, low socioeconomic status, and trouble reading social cues.

■ ■ ■

Q: Is it just a popular notion that a lot of prisoners have ADD? Is there a link?

A: It is true that many prisoners have ADD. Frank Elliot, the father of behavioral neurology, studied this association in the 1950s and found that more than 80 percent of chronic repeat offenders had learning problems and childhood histories consistent with what we would today call ADD. However, they also would have met the criteria for conduct disorder and oppositional defiant disorder.

Impulsivity, high energy, frustrations, risk-taking behavior, and low self-esteem all add to the likelihood that the ADD-er can end up in a troubled situation. Unfortunately, because of the restrictions on doing research on a jailed population, and out of respect for their privacy, the percentage of prisoners who actually have been diagnosed with ADD remains a mystery today. It is estimated that 50 to 80 percent of prisoners have ADD as a component of their psychiatric picture. Treatments available for prisoners with this condition remain spotty and unheralded. Undoubtedly, this is another troubling, unaddressed health issue in the prison population and its investigation might result in a big cost-benefit savings for society.

■ ■ ■

Q: Do parent management training and cognitive-behavioral therapy work to reduce aggression?

A: I have seen these techniques radically lower parent-child struggles in a number of households. Parents are often taught in the home, with the child present. A few meetings can help reduce the anger and stress in a fairly out-of-control environment.

One of the many contributions of Russell Barkley and Arthur Anastopoulos is their work on the use of parent training. Barkley's book, *Defiant Children: A Clinician's Manual for Parent Training*, is a must for therapists and interested parents. He and colleagues have developed highly regarded workbooks and audio- and videotapes useful for parents as well. Briefly, cognitive behavioral therapy involves training the child to verbalize to himself the specifics of a problem situation, which then leads to a cognitive focus on the steps necessary to resolve the problem at hand.

A parent training course involves from eight to twelve weekly sessions. The basic principles are to teach parents about ADD and its many faces, identifying problems in the home and giving confidence to the parents that they can do something about their child's behavior. Too often parents are demoralized and believe they are failures as parents. Parent Management Training can help restore their confidence and give them tools to apply. The training teaches the parents in depth about ADD and provides basic instruction in behavioral management technique, which is used to change behavior patterns by reinforcing good behavior and punishing bad behavior. They are taught skills in positively focusing their attention, that is, they are taught to notice and reward the positive behaviors of their children with an increase in attention and praise. They are taught to develop an appropriate token system whereby the child can earn or lose tokens or points so that when enough are accumulated they earn a predetermined award such as playing Nintendo for a prescribed period of time, being able to use the family car, etc. They learn to use "time outs," in which the child goes to his room when his behavior is out of hand or unacceptable. The combination of Parent Management Training and medication seems to be particularly effective with aggressive ADD children.

.17.

The Doctors' Dilemmas

QUESTIONS FROM

HEALTH PROFESSIONALS

ON THE TREATMENT OF ADD

■ ■ ■

Q: How do you modify traditional insight-oriented psychotherapy when working with adults who have ADD?

A: You need to be more directive and interactive. You need to be more like a coach than a traditional, neutral therapist. While the "blank screen" model works well with patients who do not have problems in focusing, ADD patients need more structure and direction than the blank-screen therapist provides.

I have found the following steps helpful in psychotherapy. First, try to identify goals with your patient. Adults with ADD often are adrift, unaware of their long-term goal in life. By sticking with the question "What do you want?" the therapist can help the patient reach an answer.

Once a goal has been identified, remind your patient of it from session to session, and inquire as to what steps he is taking to reach the goal. Our patients with ADD often forget their goals, not because they unconsciously are avoiding them, but because of their ADD. They forget what they are working toward. They forget what they want in life. It may sound rudimentary, but it can help a great deal for you to remind your patient of what he has stated he wants and to inquire as to his progress. This should not be done in a nagging fashion; nor, however, should the therapist be without skepticism. If the patient says, for example, "My proposal for that marketing idea? Oh, I've got that covered," the therapist should press on. He should ask a follow-up like, "Do you really have it covered, or are you just reassuring me and you that you *will* have it covered?"

This kind of prodding might feel too persistent with most patients; however, it is just what ADD patients need. They need help in bearing the tension of saying, "No, I do not have it covered. The mere mention of that proposal brings a knot to my stomach. I have been meaning to do it for weeks but I haven't gotten to it yet. I hate to think about it. It makes me crazy to think about it. So, instead of thinking about it, I will tell you and tell myself that I have it covered. That way, the bad feeling will go away." By your asking to know more, you, the therapist, join the patient in the effort to stay with the bad feeling of the proposal not yet being acted upon. In staying with that bad feeling, the patient can begin to plan how to complete the proposal, instead of reflexively avoiding it.

In addition to identifying goals, these patients also need help with identifying feelings. This is true with most patients in psychotherapy, but it is particularly true with those who have ADD. They often do not know what they are feeling. Or they have a delayed reaction, so they only know what they are feeling hours after the stimulus has passed. This can be frustrating for them, and confusing for those around them. Imagine an interchange like this:

> JOHN: I'm furious.
>
> JILL: Why?
>
> JOHN: Because you didn't back me up in that argument with Henry and Beth.
>
> JILL: But that was last week.
>
> JOHN: I know. But it just hit me now how mad it made me.
>
> JILL: You're telling me now you're mad at me about something that happened last week, only last week you said nothing about it? How about last month—is there anything from back then I should be worrying about? Last year? How about then?

The delayed recognition of feelings is a problem a therapist can help.

While you may modify traditional psychotherapy in certain ways with ADD patients, keep in mind also that they often need the opportunities for emotional exploration that insight-oriented therapy provides. In other words, don't throw out the therapy baby with the bath water. Make some changes, but preserve what is central.

■ ■ ■

Q: One of my patients who has ADD has a tendency to suddenly lose perspective. He'll be doing fine, then one day the whole world will look black, based upon a trivial slight or perceived failure. Is this typical, and what approach works from the therapist's standpoint?

A: It is very common. Why the sudden loss of perspective is so common in ADD I do not know, but I see it all the time. I'll bet there is a neurological basis for it. It is as if the train just runs off the track. The individual may be going along, having pleasant, productive thoughts, enjoying the morning at work or the afternoon at home or the drive to the country, when out of nowhere—whammo!—he or she plunges into pain. The thoughts are whirring along their neural circuits smoothly and powerfully, like the smoothest modern train, when suddenly there is no more track. The circuit breaks. The thoughts pile on top of one another in a big crash, and there is psychic blood everywhere.

The therapist does his best to put the train back on the track rather than analyze why it ran out of track. It is very difficult for the patient himself to do this. He is struggling in the wreckage, but it is not so difficult for the therapist to help him. The key technique is reassurance.

Reassurance may have a bad name in some kinds of psychotherapy. It may seem superficial or ineffective. The therapist may think it is better for the patient to learn how to reassure himself or herself, rather than the therapist to offer this balm. In addition, the therapist may fear that the reassurance will become addicting, the patient wanting more and more. For many patients, this may be true.

However, for patients with ADD, reassurance puts the train back on track. Reassurance restores perspective. Reassurance staves off unnecessary pain. It is true that it must be supplied over and over again, but so must many essentials in life, like food and water. For individuals with ADD, reassurance belongs in the same category with food and water.

The reassurance is best if given freely and simply. Short phrases do best, such as "That's OK, you've dealt with this before," or "Don't worry about him. You know how he is," or "You've demonstrated many times how smart you are," or "You really do look good," or "I don't think you have anything to worry about on that score," or "You won't be alone out there," or "For you, it's a piece of cake," or "From what you've told me, I don't think you have a thing to worry about." These kinds of reassurance can act rapidly and effectively to give balance to a piled-up mind.

People with ADD are usually starved for reassurance (although they may be too proud to admit it), and they thrive on it when they get it.

■ ■ ■

Q: Do you ever see psychosis in ADD?

A: Yes. Usually the patient has some other diagnosis as well as ADD, such as manic-depressive or bipolar disorder, or paranoia, or some other condition with which psychosis is often associated. Psychosis in a patient with ADD alone is rare.

■ ■ ■

Q: When is group therapy indicated for adults with ADD?

A: A support group of some sort is always helpful. Adults with ADD gain knowledge, reassurance, insight, and a sense of community from a group. They also get social feedback. They hear from others how they themselves are coming across. This is valuable information, as most people with ADD are poor self-observers, often quite unaware of their impact on others.

■ ■ ■

Q: I have seen a few patients who at first I thought had a narcissistic personality disorder but then I realized had ADD. Have you heard this from others?

A: Yes. ADD can look like narcissism, or self-centeredness, because the individual is not paying attention to other people. He *looks* as if he is just paying attention to himself. However, if you could look into his mind you would find distraction rather than self-absorption. In fact, most people with ADD are quite well attuned to others—when they can focus.

Other personality disorders that can look like ADD include (1) passive-aggressive personality, in that the individual can feel as if he is not paying attention or following through out of passivity, (2) histrionic personality, in that the distractibility of ADD can mimic the dissociative state one finds in histrionic personalities, and (3) antisocial personality, in that the impulsivity of ADD can lead to certain antisocial behaviors.

■ ■ ■

Q: You stress the importance of a balanced treatment regimen. But honestly, isn't medication the key?

A: The longer I treat ADD—in both children and adults—the more convinced I am that a balanced treatment plan is essential. Medication alone is insufficient.

While medication gives you a quick burst of improvement at the outset of treatment, you need education, structure, and other kinds of support to maintain that improvement over time.

To give medication without addressing the patient's need to learn about ADD, or to give medication without also instructing the patient on methods of reorganizing or rethinking his or her lifestyle, or to give medication without exploring the need for psychotherapy or coaching is like offering a lawn mower to someone whose backyard has become a jungle. It may be a start, but the patient needs a lot more than that! He or she needs help understanding how the jungle got there and how to keep it from growing back; needs teams of workers to chop down vines and dig up trees and remove snakes and lizards and crocodiles and whatever other dangerous species have crawled into their backyard. Once the major work has been done, the lawn mower may become the mainstay of treatment, but there is no way it will ever be enough, by itself, to maintain the yard. The patient–homeowner also needs knowledge. And some water, fertilizer, and encouragement as well.

While extremely useful, medication alone is never enough.

■ ■ ■

Q: When I have heard you talk about coaching, encouragement, and reassurance in treating adults with ADD, I worry that you are oversimplifying human nature. I wish it were so simple! You make it sound as if all these people need is a cold shower and a run around the block.

A: I understand your objection, and when I started treating ADD, I would have agreed with you. Human nature is devilishly complex, and complex solutions are more to be trusted than simple ones.

However, I have found that while ADD is by no means a simple condition, some of the treatments that help most are simple indeed. Exercise is one of these. A shock to the system to change one's mind-set is another. Put those two together and what do you have? A run around the block and a cold shower.

Those of us who believe in psychotherapy—and I count myself as one—have perhaps dismissed these simple solutions too quickly. They do not oppose traditional psychotherapy; they complement it.

If a patient with ADD is stuck by himself in a brooding, ruminative funk, I honestly think he will do better to go for a run and take a shower than to introspect further. Then, at some later point when he has reequilibrated, we can investigate the psychodynamic basis of the funk.

Coaching, reassurance, and encouragement, as well as exercise and cold showers, deserve even the most sophisticated clinician's respect as highly effective and valuable tools for promoting growth and easing pain.

■ ■ ■

Q: I agree that many of my patients need explicit tips on how to get organized. My problem is, I don't feel comfortable giving those tips myself. I don't even feel qualified! What can you suggest?

A: I have several consultants to whom I refer my patients for help with organization. For a reasonable fee (from $30 to $75 per hour depending upon the person's qualifications) the consultant will see the patient in his or her office or even go to the patient's own office or home and tackle the specifics of organization and time management. The consultant can get into the nuts and bolts of the patient's everyday jumble in a way I cannot. Nor do I know enough about organization skills to do the job as well. My patients have had great success with these consultants. They later tell me it was a most valuable part of their treatment.

■ ■ ■

Q: How do you feel about using medication to treat an ADD patient who has a history of substance abuse?

A: I require that the substance abuse be stopped. In other words, I will not prescribe medication for ADD to someone who is actively abusing alcohol, cocaine, marijuana, or any other substance.

However, I do not think a history of substance abuse should prevent these patients from getting the treatment they need. Many adults with ADD have self-medicated with one substance or another. It makes sense to treat these people with the right medication, as one would treat any other patient. There is no evidence that medication will lead these patients back into substance abuse. In fact, the reverse is more likely true, that they are at greater risk for relapse into substance abuse if their ADD is *not* treated.

Appendix 1

FIFTY TIPS ON THE MANAGEMENT OF ADULT ADD

■ ■ ■

The following tips on the nonmedication management of adult ADD are the original fifty that appeared in *Driven to Distraction*. So many people have told us they are useful to them that we decided to reproduce them here. They are intended to accompany the new tips found in chapter 7.

Insight and Education

1. Be sure of the diagnosis. Make sure you're working with a professional who really understands ADD and has excluded related or similar conditions, such as anxiety states, agitated depression, hyperthyroidism, manic-depressive illness, or obsessive-compulsive disorder.

2. Educate yourself. Perhaps the single most powerful treatment for ADD is understanding ADD in the first place. Read books. Talk with professionals. Talk with other adults who have ADD. These may be found through ADD support groups or local or national

ADD organizations like CH.A.D.D. You'll be able to design your own treatment to fit your own version of ADD.

3. Choose a coach. It is useful for you to have a coach, for some person near to you to keep after you, but always with humor. Your coach can help you get organized, stay on task, give you encouragement, or remind you to get back to work. Friend, colleague, or therapist (it is possible, but risky, for your coach to be your spouse), a coach is someone who stays on you to get things done, exhorts you as coaches do, keeps tabs on you, and in general stands in your corner. A coach can be tremendously helpful in treating ADD.

4. Seek encouragement. ADD adults need lots of encouragement. This is in part due to many self-doubts that have accumulated over the years. But it goes beyond that. More than most people, ADD adults wither without encouragement and thrive when given it. They will often work for another person in a way they won't work for themselves. This is not "bad," it just is. It should be recognized and taken advantage of.

5. Realize what ADD is *not*—i.e., conflict with mother, unconscious fear of success, passive-aggressive personality, etc. People with ADD, of course, may have a conflict with their mother or an unconscious fear of success or have a passive-aggressive personality, but it is important to separate the ADD from these other kinds of problems because the treatment for ADD is completely different.

6. Educate and involve others. Just as it is key for you to understand ADD, it is equally if not more important for those around you to understand it—family members, coworkers, school personnel, and friends. Once they get the concept, they will be able to understand you much better and to help you reach your goals.

7. Give up guilt over high-stimulus-seeking behavior. Understand that you are drawn to high stimuli. Try to choose them wisely, rather than brooding over the "bad" ones.

8. Listen to feedback from trusted others. Adults (and children, too) with ADD are notoriously poor self-observers. They use a lot of what can appear to be denial.

9. Consider joining or starting a support group. Much of the most useful information about ADD has not yet found its way into books but remains stored in the minds of the people who have

ADD. In groups this information can come out. Plus, groups are really helpful in giving the kind of support that is so badly needed.

10. Try to get rid of the negativity that may have infested your system if you have lived for years without knowing what you had was ADD. A good psychotherapist may help in this regard.

11. Don't feel chained to conventional careers or conventional ways of coping. Give yourself permission to be yourself. Give up trying to be the person you always thought you should be—the model student or the organized executive, for example—and let yourself be who you are.

12. Remember that what you have is a neurological condition. It is genetically transmitted. It is caused by biology, by how your brain is wired. It is *not* a disease of the will, nor a moral failing, nor some kind of neurosis. It is not caused by a weakness in character, nor by a failure to mature. Its cure is not to be found in the power of the will, nor in punishment, nor in sacrifice, nor in pain. Always remember this. Try as they might, many people with ADD have great trouble accepting the syndrome as being rooted in biology rather than weakness of character.

13. Try to help others with ADD. You'll learn a lot about this condition in the process, as well as feel good to boot.

Performance Management

14. Establish external structure. Structure is the hallmark of the nonpharmacological treatment of the ADD child. It can be equally useful with adults. Once in place, structure works like the walls of the bobsled slide, keeping the speedball sled from careening off the track. Also make frequent use of lists, notes to self, color coding, rituals, reminders, and files.

15. Use pizzazz. Try to make your environment as peppy as you want it to be without letting it boil over. If your organization system can be stimulating (imagine that!) instead of boring, then you will be more likely to follow it. For example, in setting things up, try color coding. Mentioned above, color coding deserves emphasis. Many people with ADD are visually oriented. Take advantage of

this by making things memorable with color: files, memoranda, texts, schedules, etc. Virtually anything in the black-and-white of type can be made more memorable, arresting, and therefore attention-getting with color.

16. When it comes to paperwork, use the principle of O.H.I.O: Only handle it once. When you receive a document or a memo or any kind of written material, try to only handle it once. Either respond to it right away, on the spot, or throw the document away, or file it permanently. *Do not* put it in a TO DO box or pile. For people with ADD, TO DO piles might just as well be called NEVER DONE piles. They serve as little menaces around one's desk or room, silently building guilt, anxiety, and resentment, as well as taking up a lot of space. Get in the habit of acting immediately on your paperwork. Make the wrenching decision to throw something away. Or, overcome inertia and respond to it *on the spot*. Whatever you do with the document, whenever possible, only handle it once.

17. Set up your environment to reward rather than deflate. To understand what a deflating environment is, most adult ADD-ers only need to think back to school. Now that you have the freedom of adulthood, try to set things up so that you will not constantly be reminded of your limitations.

18. Acknowledge and anticipate the inevitable collapse of X percent of projects undertaken, relationships entered into, obligations incurred. Better that you anticipate these "failures" rather than be surprised by them and brood over them. Think of them as part of the cost of doing business.

19. Embrace challenges. ADD people thrive with many challenges. As long as you know they won't all pan out, as long as you don't get too perfectionistic and fussy, you'll get a lot done and stay out of trouble. Far better that you be too busy than not busy enough. As the old saying goes, if you want to get something done, ask a busy person.

20. Make deadlines. Deadlines help you focus. This was put best by Samuel Johnson, who said, "Nothing focuses the mind so wonderfully as the knowledge that a man is to be hanged in a fortnight."

21. Break down large tasks into small ones. Attach deadlines to

the small parts. Then, like magic, the large task will get done. This is one of the simplest and most powerful of all structuring devices. Often a large task will feel overwhelming to the person with ADD. The mere thought of trying to perform the task makes one turn away. On the other hand, if the large task is broken down into small parts, each component may feel quite manageable. (For example, it was only by using this technique that we managed to write this book.)

22. Prioritize rather than procrastinate. If you cannot handle it only once (tip 16), then be sure to prioritize. When things get busy, the adult ADD person loses perspective: paying an unpaid parking ticket can feel as pressing as putting out the fire that just got started in the wastebasket. Sometimes one becomes paralyzed. Prioritize. Take a deep breath. Put first things first. Then go on to the second and the third task. Don't stop. Procrastination is one of the hallmarks of adult ADD. You have to really discipline yourself to watch out for it and avoid it.

23. Accept the fear of things going too well. Accept edginess when things are too easy, when there's no conflict. Don't gum things up just to make them more stimulating.

24. Notice how and where you work best: in a noisy room, on the train, wrapped in three blankets, listening to music, whatever. Children and adults with ADD can do their best under rather odd conditions. Let yourself work under whatever conditions are best for you.

25. Know that it is OK to do two things at once: carry on a conversation and knit, or take a shower and do your best thinking, or jog and plan a business meeting. Often people with ADD need to be doing several things at once in order to get anything done at all.

26. Do what you're good at. Again, if it seems easy, that is OK. There is no rule that says you can only do what you're bad at.

27. Leave time between engagements to gather your thoughts. Transitions are difficult for ADD-ers, and minibreaks can help ease the transition.

28. Keep a notepad in your car, by your bed, and in your pocketbook or jacket. You never know when a good idea will hit you, or you'll want to remember something else.

29. Read with a pen in hand, not only for marginal notes or underlining, but for the inevitable cascade of "other" thoughts that will occur to you.

Mood Management

30. Have structured "blow-out" time. Set aside some time in every week for just letting go. Whatever you like to do—blasting yourself with loud music, taking a trip to the racetrack, having a feast—pick some kind of activity from time to time where you can let loose in a safe way.

31. Recharge your batteries. Related to number 30, most adults with ADD need, on a daily basis, some time to waste without feeling guilty about it. One guilt-free way to conceptualize it is to call it time to recharge your batteries. Take a nap, watch TV, meditate. Something calm, restful, at ease.

32. Choose "good," helpful addictions, such as exercise. Many adults with ADD have an addictive or compulsive personality that keeps them always hooked on something. Try to make this something positive.

33. Understand mood changes and ways to manage these. Know that your moods will change willy-nilly, independent of what's going on in the external world. Don't waste your time looking for someone to blame. Focus rather on learning to tolerate a bad mood, knowing that it will pass, and learning strategies to make it pass sooner. Change sets, i.e., get involved with some new activity (preferably interactive), such as a conversation with a friend, or a tennis game, or reading a book.

34. Related to number 33, recognize the following cycle which is very common among adults with ADD:

    a. Something "startles" your psychological system, a change or transition, a disappointment or even a success. The precipitant may be quite trivial, nothing more than an everyday event.

    b. This "startle" is followed by a minipanic with a sudden loss of perspective, the world being set topsy-turvy.

c. You try to deal with this panic by falling into a mode of obsessing and ruminating over one or another aspect of the situation. This can last for hours, days, even months.

To break the negative obsessing, have a list of friends to call. Have a few videos that always engross you and get your mind off things. Have ready access to exercise. Have a punching bag or pillow handy if there's extra angry energy. Rehearse a few pep talks you can give yourself, like, "You've been here before. These are the ADD blues. They will soon pass. You are OK."

35. Learn how to name your feelings. Many people with ADD, particularly men, get frustrated and angry because they cannot put their feelings into words. With practice and coaching, this is a skill that can be learned.

36. Expect depression after success. People with ADD commonly complain of feeling depressed, paradoxically, after a big success. This is because the high stimulus of the chase or the challenge or the preparation is over. The deed is done. Win or lose, the adult with ADD misses the conflict, the high stimulus, and feels depressed.

37. Learn symbols, slogans, sayings as shorthand ways of labeling and quickly putting into perspective slip-ups, mistakes, or mood swings. When you turn left instead of right and take your family on a twenty-minute detour, it is better to be able to say, "There goes my ADD again," than to have a six-hour fight over your unconscious desire to sabotage the whole trip. These are not excuses. You still have to take responsibility for your actions. It is just good to know where your actions are coming from and where they're not.

38. Use "time-outs," as with children. When you are upset or overstimulated, take a time-out. Go away. Calm down.

39. Learn how to advocate for yourself. Adults with ADD are so used to being criticized, they are often unnecessarily defensive in putting their own case forward. Learn to get off the defensive.

40. Avoid premature closure of a project, a conflict, a deal, or a conversation. Don't "cut to the chase" too soon, even though you're itching to.

41. Try to let a successful moment last and be remembered and become sustaining over time. You'll have to train yourself consciously and deliberately to do this because you'll naturally tend to forget your successes as you brood over your shortcomings or pessimistically anticipate the worst.

42. Remember that ADD usually includes a tendency to overfocus or hyperfocus at times. This hyperfocusing can be used constructively or destructively. Be aware of its destructive use: a tendency to obsess or ruminate over some imagined problem without being able to let it go.

43. Exercise vigorously and regularly. You should schedule exercise into your life and stick with it. It helps work off excess energy and aggression in a positive way, it allows for noise reduction within the mind, it stimulates the hormonal and neurochemical system in a most therapeutic way, and it soothes and calms the body. When you add all that to the well-known health benefits of exercise, you can see how important exercise is. Make it something fun so you can stick with it over the long haul, i.e., the rest of your life. One particular form of exercise, sexual activity, is very good for ADD.

Interpersonal Life

44. Make a good choice in a significant other. Obviously, this is good advice for anyone. But it is striking how the adult with ADD can thrive or flounder depending on the choice of mate.

45. Learn to joke with yourself and others about your various symptoms, from forgetfulness to getting lost all the time to being tactless or impulsive. If you can bring a sense of humor to your failings, others will forgive you much more quickly.

46. Schedule activities with friends. Adhere to these schedules faithfully. It is crucial for you to keep connected to other people.

47. Find and join groups where you are liked, appreciated, understood, enjoyed. Even more than most people, people with ADD take great strength from group support.

48. Don't stay too long where you *aren't* understood or appreciated. Jut as people with ADD gain a great deal from supportive

groups, they are particularly drained and demoralized by negative groups, and they have a tendency to stay with them too long, vainly trying to make things work out, even when all the evidence shows they can't.

49. Pay compliments. Notice other people. In general, get social training if you're having trouble getting along with people.

50. Set social deadlines. Without deadlines and dates, your social life can atrophy. Just as you will be helped by structuring your business week, so, too, you will benefit from keeping your social calendar organized. This will help you stay in touch with friends and get the kind of social support you need.

Appendix II

■ ■ ■

1. Get an accurate diagnosis. This is the starting point of all treatment for ADD.

2. Educate the family. All members of the family need to learn the facts about ADD as the first step in the treatment. Many problems will take care of themselves once all family members understand what is going on. The education process should take place with the entire family, if possible. Each member of the family will have questions. Make sure all these questions get answered.

3. Try to change the family "reputation" of the person with ADD. Reputations within families, like reputations within towns or organizations, keep a person in one set or mold. Recasting the reputation of the person with ADD within the family can set up brighter expectations. If you are expected to screw up, you probably will; if you are expected to succeed, you just might. It may be hard to believe at first, but having ADD can be more a gift than a curse. Try to see and develop the positive aspects of the person with ADD, and try to change his family reputation to accentuate these positive aspects. Remember, this person usually brings a special something to

the family, special energies, special creativity, special humor. He (or she) usually livens up any gathering he attends, and even when he is disruptive, it's usually exciting to have him around. He punctures bombast and does not tolerate fools. He is irreverent and not afraid to speak his mind. He has a lot to give, and the family, more than any group of people, can help him reach his potential.

4. Make it clear that ADD is nobody's fault. It is not Mom's or Dad's fault. It is not brother's or sister's fault. It is not Grandmother's fault, and it is not the fault of the person who has ADD. It is nobody's fault. It is extremely important this be understood and believed by all members of the family. Lingering feelings that ADD is just an excuse for irresponsible behavior or that ADD is caused by laziness will sabotage treatment.

5. Also make it clear that ADD is a family issue. Unlike some medical problems, ADD touches everybody in the family in a daily, significant way. It affects early-morning behavior, it affects dinner-table behavior, it affects vacations, and it affects quiet time. Let each member of the family become a part of the solution, just as each member of the family has been a part of the problem.

6. Pay attention to the "balance of attention" within the family. Try to correct any imbalance. Often, when one child has ADD, his siblings get less attention. The attention may be negative, but the child with ADD often gets more than his share of parents' time and attention day in and day out. This imbalance of attention can create resentment among siblings, as well as deprive them of what they need. Bear in mind that being the sibling of a child with ADD carries its own special burdens. Siblings need a chance to voice their concerns, worries, resentments, and fears about what is going on. Siblings need to be allowed to get angry as well as to help out. Be careful not to let the attention in the family become so imbalanced that the one person with ADD is dominating the whole family scene, defining every event, coloring every moment, determining what can and cannot be done, controlling the show.

7. Try to avoid the Big Struggle. A common entanglement in families where ADD is present but not diagnosed, or diagnosed but unsuccessfully treated, the Big Struggle pits the child with ADD against his parents, or the adult with ADD against his spouse, in a

daily struggle of wills. The negativity that suffuses the Big Struggle eats away at the whole family. Just as denial and enabling can define the alcoholic family, so can the Big Struggle define (and consume) the ADD family.

8. Once the diagnosis is made, and once the family understands what ADD is, have everybody sit down together and negotiate a deal. Using the principles outlined earlier, try to negotiate your way toward a "game plan" that everyone in the family can buy into. To avoid the family gridlock of the Big Struggle, or to avoid an ongoing war, it is best to get into the habit of negotiation. This can take a lot of work, but over time some kind of negotiated settlement can usually be reached. The terms of the settlement should be made explicit; at best they should be put into writing so they can be referred to as needed. They should include concrete agreements by all parties as to what is promised, with contingency plans for meeting and not meeting the goals. Let the war end with a negotiated peace.

9. If negotiation bogs down at home, consider seeing a family therapist, a professional who has experience in helping families listen to each other and reach consensus. Since families are sometimes explosive, it can be very helpful to have a professional around to keep the explosions under control. Also consider buying a book to help in negotiation, such as Fisher and Ury's *Getting to Yes*.

10. Within the context of family therapy, role-playing can be helpful to let members of the family show each other how they see them. Since people with ADD are very poor self-observers, watching others play them can vividly demonstrate behavior they may be unaware of rather than unwilling to change. Video can help in this regard as well.

11. If you sense the Big Struggle is beginning, try to disengage from it. Try to back away. Once it has begun, it is very hard to get out of. The best way to stop it, on a day-to-day basis, is not to join it in the first place. Beware of the struggle's becoming an irresistible force.

12. Give everyone in the family a chance to be heard. ADD affects everyone in the family, some silently. Try to let those who are in silence speak.

13. Try to break the negative process and turn it into a positive

one. Applaud and encourage success when it happens. Try to get everyone pointed toward positive goals, rather than gloomily assuming the inevitability of negative outcomes. One of the most difficult tasks a family faces in dealing with ADD is getting onto a positive track. However, once this is done, the results can be fantastic. Use a good family therapist, a good coach, whatever—just focus on building positive approaches to each other and to the problem.

14. Make it clear who has responsibility for what within the family. Everybody needs to know what is expected of him or her. Everybody needs to know what the rules are and what the consequences are.

15. As a parent, avoid the pernicious pattern of loving the child one day and hating him the next. One day he exasperates you and you punish him and reject him. The next day he delights you and you praise him and love him. It is true of all children, but particularly true of those with ADD, that they can be little demons one day and jewels of enchantment the next. Try to keep an even keel in response to these wide fluctuations. If you fluctuate as much as the child, the family system becomes very turbulent and unpredictable.

16. Make time for you and your spouse to confer with each other. Try to present a united front. The less you can be manipulated the better. Consistency helps in the treatment of ADD.

17. Don't keep ADD a secret from the extended family. It is nothing to be ashamed of, and the more the members of the extended family know about what is going on the more help they can be. In addition, it would not be unlikely for one of them to have it and not know about it as well.

18. Try to target problem areas. Typical problem areas include study time, morning time, bedtime, dinnertime, times of transition (leaving the house and the like), and vacations. Once the problem area has been explicitly identified, everyone can approach it more constructively. Negotiate with each other as to how to make it better. Ask each other for specific suggestions.

19. Have family brainstorming sessions. When a crisis is not occurring, talk to each other about how a problem area might be dealt with. Be willing to try anything once to see if it works. Approach problems as a team with a positive, can-do attitude.

20. Make use of feedback from outside sources—teachers, pediatrician, therapist, other parents and children. Sometimes a person won't listen to or believe something someone in the family says, but will listen to it if it comes from the outside.

21. Try to accept ADD in the family just as you would any other condition and normalize it in the eyes of all family members as much as possible. Accommodate to it as you might a family member's special talents or interests, like musical ability or athletic skills, whose development would affect family routines. Accommodate to it, but try not to let it dominate your family. In times of crisis this may not seem possible, but remember that the worst of times do not last forever.

22. ADD can drain a family. ADD can turn a family upside down and make everybody angry at everybody else. Treatment can take a long while to be effective. Sometimes the key to success in treatment is just to persist and to keep a sense of humor. Although it is hard not to get discouraged if things just seem to get worse and worse, remember that the treatment of ADD often seems ineffective for prolonged periods. Get a second consultation, get additional help, but don't give up.

23. Never worry alone. Try to cultivate as many supports as possible. From pediatrician to family doctor to therapist, from support group to professional organization to national conventions, from friends to relatives to teachers and schools, make use of whatever supports you can find. It is amazing how group support can turn a mammoth obstacle into a solvable problem, and how it can help you keep your perspective. You'll find yourself saying, "You mean we're not the only family with this problem?" Even if this does not solve the problem, it will make it feel more manageable, less strange and threatening. Get support. Never worry alone.

24. Pay attention to boundaries and overcontrol within the family. People with ADD often step over boundaries without meaning to. It is important that each member of the family know that he or she is an individual, and not always feel under the collective will wielded by the family. In addition, the presence of ADD in the family can so threaten parents' sense of control that one or another parent becomes a little tyrant, fanatically insisting on control over all

things all the time. Such a hypercontrolling attitude raises the tension level within the family and makes everybody want to rebel. It also makes it difficult for family members to develop the sense of independence they need to have to function effectively outside the family.

25. Keep up hope. Hope is a cornerstone in the treatment of ADD. Have someone in mind whom you can call who will hear the bad news but also be able to pick up your spirits. Always bear in mind the positive aspects of ADD—energy, creativity, intuition, good-heartedness—and also bear in mind that many, many people with ADD do very well in life. When ADD seems to be sinking you and your family, remember that things can get better.

Families in general have tremendous power both to heal and to inflict pain. If the family is willing to cast a new eye upon a chronically wounded member, if the family is willing to heal him, it can do so better than all the medications, therapies, and incantations ever devised. However, if the family is unwilling to look differently upon one of its members, if the family instead sneers and snorts, "Just another one of your lame excuses! Why don't you just shape up?" then the family can undermine whatever good treatment he may receive. Few of us ever outgrow the power of our families both to deflate us and to fill us up. Few of us ever get past the wish for love and approval from mother or father, sibling or kin. That wish can be used in our favor, to support us as the wish is granted, or it can be used in our destruction as the wish is perpetually denied.

For the family to use its considerable power to heal, it must be willing to accept the challenge of change. All groups, especially families, feel threatened by a change in the status quo, no matter how bad the status quo may be. As the person with ADD seeks to change, he is also asking his family to change with him. This is never easy. It is not the bad family that has a hard time with change; it is all families. But with education and information as guides, with encouragement and support as reinforcers, most families can successfully adapt. As there is less suffering in the family system, life at home can even be fun.

Appendix III

TWENTY-FIVE TIPS ON THE MANAGEMENT

OF ADD IN COUPLES

■ ■ ■

The following guidelines or "tips" might be helpful in dealing with issues in couples where one partner has ADD. These tips offer a starting point for discussion. The best way to use them is to read them out loud, together. If a suggestion seems relevant to you, pause over it and discuss it. As you do this, you can begin to set up your own way of dealing with ADD in your relationship. The keys to it all, as is the case with most problems in couples, are improving communication and resolving the power struggle.

1. Make sure you have an accurate diagnosis. Once you are sure of the diagnosis, learn as much as you can about ADD. There is an increasing body of literature out on the topic. The more you and your mate know, the better you will be able to help each other. The first step in the treatment of ADD is accurate diagnosis and education.

2. Keep a sense of humor! If you let it be, ADD can be really funny at times. Don't miss out on the chance to laugh when the laugh is there. At that psychological branch point we all know so well—ADD or no ADD—when the split-second options are to get mad, cry, or laugh, go for the laughter. Humor is a key to a happy life with ADD.

3. Declare a truce. After you have made the diagnosis and have done some reading, take a deep breath and wave the white flag. You both need some breathing space to begin to get your relationship on new footing. You may need to ventilate a lot of stored-up bad feeling. Do that, so you won't lug it with you everywhere.

4. Set up a time for talking. You will need some time to talk to each other about ADD—what it is, how it affects your relationship, what each of you wants to do about it, what feelings you have about it. Don't do this on the run—i.e., during TV commercials, while drying dishes, in between telephone calls, etc. Set up some time. Reserve it for yourselves.

5. Spill the beans. Tell each other what is on your mind. The effects of ADD show up in different ways for different couples. Tell each other how it is showing up between you. Tell each other just how you are being driven crazy, what you like, what you want to change, what you want to preserve. Get it all out on the table. Try to say it all before you both start reacting. People with ADD have a tendency to bring premature closure on discussions, to go for the bottom line. In this case, the bottom line is the discussion itself.

6. Write down your complaints and your recommendations. It is good to have in writing what you want to change and what you want to preserve. Otherwise you'll forget.

7. Make a treatment plan. Brainstorm with each other as to how to reach your goals. You may want some professional help with this phase, but it is a good idea to try starting it on your own.

8. Follow through on the plan. Remember, one of the hallmarks of ADD is insufficient follow-through, so you'll have to work to stick with your plan.

9. Make lists for each other. Try to use them constructively, not as threats or evidence in arguments of what you have requested that hasn't been done.

10. Use bulletin boards. Messages in writing are less likely to be forgotten. Of course, you have to get in the habit of looking at the bulletin board!

11. Put notepads in strategic places such as by your bed, in your car, in the bathroom and kitchen.

12. Consider writing down what you want the other person to

do and give it to him or her in the form of a list every day. This must be done in a spirit of assistance, not of dictatorship. Keep a master appointment book for both of you. Make sure each of you checks it every day.

13. Take stock of your sex lives in light of ADD. As was mentioned earlier, ADD can affect sexual interest and performance. It is good to know the problems are due to ADD, and not something else.

14. Avoid the pattern of mess-maker and cleaner-upper. You don't want the non-ADD partner to "enable" the ADD partner by cleaning up all the time, in the manner that the nonalcoholic spouse may "enable" the alcoholic spouse by covering up all the time. Rather, set up strategies to break this pattern.

15. Avoid the pattern of pesterer and tuner-outer. You don't want the non-ADD partner to be forever nagging and kvetching at the ADD partner to pay attention, get his or her act together, come out from behind the newspaper, etc. People with ADD frequently need a certain amount of "down time" every day to recharge their batteries. It is better that this time be negotiated and set aside in advance rather than struggled over each time it comes up.

16. Avoid the pattern of the victim and the victimizer. You don't want the ADD partner to present himself or herself as a helpless victim left at the merciless hands of the all-controlling non-ADD mate. This dynamic can evolve easily if you aren't careful. The ADD person needs support and structure; the non-ADD mate tries to provide these. Unless there is open and clear communication about what is going on, the support and structure can feel like control and nagging.

17. Avoid the pattern of master and slave. Akin to number 16. However, in a funny way it can often be the non-ADD partner who feels like the slave to his or her mate's ADD. The non-ADD partner can feel that the symptoms of ADD are ruining the relationship, wrapping around it like tentacles, daily disrupting what could be, and once was, an affectionate bond.

18. Avoid the pattern of a sadomasochistic struggle as a routine way of interacting. Prior to diagnosis and intervention, many couples dealing with ADD spend most of their time attacking and

counterattacking each other. One hopes to get past that and into the realm of problem-solving. What you have to beware of is the covert pleasure that can be found in the struggle. ADD is exasperating; therefore, you can enjoy punishing your mate by fighting with him or her. Try, rather, to vent your anger at the disorder, not at the person. Say "I hate ADD" instead of "I hate you," or say "ADD drives me crazy" instead of "You drive me crazy."

19. In general, watch out for the dynamics of control, dominance, and submission that lurk in the background of most relationships, let alone relationships where ADD is involved. Try to get as clear on this as possible, so that you can work toward cooperation rather than competitive struggle.

20. Break the tapes of negativity. Many people who have ADD have long ago taken on a resigned attitude of "There's no hope for me." The same can happen to both members of the couple. As will be mentioned in many places throughout this book, negative thinking is a most corrosive force in the treatment of ADD. What I call the "tapes of negativity" can play relentlessly, unforgivingly, endlessly in the mind of the person with ADD. It is as if they click on as the sun rises and click off only when the unconsciousness of sleep shuts them down. They play, over and over, grinding noises of "You can't," "You're dumb," "It won't work out," "Look how far behind you are," "You're just a born loser." The tapes can be playing in the midst of a business deal, in the reverie of a car ride home, or they can take the place of making love. It is hard to be romantic when you are full of negative thoughts. The thoughts seduce you, like a satanic mistress, into "loving" them instead. These tapes are very difficult to stop, but with conscious and sustained effort, they can be smashed.

21. Use praise freely. Encouragement, too. Begin to play positive tapes. Find something positive to say about your mate or about yourself every day. Build each other up consciously, deliberately. Even if it feels hokey at first, often as exercise feels goofy at first, over time it will feel good and have a sustaining effect.

22. Learn about mood management. Anticipation is a great way to help anyone deal with the highs and lows that come along. This is especially true in ADD. If you know in advance that when you say

"Good morning, honey!" the response you get might be "Get off my back, will you!" then it is easier to deal with that response without getting a divorce. And if the other member of the couple has learned something about his or her moods, the response to "Good morning, honey!" might be "I'm in one of my ADD funks," or something like that, instead of an attack on the other person.

23. Let the one who is the better organizer take on the job of organization. There's no point in flogging yourself with a job you can't do. If you can't do the checkbook, don't do the checkbook. If you can't do the kids' clothes shopping, then don't do the kids' clothes shopping. That's one of the advantages of being in a couple. You have another person to help out. However, the job the other person does instead of you must then be adequately appreciated, noticed, and reciprocated.

24. Make time for each other. If the only way you can do this is by scheduling it, then schedule it. This is imperative. Many people with ADD slip away like quicksilver: now you have them, now you don't. Clear communication, the expression of affection, the taking up of problems, playing together and having fun—all these ingredients of a good relationship cannot occur unless you spend time together.

25. Don't use ADD as an excuse. Each member of the couple has to take responsibility for his or her actions. On the other hand, while one mustn't use ADD as an excuse, knowledge of the syndrome can add immeasurably to the understanding one brings to the relationship.

Appendix IV

WHERE TO GO FOR HELP

■ ■ ■

If you believe that you, or someone you know, may have ADD, and you would like additional information, a good place to start is your own physician. If your doctor is not expert on the syndrome, he or she can probably point you in the right direction. The local medical society or psychological society is another good resource, as is any medical school in your area. The departments of psychiatry, psychology, child psychiatry, neurology, pediatrics, and family medicine would be most likely to have experts.

If you still have trouble finding help, we offer this appendix as an additional resource. However, we cannot emphasize too strongly the following point: *Do not diagnose and treat yourself. Get professional consultation.*

ORGANIZATIONS TO CONTACT FOR INFORMATION ABOUT ADD

Attention Deficit Disorder Association (ADDA)
P.O. Box 488
West Newbury, MA 01985

ADDA sponsors the activities of the ADDult Support Network, *ADDult News,* and *Challenge* (see below).

Adult ADD Association
1225 East Sunset Drive, Suite
   640
Bellingham, WA 98226-3529
(206) 647-6681

Adult Attention Deficit Foun-
   dation
132 North Woodward Avenue
Birmingham, MI 48009
(313) 540-6335

Adult ADHD Clinic
University of Massachusetts
   Medical Center
Department of Psychiatry
55 Lake Avenue North
Worcester, MA 01655
(508) 856-2552
This clinic, under the direction
   of Kevin Murphy, Ph.D.,
   serves adults. U. Mass. also
   has an internationally famous
   clinic for treatment and research in childhood ADD
   under the guidance of Russell Barkley, Ph.D.

CH.A.D.D.
(Children and Adults with At-
   tention Deficit Disorder)
499 Northwest 70th Avenue,
   Suite 308
Plantation, FL 33317
(305) 587-3700
Fax: (305) 587-4599
CH.A.D.D. is the national and
   international nonprofit

parent-support organization
   for children and adults with
   ADD.

National Coaching Network
Box 353
Lafayette Hill, PA 19444
The mission of the NCN is to
   provide information about
   ADD coaching and to be a
   forum for discussion/educa-
   tion within the community
   of professional ADD coaches.
   For information about ADD
   coaching, send $3 and a self-
   addressed, stamped, business
   envelope.

SOME STATE ADVOCACY
GROUPS

ADD Advocacy Group
8091 South Ireland Way
Aurora, CO 80016
(303) 690-7548

CH.A.D.D. National State Net-
   working Committee
499 Northwest 70th Avenue,
   Suite 308
Plantation, FL 33317
(305) 587-3700
This committee offers guidance
   and expertise in the formation of CH.A.D.D. state
   councils throughout the
   country, which can serve as
   advocacy groups.

ORGANIZATIONS TO CONTACT FOR INFORMATION ABOUT LEARNING
DISABILITIES AND DYSLEXIA

Orton Dyslexia Society
8600 LaSalle Road
Baltimore, MD 21204-6020
(301) 296-0232
A great and proud organization
full of dedicated individuals,
the Orton Dyslexia Society
has stood strong for many
decades advocating for research, education, and equal-
ity. A packet of information on
dyslexia is available for $4.00.

ERIC Clearinghouse on Adult
Career and Continuing Education
(800) 848-4815
This "hotline" can provide important information about
employment possibilities, career changes, educational resources, etc.

National Network of Learning
Disabled Adults
(602) 941-5112

National Center for Learning
Disabilities
381 Park Avenue South, Suite
1420
New York, NY 10016
(212) 545-7510

National Information Center
for Children and Youth with
Disabilities (NICHY)

P.O. Box 1492
Washington, DC 20013-1492

Northeast Conference on
Learning Disabilities and
Mental Health
P.O. Box 271336
West Hartford, CT 06127-
1336
(203) 232-6112
Annual conference with work-
shops, research presentations,
and topics related to
LD/ADD and MH. Spon-
sored by the Learning Dis-
abilities Association of
Connecticut, 139 North
Main Street, West Hartford,
CT 06107.

Self-Help Clearing House
St. Claire's Riverside Medical
Center
Pocono Road
Denville, NJ 07834
(201) 625-9565
Provides local and national re-
ferral services and carries
support-group listings.

Learning Disabilities Association of America
4156 Library Road
Pittsburgh, PA 15234
(412) 341-1515

National Center for Law and
Learning Disabilities
P.O. Box 368
Cabin John, MD 20818
(301) 469-8308
Fax (301) 469-9466

NEWSLETTERS

The ADHD Report
Guilford Publications
Russell Barkley, Editor
To subscribe call, toll free,
(800) 365-7006
This is a superb newsletter,
edited by one of the fore-
most authorities on the subject. It is a must for any
parent, clinician, school official, or individual who wants
to stay current with new developments in the field.

ADDendum [for adults with
ADD]
c/o C.P.S.
5041-A Backlick Road
Annandale, VA 22003
Paul Jaffe, Editor
This quarterly publication for
adults with ADD includes reviews of recent research, in-
terviews and articles by
leading researchers and clinicians specializing in adult
ADD, question-and-answer
columns, and articles and poetry written by adults with

ADD. In addition, *ADDen-
dum* has available a nationwide listing of adult ADD
support groups.

ADDult News
c/o Mary Jane Johnson
ADDult Support Network
2620 Ivy Place
Toledo, OH 43613
This newsletter includes sub-
stantive articles about issues
relevant to adults with ADD,
as well as a listing of resources and support-group
announcements. *ADDult
News* welcomes letters, comments, personal stories,
poems and artwork.
This publication is available at a
cost of $12.00 per year for
four issues.

CH.A.D.D.ER and
    CH.A.D.D.ER BOX
CH.A.D.D. National Head-
quarters
499 Northwest 70th Avenue,
Suite 308
Plantation, FL 33317
(305) 587-3700
Fax: (305) 587-4599
CH.A.D.D.ER: A biannual,
twenty-five-page-plus
newsletter that frequently
contains articles written by
leading researchers and clinicians for adults with ADD.

CH.A.D.D.ER BOX: A monthly newsletter with several issues per year devoted solely to adult ADD concerns.

Challenge
P.O. Box 448
West Newbury, MA 01985
A bimonthly published by ADDA, this newsletter occasionally has articles about ADD in adults.

The Rebus Institute Report
1499 Bayshore Boulevard,
Suite 146
Burlingame, CA 94010
A quarterly newsletter published by the Rebus Institute, a nonprofit research institute devoted to the study and dissemination of information related to adults with learning difficulties and ADD. The newsletter includes employment-related issues, ADA (see below) information, book reviews, news reports, and announcements.

OFFICES TO CONTACT FOR INFORMATION ABOUT THE AMERICANS WITH DISABILITIES ACT, EQUAL EMPLOYMENT OPPORTUNITY ISSUES, AND EDUCATIONAL RIGHTS ACCORDING TO PL94-142 (ALSO CALLED INDIVIDUALS WITH DISABILITIES EDUCATION ACT—IDEA) AND SECTION 504

Equal Employment Opportunity Commission
1801 L Street, NW
Washington, DC 20507
(202) 663-4900
(800) 800-3302
Contact the EEOC about employment issues related to the Americans with Disabilities Act. Title 1 of ADA prevents an employer from discriminating against a qualified individual with a mental or physical disability with regards to job-application procedures, hiring, discharge, compensation, advancement, job training, and other conditions and privileges of employment.

Department of Justice
Office of Americans with Disabilities Act
Civil Rights Division
P.O. Box 66118
Washington, DC 20035
(202) 514-0301

Contact the Department of Justice about "public accommodation" issues, as defined by the Americans with Disabilities Act. Title III of the act prohibits any private entity that owns, leases, or operates a place of public accommodation (e.g., restaurants, retail stores, colleges, and graduate schools) from discriminating against an individual on the basis of disability.

Office of Civil Rights
U.S. Department of Education
400 Maryland Avenue, SW
Washington, DC 20202-4135
(202) 401-3020
Contact OCR with issues pertaining to Section 504 of the Rehabilitation Act (1973),

and the Individuals with Disabilities Education Act (IDEA), both of which provide guidelines for the rights of individuals with ADD in public school settings.

The Rebus Institute
1499 Bayshore Boulevard,
Suite 146
Burlingame, CA 94010
The Rebus Institute has printed information about the relevance of ADA to LD and ADD adults, especially as to how the new act relates to employment situations.

Job Accommodation Network
Box 468
Morgantown, WV 25505
(800) 526-7234
(800) ADA-WORK

READINGS AND REFERENCES ABOUT ADD

The following list contains books and other resources that we think will be helpful in learning more about ADD and LD in adults and children. It is only a sample, however, of the many excellent and informative publications that are available about attention deficit disorder. Perhaps it can serve as your starting point. The books are presented alphabetically by author, with the exception of the first one.

Driven to Distraction: Recognizing and Coping with Attention Deficit Disorder from Childhood through Adulthood. Edward M. Hallowell and John J. Ratey. Pantheon, New York, 1994. Told mainly through stories of children, adults, couples, and families, this book is an introduction to the world of ADD. It emphasizes the emotional experience of ADD, as well as practical tips on how to deal with it.

Inside Attention Deficit Disorder. Susan Alfultis. 1991. Subtitled "A Collection of Thoughts and Feelings on ADD by an Adult Who Lives It," this personal account of ADD is thought-provoking and helpful. Available through ADDA.

Attention Deficit Hyperactivity Disorder: A Handbook for Diagnosis and Treatment. Russell Barkley, Ph.D. Guilford Publications, New York, 1990. This comprehensive text details the history of ADD, the developmental course of the disorder, its relation to cognitive and emotional maturation, its impact on the family, and its implications for adulthood. It discusses evaluative, diagnostic, and treatment methodologies, and provides a solid understanding of the research that has been done in the field.

ADHD: What Do We Know? and *ADHD: What Can We Do?* Two videos by Russell Barkley, Ph.D., available through Guilford Press Videos, Guilford Publications, Inc., 72 Spring Street, New York, NY 10012.

Psychiatric Aspects of Minimal Brain Dysfunction in Adults. Leopold Bellak, editor. Grune & Stratton, New York, 1979. This book was written before MBD and ADD were taken to be much the same thing. A classic in the field, the book is now out of print.

CH.A.D.D.ER, Special Edition: The Adult with ADD, written specifically about adult issues, available through CH.A.D.D.

Maybe You Know My Kid: A Parent's Guide to Identifying, Understanding and Helping Your Child with Attention Deficit Disorder. Mary Cahill Fowler. Birch Lane Press, New York, 1990. Takes the reader on one family's journey toward discovering their child was not willfully misbehaving, but had attention deficit hyperactivity disorder. May help the adult in identifying childhood patterns consistent with ADD.

Ritalin: Theory and Patient Management. Lawrence L. Greenhill, M.D., and Betty B. Osman, Ph.D., editors. 1991. Mary Ann Liebert Press, 1651 3rd Avenue, New York, NY 10128. A reference book on the many issues related to the use of Ritalin: the action of Ritalin on the central nervous system, the use of Ritalin to decrease impulsive behavior and increase cognitive performance, the pharmacological treatment of ADD in adults, and many more chapters by leaders in the field.

Attention Deficit Disorder: A Different Perception. Thom Hartmann. Underwood-Miller, Novato, Calif., 1993. An interesting theory. Thom Hartmann has done a great deal to help "normalize" ADD. He is an innovative thinker and a good writer.

Hyperactive Children Grown Up. Lily Hechtman, Ph.D. and Gabrielle Weiss, Ph.D. Guilford Press, New York, 1986. Hechtman and Weiss have followed children with ADD for the past three decades. The book summarizes the findings of their landmark longitudinal studies and integrates their findings with that of other research in the field.

Trauma and Recovery. Judith Lewis Herman, M.D. Basic Books, New York, 1992. While not touching on ADD, this moving book discusses trauma as well as any book has. Since many people with learning disabilities or attention deficit disorder also have a history of trauma, we mention this book here.

Learning Disabilities: Proceedings of the National Conference. James F. Kavanaugh and Tom J. Truss, editors. York Press, Parkton, Md., 21120, 1988. Excellent collection.

You Mean I'm Not Lazy, Stupid, or Crazy?!: A Self-help Book for Adults with Attention Deficit Disorder. 1993. Kate Kelly and Peggy Ramundo. Tyrell and Jerem Press, Box 20089, Cincinnati, OH, 45220. Written by and for ADD adults, this book includes tips on coping with, organizing, and living the life of an ADD adult.

Attention Deficit Disorder and the Law: A Guide for Advocates. Peter S. Latham, J.D., and Patricia H. Latham, J.D. 1992. A clear and comprehensive overview of the rights of ADD individuals according to PL 94-142, IDEA, the Social Security Act, ADA, federal, state, and case law. Available through JKL Communications, 1016 16th Street, NW, Suite 700, Washington, DC 20036.

Keeping a Head in School. Mel Levine, M.D. Educators Publishing Service, Cambridge, Mass., 1991. This book offers practical advice, studying strategies, and hope for the grammar-school and high-school student with ADD. Includes an overview of learning disabilities and problems, an explanation of different learning styles, and creative methods that can be employed to accomplish goals.

Diagnosing Learning Disorders: A Neuropsychological Framework, Bruce B. Pennington. Guilford Press, New York, 1991. A superb overview. Written more for the professional than the lay reader.

ADD and the College Student: A Guide for High School and College Students with Attention Deficit Disorder. Patricia O. Quinn, M.D., editor. Magination Press, New York, 1994. A practical guide in a field where much guidance is needed.

The Boy Who Couldn't Stop Washing. Judith Rapoport. E. P. Dutton, New York, 1989. This book articulates the etiology, and the trauma, of obsessive-compulsive disorder. It has struck many chords for adults with ADD.

Smart Kids with School Problems: Things to Know and Ways to Help. Priscilla Vail. New American Library, New York, 1987. *Learning Styles: Food for Thought and 130 Practical Tips.* Priscilla Vail, Modern Learning Press, Rosemont, N.J., 1993. *Emotion: The On/Off Switch for Learning.* Priscilla Vail, Modern Learning Press, Rosemont, N.J., 1994. Priscilla Vail brings a special combination of warmth, hard-nosed practicality, and strong prose to all her writing. These three titles are but a suggested sample.

Attention Deficit Disorders in Adults: Practical Help for Sufferers and Their Spouses. Lynn Weiss, Ph.D. Taylor Publishing Company, Dallas, 1992. Emphasizes the ways in which ADD symptoms appear in adults. Reviews treatment and coping strategies and includes a list of clinicians across the country who are specializing in treating adults with ADD.

The Hyperactive Child, Adolescent, and Adult. Paul Wender, M.D. Oxford University Press, New York, 1987. Dr. Wender, one of the true innovators in all of contemporary psychiatry and a pioneer in the field of ADD, presents here an overview of ADD in childhood, adolescence, and adulthood. He discusses evaluation procedures and treatment approaches developed from his lifetime of work in the field. Written for the parent, healthcare professional, or adult with ADD.

EDUCATIONAL VENDORS

A.D.D. WareHouse
300 Northwest 70th Avenue,
   Suite 102
Plantation, FL 33317
(305) 792-8944

The Attention Deficit Resource
   Center
1344 Johnson Ferry Road,
   Suite 14
Marietta, GA 30068

SUPPORT GROUPS

We are grateful to Lisa Poast of Bellingham, WA, for putting together the following list of support groups for adult ADD around the country. The list cannot be complete, because new groups are being formed all the time. However, the list was updated in August 1994, so it is as current as was possible for the publication of this book.

ALABAMA
   Birmingham
John Larson
(205) 823-5910

ALASKA
   Anchorage
Anchorage CH.A.D.D.
(907) 338–1491

ARIZONA
   Ahwatukee (Phoenix area)
South Mountain CH.A.D.D.
(602) 820–4435

Jeri Goldstein, M.C., R.N.
(602) 345–6622

   Bullhead City
Northwestern Arizona
CH.A.D.D.
(602) 763–7346

   *Glendale (Phoenix
   area)*
Attention Deficit Disorder
Clinic
(602) 863–7950

Prescott
Families with Attention Deficit
Disorder
(602) 636–5160
Scottsdale
Attention Deficit Disorder
Clinic
(602) 423–7770
Tucson (Northeast)
Steven Ledingham
A.S.K. about ADD
(602) 749–5465
(602) 621–3149
Tucson
CH.A.D.D. of Tucson
(602) 797–2162

Della Mays, Adult Coordinator
(602) 887–0978

CALIFORNIA
Alameda County
CH.A.D.D. of Alameda County
(510) 581–9941
Arcadia (Pasadena area)
Melissa Thomasson, Ph.D.
(818) 301–7977
Contra Costa County
Pat and Monte Churchill
(510) 825–4938
*Encinitas (north of
San Diego)*
Coastal North County
CH.A.D.D.
(619) 259–5325

Laguna Beach
CH.A.D.D. of Laguna Beach
(714) 457–2125
Long Beach
Patreen Bower, M.S., M.F.C.C.
Sue Griffith, M.A., Psy. Asst.
(714) 953–8220
Mountain View
CH.A.D.D. of Mid–Peninsula
(415) 969–6233
Needles
(see Bullhead City, Arizona
listing)
Newport Beach
Joan Andrews, L.E.P.
(714) 476–0991
Roseville
(Sacramento area)
CH.A.D.D. of Roseville &
Greater Sacramento
(916) 782–5661

Milton Lucius, Ph.D.
(916) 933–5217

John R. Capel, Ph.D.
(916) 488–5788
San Diego
Andrea Little
Roland Rotz, Ph.D.
Learning Development Services
(619) 276–6912
San Francisco
San Francisco/N. Peninsula
CH.A.D.D.
(415) 994–2438

San Jose
Karen Neale, M.A.
(408) 395–1348
San Rafael
MATRIX
(415) 499–3877

David Hayes
Adult Coordinator
(415) 435–0994
Simi Valley
CH.A.D.D. of the Conejo
Valley
(805) 520–4943
Ukiah
Mendocino County/
Redwood Empire CH.A.D.D.
(707) 462–1133
Wildomar
CH.A.D.D. of Temecula Valley
(909) 674–8052

CALIFORNIA SPOUSE
SUPPORT GROUPS
Arcadia (Pasadena area)
Melissa Thomasson, Ph.D.
(818) 301–7977
Contra Costa County
Monte Churchill
(510) 825–4938
*Folsom (Sacramento
area)*
Milton Lucius, Ph.D.
(916) 933–5217
Simi Valley
CH.A.D.D. of the Conejo Valley
(805) 520–4943

COLORADO
Boulder
John Cizman
(303) 786–8112
Colorado Springs
CH.A.D.D. of Colorado Springs
(719) 597–9857
Denver
Don Lambert
(303) 424–5272
Denver (Metro North)
Harry Orr
(303) 458–5675
(303) 424–3116
Fort Collins
Maxine Jarvi
(303) 223–1338
(970) 223–1338
effective 4/2/95
Lakewood (Denver area)
Mile Hi CH.A.D.D.
(303) 936–7821
Littleton
(Metro South Denver)
Dennis Smith
(303) 790–2354
*For additional listings in
Colorado, contact:*
Ralph Myers, Editor
ADD VANTAGE
(303) 287–6944

CONNECTICUT
Avon (Hartford area)
CH.A.D.D. of the Farmington
Valley
(203) 651–3880

East Hampton
CH.A.D.D. of East Hampton
Cathy Ziegler, Coordinator
(203) 267–6807

Liz Johnson, Co–coordinator
(203) 873–1733
Mansfield
Mansfield CH.A.D.D.
(203) 429–2582

Paul Kalajain, Adult Coordinator
(203) 487–1920
New Haven
CH.A.D.D. of New Haven
County
(203) 888–1434
New Milford
(north of Danbury)
CH.A.D.D. of Candlewood
Valley
(203) 350–9484
Rocky Hill
Joel Shusman
(203) 257–3221
Waterford
CH.A.D.D. of Southeastern
Connecticut
(203) 443–2500
(203) 444–0263

CONNECTICUT SPOUSE
SUPPORT GROUPS
Avon (Hartford area)
CH.A.D.D. of the Farmington
Valley
(203) 651–3880

DELAWARE
Wilmington
Lizbee Mahoney, Adult
Coordinator
CH.A.D.D. of Brandywine
Valley
(302) 478–8202

FLORIDA
Fort Walton Beach
Okaloosa County CH.A.D.D.
(904) 863–2459
Jacksonville
CH.A.D.D. of Duval
(904) 390–0866

Bethann P. Vetter,
Adult Coordinator
(904) 731–7230
Orlando
CH.A.D.D. of Seminole
County
(407) 324–1442
Pembroke Pines
CH.A.D.D. of South Broward
& North Dade Counties
(305) 680–0799
Plantation
CH.A.D.D. of West Broward
(305) 721–8793
Tampa
Hillsborough County
CH.A.D.D.
(813) 852–8075

GEORGIA
Atlanta (Buckhead)
L.D. Adults of Georgia
(404) 514–8088

Decatur (Atlanta area)
Joan Teach, Ph.D.
(404) 378–6643

ILLINOIS
Bloomington
Ron Ropp, Rel.D.
(309) 829–0751
*Chicago
(Northwest Suburban)*
CH.A.D.D. of Northwest
Suburban Chicago
(708) 303–1189
*Chicago (South
Suburban)*
South Suburban Chicago
CH.A.D.D.
(708) 798–9331
*Chicago (Southwest
Suburban/Will County)*
ADAPPT
(708) 361–3387
Frankfort
ADD-ONS, Ltd.
Mary P. Daum, President
(815) 469–8567
Freeport
Freeport Area CH.A.D.D.
(815) 235–8019
Peoria
Deborah Dornaus
(309) 693–0038
Rockford
CH.A.D.D. of Rockford
(815) 968–5640

Gary Hubbard, M.S., L.M.F.T.
(815) 282–1800

*For additional listings in
Illinois, contact:*
Illinois State ADD Council
(708) 361–4878

INDIANA
Bloomington
Abilities Unlimited
(812) 332–1620
*Fortville
(Indianapolis Eastside)*
ADDults of Central Indiana
(317) 649–2871
Greensburg
Tree City CH.A.D.D.
(812) 663–6877
*Portage
(Northwest Indiana)*
David Shultz
(219) 232–6690

Teresa Gross
(219) 465–0447
Richmond
Rita Spoonamore
Adult Attention Deficit
Disorder Support
(317) 966–0221

IOWA
Iowa City
CH.A.D.D. of Iowa City
(319) 656–3043

Don Walker, Adult Coordinator
(319) 337–5201

KANSAS
Overland Park
Avner Stern, Ph.D.
(913) 469–6510

Prairie Village
ADD/ADHD Education &
Resource Association
(913) 362–6108

KANSAS SPOUSE
SUPPORT GROUPS
Prairie Village
ADD/ADHD Education &
Resource Association
(913) 362–6108

KENTUCKY
Lexington
CH.A.D.D. of the Bluegrass
(606) 272–2166

Nancy Blakley, Adult
Coordinator
(606) 223–3074
Paducah
CH.A.D.D. of Western
Kentucky
(502) 488–2252

LOUISIANA
*New Orleans
(Northern area)*
River Parish CH.A.D.D.
(504) 467–4983

MAINE
Scarborough
Lindy Botto
(207) 883–2528

MARYLAND
Bel Air
CH.A.D.D. of Harford
(410) 569–3532

Frederick
Frederick County CH.A.D.D.
(301) 898–3912
Rockville
CH.A.D.D. of Montgomery
County
(301) 869–3628

Kathleen G. Nadeau, Ph.D.
(301) 718–8114

MARYLAND SPOUSE
SUPPORT GROUP
Rockville
CH.A.D.D. of Montgomery
County
(301) 869–3628

Kathleen G. Nadeau, Ph.D.
(301) 718–8114

MASSACHUSETTS
Greenfield
CH.A.D.D. of Western
Massachusetts
(413) 665–2108
(413) 648–9801

Lori Roy, Adult Coordinator
(413) 773–5545
Lynn
North Shore Adults and
Children with ADD
(617) 599–6818

Linda Harrison
(508) 777–4077
Plymouth
Linda Greenwood
(508) 747–2179

Weston (Boston area)
John Patrick Moir
(603) 881-5540

MICHIGAN
Ann Arbor
Jim Reisinger
ADDult Information Exchange
Network
(313) 426-1659
    Clinton Township/
    Pontiac/Royal Oak/Troy
Kathleen Van Howe
Adult ADD Awareness
(810) 939-1112
    Cadillac
North Central Michigan
CH.A.D.D.
(616) 779-0482

Adult Coordinator
(616) 775-3754
    Chesterfield
    (Macomb County)
Chesterfield CH.A.D.D.
(810) 949-7890
    Grosse Pointe
Gerhard W. Heinen
(313) 886-8907
    Lansing
Sue Wallace
(517) 627-3387

Jennifer Bramer, Ph.D., L.P.C.
Lansing Community College
Counseling Services
Department
(517) 483-1184

Novi
Fred Michaelson
(810) 348-2656

MINNESOTA
    Minneapolis
William Ronan, LICSW
(612) 933-3460

MISSOURI
    Kansas City
(see Overland Park and Prairie
Village, Kansas listings)
    St. Louis
Barb Rosenfeld, Adult
Coordinator
Attention Deficit Disorder
Association of Missouri
(314) 963-4655
    St. Louis area
DePaul Health Center/Adults
with ADD Support Group
(314) 344-7224
    St. Louis Park
    (Minneapolis area)
Twin Cities CH.A.D.D.
(612) 922-5761

MISSOURI SPOUSE
SUPPORT GROUPS
    Kansas City
(see Prairie, Kansas listing)

MONTANA
    Great Falls
Dennis Patton
(406) 454-1964
    Great Falls
David Walker
(406) 727-2137

Havre
Cherie Miller
New World
(406) 265–1871
Kalispell
Flathead Valley CH.A.D.D.
(406) 257–5450

NEW HAMPSHIRE
Concord
Sarah Brophy, Ph.D.
(603) 226–6121
Nashua
John Patrick Moir
(603) 881–5540

NEW JERSEY
Fair Haven
Robert LoPresti, Ph.D.
Adult ADD Self-Help
Support Group
(908) 842–4553
Washington Township
(Gloucester County)
CH.A.D.D. of Washington
Township
(609) 582–5717

NEW JERSEY SPOUSE
SUPPORT GROUPS
Fair Haven
Robert LoPresti, Ph.D.
Adult ADD Self-Help
Support Group
(908) 842–4553

NEW MEXICO
Albuquerque
Attention Deficit Disorder Clinic
(505) 243–9600

Las Cruces
Dona Ana County CH.A.D.D.
(505) 523–5076
Adult Coordinator
(505) 523–8770

NEW YORK
Buffalo area
CH.A.D.D. of Western
New York
(716) 626–4581
Hautpauge
(Eastern Long Island)
CH.A.D.D. of Suffolk County
(516) 751–6989
Long Island
Joan B. Ells
(516) 244–3665
Manhattan
Barbara Andersen
(914) 476–0965
Queens
Forest Hills/Flushing
CH.A.D.D.
(718) 969–0549
Rochester
Greater Rochester Attention
Deficit Disorder Association
(GRADDA)
(716) 251–2322
Utica
CH.A.D.D. of Mohawk Valley
(315) 724–4233
White Plains
CH.A.D.D. of Westchester
County
(914) 278–3020

Susan G. Salit, M.S.W., Adult
Coordinator
(914) 472–2935

Charlotte Tomaino, Ph.D.
(914) 949–4055

NEW YORK SPOUSE GROUPS
Rochester
Greater Rochester Attention
Deficit Disorder Association
(GRADDA)
(716) 251–2322

NORTH CAROLINA
Charlotte
CH.A.D.D. of Mecklenburg
County
(704) 551–9120

OHIO
Eaton area
(see Richmond, Indiana listing)
Toledo
Jan Menzie
(419) 841–6603
Xenia
A.S.K. about ADD
Bettylou Huber
(513) 862–4573

Madge Jones
(513) 897–4380

OKLAHOMA
Oklahoma City
CH.A.D.D. of Central
Oklahoma
(405) 722–1233

Tulsa
Shelley Curtiss
(918) 622–1370

Juan Wilson
(918) 486–5035

**OKLAHOMA SPOUSE
SUPPORT GROUPS**
Tulsa
Cathy Holmes
(918) 369–5750

OREGON
Portland (Northwest)
ADDVENTURES Support
Group
(503) 452–5666
Portland (Northeast)
Metro–Portland CH.A.D.D.
(503) 294–9504
The Dalles
Mike Newman
(503) 296–4408

PENNSYLVANIA
Bethlehem
CH.A.D.D. of Lehigh Valley
(610) 258–9615
*Bryn Mawr (West of
Philadelphia)*
Parents Supporting Parents
Main Line CH.A.D.D.
(610) 626–2998
Harrisburg
CH.A.D.D. of the Capital Area
(717) 766–8084
Lancaster
Lancaster County CH.A.D.D.
(717) 626–0745

Lancaster
Judy Mansfield
(717) 656–9515
Malvern
Jerry McCrone
(610) 647–8807
Philadelphia
Susan Sussman, M.Ed.
(610) 825–8572
Pittsburgh
Southwest Pennsylvania
CH.A.D.D. Network Adult
ADD Support Group
(412) 531–4554

PENNSYLVANIA SPOUSE
SUPPORT GROUPS
Lancaster
Judy Mansfield
(717) 656–9515

RHODE ISLAND
Providence
Austin Donnelly
Rhode Island ADDult Support
Group
(401) 463–8778

SOUTH CAROLINA
Columbia
The Mental Health Association
in Mid-Carolina
(803) 733–5425
Seneca
CH.A.D.D. of Upstate South
Carolina
(803) 882–8370
Spartanburg
CH.A.D.D. of Spartanburg
(803) 587–8756

TENNESSEE
Knoxville
CH.A.D.D. of Greater East
Tennessee
(615) 681–1174
Nashville
ADD'sUP
(615) 292–5947

TEXAS
Austin
L.D.A. of Austin
(512) 477–5516

Jo Anne Nicholson, Adult
Coordinator
(512) 892–3736
Denton
North Texas CH.A.D.D.
(817) 383–5795
Houston (Southwest)
Karen Kasper
Houston Adult ADD Support
Group
(713) 353–3898
*For additional listings in
Texas, contact:*
Attention Deficit Disorders
Association—Southern
Region
(713) 955–3720

UTAH
Salt Lake City
Joyce Otterstrom
L.D.A. of Utah
(801) 355–2881

VIRGINIA
Arlington
Maggie Baker, Adult
Coordinator
CH.A.D.D. of Arlington/
Alexandria/Falls Church
(703) 979–0820
*Bon Aire (Richmond
area)*
CH.A.D.D. of Central Virginia
(804) 672–1308
Fairfax County
Susan Biggs, Ed.D.
(703) 642–6697
Glen Allen
CH.A.D.D. of Central
Virginia
(804) 672–1308
Newport News
Jody Lochmiller-Jones
Adult Attention Deficit &
Related Disorders Outreach
(804) 930–1931
Newport News
Peninsula Attention Deficit Disorder Association (PADDA),
Adult Chapter
(804) 874–2343

WASHINGTON
Bellingham
Lisa F. Poast
Adult ADD Association
(360) 647–6681
Kennewick
Kathy VanDyke
(509) 586–4257

Olympia
Attention Deficit Disorder
Clinic
(360) 754–4801
Seattle
W. J. McNabb, Ph.D.
(206) 609–3470
Tacoma
ADDult Support of Washington
Cynthia Hammer
(206) 752–0801 (evenings)

Brian Howell
(206) 759–2914 (days)
Vancouver
Columbia River CH.A.D.D.
(360) 750–6387

WASHINGTON SPOUSE
SUPPORT GROUPS
Bellingham
Adult ADD Association
(360) 647–6681

Linda Hallmark, M.S.
(360) 715–0341
Olympia
Pat and Helena Nagle
Attention Deficit Disorder
Clinic
(360) 754–4801

WISCONSIN
Milwaukee (Northeast)
Robert Lintereur
(414) 242–5387

Bob Fuller
(414) 377–6900

Milwaukee (Southeast)
CH.A.D.D. of Southeast Wisconsin
(414) 223–8310

Bob Roman, Adult Coordinator
(414) 291–7058 ext. 6797
*Waukesha
(Milwaukee area)*
Paul Rembas
Adult ADHD Support Group
(414) 542–6694

WISCONSIN SPOUSE
SUPPORT GROUPS
*Waukesha
(Milwaukee area)*
Amy Schley, Ph.D.
(414) 542–6694

CANADA
*Campbell River,
British Columbia*
Loring Kuhn, Adult
Coordinator
CH.A.D.D. Canada of
Campbell River
(604) 923–7405

*New Westminster,
British Columbia*
Claudette Kovacs
ADDSA (Attention Deficit
Disorder Support Association)
(604) 524–9183

Marielle Gauvin, Adult
Coordinator
(604) 524–0763
Bedford, Nova Scotia
Lida Currie
Attention Deficit Association of
Nova Scotia
(902) 835–2343
Ottawa, Ontario
CH.A.D.D. Canada of the
National Capital Region
(613) 722–8482
*For additional listings of
Canadian Support Groups,
contact:*
Mark Turcotte
CH.A.D.D. Canada
(613) 231–7646

Changes and/or additions may be sent to:
Lisa F. Poast
Adult ADD Association
1225 E. Sunset Drive,
Suite 640
Bellingham, WA 98226–3529
(360) 647–6681

■ ■ ■

The Adult ADD Association wishes to thank the authors of *Answers to Distraction*, Ned Hallowell and John Ratey, for making possible this updated listing through their financial support. We thank also those individuals who so generously give of their time as volunteers to the many adults with ADD seeking referral and support.

■ ■ ■